Multinational Corporations in Indonesia and Thailand

Multinational Corporations in Indonesia and Thailand

Wages, Productivity and Exports

Edited by

Eric D. Ramstetter

and

Fredrik Sjöholm

First published 2006 by
PALGRAVE MACMILLAN
Houndmills, Basingstoke, Hampshire RG21 6XS and
175 Fifth Avenue, New York, N.Y. 10010
Companies and representatives throughout the world

PALGRAVE MACMILLAN is the global academic imprint of the Palgrave
Macmillan division of St. Martin's Press, LLC and of Palgrave Macmillan Ltd.
Macmillan® is a registered trademark in the United States, United Kingdom
and other countries. Palgrave is a registered trademark in the European
Union and other countries.

ISBN-13: 978–1–4039–9878–1 hardback
ISBN-10: 1–4039–9878–7 hardback

This book is printed on paper suitable for recycling and made from fully
managed and sustained forest sources.

A catalogue record for this book is available from the British Library.

Library of Congress Cataloging-in-Publication Data
Multinational corporations in Indonesia and Thailand : wages,
    productivity and exports / edited by Eric D. Ramstetter & Fredrik Sjöholm.
        p.   cm.
    Includes bibliographical references and index.
    ISBN 1–4039–9878–7 (cloth)
    1. International business enterprises—Indonesia.   2. International
    business enterprises—Thailand.   3. Industrial productivity—Indonesia.
    4. Industrial productivity—Thailand.   5. Wages—Indonesia.
    6. Wages—Thailand.   7. Exports—Indonesia.   8. Exports—Thailand.
    I. Ramstetter, Eric D., 1956–   II. Sjöholm, Fredrik, 1966–
    HD2904.M85 2006
    338.8′88593—dc22   2005056728

10   9   8   7   6   5   4   3   2   1
15 14 13 12 11 10 09 08 07 06

Printed and bound in Great Britain by
Antony Rowe Ltd, Chippenham and Eastbourne

Contents

List of Tables and Figures

Tables

Figures

Foreword

This book examines how foreign multinational corporations (MNCs) affect wages, productivity and exports in Southeast Asia's two largest economies, Indonesia and Thailand. The primary contribution of this book is to summarize important results from numerous micro analyses of these issues in large samples of manufacturing plants in the two economies. As far as we know, this is the first book to focus primarily on micro analysis of these issues in Southeast Asia. This allows the book to address numerous important questions (see Chapter 1) in much greater detail than previously possible. The book also describes how the micro analyses are related to the evolution of MNCs' activities, as well as the Indonesian and Thai economic policies that affected those activities.

The book is the result of a project organized by the International Centre for the Study of East Asian Development (ICSEAD), Kitakyushu, Japan, between April 2000 and March 2003. All of the chapters in the book represent revised syntheses of several papers first presented at project workshops held at ICSEAD on 4–5 August 2001, 22–23 March 2002 and 28 March 2003, and/or made available in ICSEAD's working paper series. A number of the project's more technical papers were also published in academic journals and books. In contrast to these more technical contributions, this volume is designed to summarize the issues involved in a way that is easily accessible to a wider audience including academics and students in economics, business, political science and related fields, as well as policy-makers and business professionals.

This book could not have been completed without the help of numerous individuals, all of whom we cannot mention here for lack of space. First and foremost, we thank the authors whose papers are included in the volume for their patience and hard work as we put this volume together. Robert E. Lipsey also provided key advice on overall project design. Second, we are indebted to the present and previous directors of ICSEAD, Shoichi Yamashita and Shinichi Ichimura, for devoting sufficient resources to see the project through and for valuable advice along the way. Third, in addition to the authors of the chapters of this volume, we are grateful to those who helped shape the volume by contributing papers and/or serving as discussants at the March 2002 and/or the March 2003 meetings, namely, Shinichi Ichimura, Fukunari Kimura, Kozo Kiyota, Hiro Lee, Hiroshi Ono, Hitoshi Osaka,

Craig R. Parsons, Phan Minh Ngoc, Johzen Takeuchi, Tran Van Tho, Wang Wen-Thuen and Shoichi Yamashita. Several observers at these meetings, including Sumira Ohashi, Kiyotaka Sato and Zane Spindler, also contributed to the discussions that authors benefited from when revising the papers that underlie this volume. Fourth, the support staff at ICSEAD, especially Megumi Arima and Saori Koishi, provided invaluable logistical assistance throughout the project for which we are also very thankful.

Fifth, we are grateful to the following publishers for granting us permission to reproduce information from the authors' previously published papers as follows:

Blackwell Publishing for permission to reproduce Table 7.7 from Fredrik Sjöholm (2003) 'Which Indonesian Firms Export? The Importance of Foreign Networks', *Papers in Regional Science*, 82: 333–50, Table 2.

Elsevier Ltd. for permission to excerpt Tables 3.8 and 5.4 from Eric D. Ramstetter (2004) 'Labor Productivity, Wages, Nationality, and Foreign Ownership Shares in Thai Manufacturing, 1996–2000', *Journal of Asian Economics*, 14: 861–84, Tables 3–4.

Taylor & Francis, Ltd. for permission to excerpt Tables 4.1, 4.2 and 4.3 from Sadayuki Takii and Eric D. Ramstetter (2005) 'Multinational Presence and Labour Productivity Differentials in Indonesian Manufacturing, 1975–2001', *Bulletin of Indonesian Economic Studies*, 41: 221–42, Tables 1–5 (http://www.tandf.co.uk).

University of Chicago Press for permission to reproduce Table 6.9 from Keiko Ito (2004a) 'Foreign Ownership and Productivity in the Indonesian Automobile Industry: Evidence from Establishment Data for 1990–1999', in Takatoshi Ito and Andrew K. Rose, eds, *Growth and Productivity in East Asia*, Chicago and London: University of Chicago Press, pp. 229–70, Table 7.11.

Finally, although we are most grateful for the assistance of those mentioned above, the editors and authors of this volume are solely responsible for the content of the volume and all opinions expressed.

Eric D. Ramstetter, ICSEAD
Fredrik Sjöholm, Stockholm School of Economics
October 2005

List of Contributors

Keiko Ito
Associate Professor
Faculty of Economics, Senshu
University
2-1-1 Higashi-mita, Tama-ku
Kawasaki, Kanagawa 214-8580
Japan

Robert E. Lipsey
Director, New York Office
National Bureau of Economic
Research
365 Fifth Avenue, 5th Floor
New York, New York, 10016-4309
USA

Atsuko Matsuoka-Movshuk
Consultant
Toyama
Japan

Oleksandr Movshuk
Associate Professor
Department of Economics
University of Toyama
Toyama 930-8555
Japan

Eric D. Ramstetter
Research Professor
11-4 Otemachi, Kokurakita-ku
International Centre for the Study
of East Asian Development
Kitakyushu 803-0814
Japan
and

Visiting Professor
Graduate School of Economics
Kyushu University
Fukuoka 812-8581
Japan

Fredrik Sjöholm
Associate Professor
Stockholm School of Asian Studies
Stockholm School of Economics
Sveavägen 65
P.O. Box 6501, S-113 83 Stockholm
Sweden

Sadayuki Takii
Research Associate Professor
11-4 Otemachi, Kokurakita-ku
International Centre for the Study
of East Asian Development
Kitakyushu 803-0814
Japan
and
Visiting Associate Professor
Graduate School of Economics
Kyushu University
Fukuoka 812-8581
Japan

Masaru Umemoto
Research Assistant Professor
11-4 Otemachi, Kokurakita-ku
International Centre for the Study
of East Asian Development
Kitakyushu 803-0814
Japan

Part I
Introduction and Overview

1
The Issues

Eric D. Ramstetter and Fredrik Sjöholm

1.1   Multinationals and the questions they raise

Much of the interest in the effects of foreign-owned multinational corporations (MNCs), aside from their broad impacts on growth and development, concerns the effects on labour markets.[1] Indeed, the assertion that MNCs unfairly exploit workers in developing economies is one of the core concerns expressed by anti-globalization activists (Stiglitz 2003; Bhagwati 2004). One clear example of labour management failures was the 1993 fire at the Kader Industrial (Thailand) factory, where poor safety standards contributed to the deaths of at least 188 employees and the injury of many others (Brown 2001). On the other hand, among academics who have researched the activities of MNCs in developing economies (e.g. United Nations Conference on Trade and Development 1994; Moran 2001; Moran et al. 2005), there is a growing consensus that MNCs impart substantial direct and indirect benefits to workers and local firms in developing economies. The most obvious way in which MNCs could benefit workers is by paying relatively high wages. Correspondingly, the chapters in Part II of this book examine the effects of manufacturing MNCs on wages in Indonesia and Thailand.

Effects on labour markets are also closely interrelated to other important effects of MNCs. For example, productivity levels are generally thought to be relatively high in MNCs compared to local firms or plants. Moreover, positive productivity spillovers are hypothesized to result in relatively high productivity in local firms or plants which operate in industries where there is a relatively large MNC presence. In addition to being important in their own right, these productivity effects can also facilitate higher labour productivity and thus higher wages in both the MNCs and local firms or plants. Thus, Part III of this book analyses the effects of MNCs on productivity.

Exporting is another important activity to which MNCs impart important effects and yet another channel through which MNCs affect labour markets in host economies. Part IV of the book analyses MNCs' contributions to host economy exports, focusing on the question of whether MNCs have higher export propensities than local firms or plants. Because these Southeast Asian economies are still quite labour-abundant, their exports tend to be labour-intensive, as do the exports of MNCs operating in them. Consequently, any increases in exports from MNCs, or indirectly through local firms, are likely to lead to a relatively rapid increase in the demand for labour relative to other factors of production, and thus increases in wages relative to the prices of other factors of production.

Indonesia and Thailand are the two largest economies in Southeast Asia. Moreover, Indonesia and Thailand are two of the most important hosts to MNCs, especially manufacturing MNCs, in Southeast Asia and the developing world. This makes the studies in this volume of keen interest, both within the region and elsewhere. By the mid-1990s, manufacturing MNCs became conspicuous, attracting a lot of attention in these economies and elsewhere. For example, the World Bank (1993) identified rapid industrialization, export growth, and increases in foreign direct investment (FDI) by MNCs as key elements of the so-called 'Asian miracle', and Indonesia and Thailand as two major beneficiaries of the so-called miracle. Discussions of FDI's contributions to the diffusion of technology also became prominent in the analysis of economic growth.[2] At the micro level, Dobson and Chia (1997) highlighted how the manufacturing MNCs contributed to increasing trade and greater integration in the East Asian region during the first half of the 1990s.

In 1997–98, the Asian financial crisis had severe effects on both Indonesia and Thailand. However, manufacturing FDI continued to grow in Thailand for years after the crisis and manufacturing MNCs continued to expand production and employment in Indonesia (see details in section 1.3). Thus, acquiring a better understanding of MNCs in these two countries continues to be a priority for academics, policy-makers and business professionals alike.

In the late 1990s and the early part of the twenty-first century, increased access to micro data led to a number of rather technical papers, several of them written as part of the research project that led to this book, which analysed manufacturing MNCs in both Indonesia and

Thailand.[3] The primary contribution of this book is to systematically and succinctly analyse the important results of several papers written by the authors as part of a research project focusing on micro analyses of manufacturing MNCs for Indonesia and Thailand in the 1990s. The chapters in this volume have also been written to be accessible to a wide audience, including academics in all related fields, policy-makers and business professionals alike. As far as we know, this is the first volume to focus on micro analyses of MNCs in Southeast Asia, which facilitates investigation of several important questions in much more detail than previously possible:

1. Do MNCs pay higher wages, have higher productivity levels or have higher export propensities than locally owned plants? Do these differences exist after accounting for factors such as a plant's industry affiliation, geographical location, factor intensities, trade orientation and worker education levels?
2. Do wage levels, productivity levels and export propensities in MNCs have any relationship to the foreign ownership share in the MNC? Alternatively, is there any relationship to the home country of the parent?
3. Are there wage or productivity spillovers from MNCs to local plants? In other words, does the extent of foreign ownership or changes in the extent of foreign ownership in an industry affect wage levels or productivity levels in locally owned establishments in that industry?
4. Do the plants acquired by MNCs tend to have high wages or other distinguishing characteristics before the takeover? How does takeover by an MNC affect wages in the plant taken over or other plants in the industry and/or region? How does this compare with wages in plants established by greenfield investment?

1.2 Multinationals and host developing economies: some analytical principles

MNCs can have profound effects on the economies of host developing countries, some of the most obvious occurring in the labour market. For instance, MNCs will typically expand employment in the formal labour market. Governments in developing countries often have trouble generating enough employment to absorb rapidly increasing labour forces and might therefore encourage inflows of FDI from MNCs. This has been an important consideration in both Indonesia and Thailand, and an especially pressing one in Indonesia after the 1997–98 crisis, when growth slowed markedly. The formal-sector jobs created by MNCs are often coveted by workers (and policy-makers), not only because they pay more than informal sector jobs, but because they often pay more than formal-sector jobs in local firms.

MNCs may choose to pay relatively high wages for several possible reasons. For example, Dunning's (1988, 1993) popular theory of the multinational corporation stresses the importance of ownership advantages as a determinant of a firm's competitiveness in foreign markets. At the most basic level, ownership advantages influence a firm's ability to overcome numerous cost disadvantages relative to local firms in host markets and become an MNC. Ownership advantages include the possession of firm-specific assets (Markusen 1991) such as patents, proprietary marketing networks and brand names, as well as specific technologies, management techniques and distribution systems. Knowledge regarding many of these assets becomes embodied in a firm's workforce and MNCs may seek to reduce the risk of losing control over firm-specific assets by paying high wages and minimizing labour turnover. These considerations are likely to be most important regarding various white-collar workers, especially top-level employees and various specialists.

Other theorists (e.g. Casson 1987; Rugman 1980, 1985) argue that ownership advantages are not required for a firm to become an MNC, and that internalization advantages (Dunning's terminology) constitute the key determinant.[4] However, theorists generally agree that MNCs do tend to possess relatively large amounts of the firm-specific assets described above. Moreover, to the extent that the ability to internalize transactions depends on the skills of a firm's labour force, internationalization can also explain MNCs' desire to reduce turnover and thus pay relatively high wages.

On the other hand, MNCs' affiliates often report difficulties securing adequate labour supplies. These difficulties were conspicuous in Thailand in the mid-1990s when shortages of skilled labour were particularly severe (Ramstetter 1997). Part of the reason for this could be that differences in business culture in MNCs and local firms make it difficult for MNCs to harmonize their labour management practices with local norms. Problems can become especially acute when the MNCs involved use management techniques that vary from perceived international norms such as in the case of Japanese MNCs in Southeast Asia during the 1980s (Koike and Inoki 1990; Yamashita 1991). Apprehension regarding MNCs can create a preference for local firms among workers and make it necessary for MNCs to pay relatively high wages to woo workers away from local firms that use more commonly accepted labour management practices. Still other studies suggest that the tendency for MNCs to pay relatively high wages is related to rent-sharing arrangements among MNCs (Budd et al., 2005), relatively volatile labour demand in MNCs (Fabri et al., 2003), and compensation for a higher closure rate among MNCs (Bernard and Sjöholm, 2003).

If MNCs possess ownership advantages or relatively large amounts of firm-specific assets, productivity will be higher in MNCs than in local firms in countries like Indonesia and Thailand because local firms are predominantly non-MNCs. MNCs possess most of the world's advanced technologies, they conduct almost all of the private research and development in the world, and they are typically more capital-intensive than locally owned firms are. All of these characteristics suggest that MNCs should have relatively high levels of labour productivity or total factor productivity, which is another reason why they could pay higher wages than local firms with lower productivity. However, this does not explain why a wage differential might persist after accounting for differences in productivity or related factors such as factor intensities.

MNC presence is also hypothesized to affect productivity in local firms. Such effects, often called spillovers, can arise if technologies in MNCs become available to local firms. Although MNCs may try to prevent the leakage of technologies as described above, there are also instances where MNCs encourage the spread of technologies, for instance through support of local suppliers. Labour mobility between MNCs and local firms is another means through which knowledge of technologies and other firm-specific assets can be spread. A final means by which MNCs can facilitate spillovers is by increasing competitive pressure to the point that local firms are forced to put greater emphasis on increasing productivity themselves. In this context, it is important that technologies used by most firms in Indonesian and Thai manufacturing, including MNCs, are still relatively standardized. This makes it very difficult for MNCs to keep their technologies proprietary and at the same time makes it relatively easy for local firms to imitate MNCs. Accordingly, the magnitude of spillovers is often hypothesized to depend on the extent of the technological gaps between MNCs and local plants, among other factors (see Chapter 4, for example).

If MNCs are more productive than local plants they may also be better able to produce products that can compete on export markets. Perhaps more importantly, some of the most important firm-specific assets controlled by MNCs relate to their international marketing networks or access to networks controlled by trading firms and the like. This lowers the transactions costs related to exporting in MNCs compared to local firms. Transactions costs associated with exports are substantial and include costs related to adapting to consumer preferences in foreign markets, identifying major competitors, and securing distribution channels. Moreover, many MNCs utilize their networks of affiliates to gather related information and minimize these transactions costs. This is another important reason why MNCs are more likely to export larger portions of their output than local firms and the growth of MNCs is likely to lead to relatively rapid growth of exports. In addition to being an important direct contribution itself, this change can also affect wages, as mentioned above. Because exports tend to be relatively labour-intensive in labour-abundant countries like Indonesia and Thailand, the growth of exports leads in turn to increases in the demand for labour relative to the demand for capital, and thus to an increase in wages relative to the price of capital, through a mechanism described in the *Stolper-Samuelson Theorem*.[5]

MNCs are also thought to restrict the access of uncontrolled affiliates to the MNC's firm-specific assets as another means of preventing the leakage of those assets or ownership advantages. For example, it is often argued that MNC parents are more reluctant to share their technology-related assets with minority-owned affiliates than with their majority-owned or wholly-owned affiliates (Chapters 4–5).[6] There is also a growing empirical literature suggesting that parents restrict the access of Southeast Asian affiliates in which the parent has relatively small foreign ownership shares to the MNC's exporting networks (Chapter 8).[7] Thus, in addition to asking whether the behaviour of MNCs differs from that of local firms, it is also important to ask if behaviour among MNCs depends on the foreign ownership share. This question is particularly important in some of the analyses of productivity and export effects of MNCs.

MNC parent behaviour has also been argued to differ depending on the home country of the parent. If the quality of MNCs' firm-specific assets or ownership advantages is somehow related to the nationality of the MNC parent, the standard theory would suggest a link between nationality and MNC behaviour. For example, one might expect MNCs from the most advanced industrial economies (e.g. Europe, Japan, North America) to have relatively sophisticated firm-specific assets related to technology or international marketing.[8] If that is the case, there may be a tendency for MNCs from these home countries to be more productive or export-oriented than others. Also, as mentioned above, there may be cultural considerations that affect the adaptability of MNCs to host country labour markets that vary by the nationality of both the parent and the host country.

Finally, it should be emphasized that the analytical principles described above and the empirical analyses to follow generally imply partial equilibrium models that examine one dimension of MNC involvement at a time. In other words, there is no general equilibrium attempt to simultaneously model the effects of MNCs on wages, productivity and exports, for example. Although this partial equilibrium approach represents an important conceptual shortcoming, it is probably the only practical way to utilize the advantages of the micro data assembled to analyse the issues at hand.

1.3 Multinational presence in manufacturing and economic policies

MNCs have played rather large roles in the manufacturing sectors of both Indonesia and Thailand, though patterns of MNC presence have differed somewhat between the two economies and it is not always easy to measure the extent of MNC presence. Indonesian and Thai economic policies have also influenced the patterns of MNC presence in important respects, as well as affected other aspects of MNC operations. This section reviews how MNC presence has evolved and how host country policies have affected MNCs in the two countries, because an understanding of these issues is important when interpreting the results of the micro analyses in the following chapters.

1.3.1 Patterns of multinational presence and data characteristics

It is far easier to trace how MNC presence has changed in Indonesia than in Thailand or in most other developing economies because Indonesia has conducted annual industrial surveys of large- and medium-sized manufacturing plants with twenty employees or more since 1975. These surveys have always required plants to report information on a number of key variables, including employment, value added, input usage, wage payments and foreign ownership shares.[9] Other variables, such as fixed capital stocks and export propensities, have been collected for shorter periods of time.[10]

The annual average of value added in manufacturing MNCs first increased 122 per cent between 1975–85 and 1986–91, and then skyrocketed another 249 per cent to reach US$8.1 billion in 1992–96 (Table 1.1).[11] Although there was a sharp drop in 1998 after the crisis

Table 1.1 Value added of manufacturing MNCs in Indonesia 1975–2001 (US$ millions, except per cent as noted)

Country, variable, industry	1975–85	1986–91	1992–96	1997–99	2000–01
Manufacturing	1,045	2,323	8,097	8,050	9,788
% of manufacturing GDP	11.31	12.23	18.92	20.46	26.94
Food, beverages, tobacco	132	235	620	786	708
Food	70	169	442	687	615
Textiles, apparel, leather, footwear	142	323	1,379	1,583	1,321
Textiles	125	262	622	829	601
Wood, furniture	42	159	375	288	233
Paper, printing	13	115	399	333	506
Chemicals, rubber, plastics	219	467	1,525	1,672	1,485
Chemicals	158	352	1,200	1,350	1,150
Non-metallic mineral products	105	94	329	276	390
Basic metals	46	249	761	338	318
Metal products, machinery	219	613	2,439	2,449	4,536
Metal products	62	177	548	403	421
General machinery	22	41	148	206	215
Electric & precision machinery	95	120	767	1,216	2,082
Electric machinery	94	118	742	1,146	2,031
Transportation machinery	40	276	977	624	1,819
Miscellaneous manufacturing	127	67	271	324	291

Note: General machinery includes a few plants in office and computing machinery, for example, 8 in 2000 and 9 in 2001, with average value added amounting to US$1.8 million in 2000–1.

Sources: BPS-Statistics (various years); International Monetary Fund (2005); Takii and Ramstetter (2004: Appendix Tables 3d, 3e).

broke (to US$5.7 billion; Takii and Ramstetter 2004; International Monetary Fund 2005), the average for 1997–99 was only slightly (1 per cent) lower than the previous period. Subsequently, there was another small increase (22 per cent) to US$9.8 billion in 2000–01. Trends in the value added of MNCs were similar to trends in overall manufacturing. Changes in MNCs' share of manufacturing GDP were thus less pronounced, increasing only slightly from 11 per cent in 1975–85 to 12 per cent in 1986–91, for example. Subsequently, the share rose to 19 per cent in 1992–96 and 20 per cent in 1997–99, and then to 27 per cent in 2000–01. Recent trends also reflect a decline in the US dollar value of manufacturing GDP after the crisis, which was related to the large currency depreciation.

Metal products and machinery has always been the largest major industry category of MNC production in Indonesia and its share of the total increased from about one-fifth in 1975–85 to 26–30 per cent in

1986–99 and then almost one-half in 2000–01 (Table 1.1). Electric and precision machinery and transportation machinery have always been the largest industries in this category and accounted for the vast majority of the growth in the industry. By 2000–1, these two industries each accounted for about one-fifth of all MNC value added, a substantial increase over previous years. MNC production was also large in chemicals, accounting for about one-sixth of the MNC total in most of the 1975–2001 period. MNC production was also substantial in food, textiles and metal products.

In the Thai case, the only official compilations of data on the activities of manufacturing MNCs refer to FDI inflows as reported in balance of payments statistics (Bank of Thailand 2005). The recipient MNC affiliate can use an increase in the stock of FDI (the stock of equity and loans remitted from the MNC parent and affiliated companies) to finance purchases of fixed assets or other (usually financial) assets, or to finance reductions in equity or loans from other sources. Thus, FDI is more an indicator of investor confidence among MNC parents and related companies than an indicator of real activity (e.g. production or employment) in the MNCs operating in Thailand.

In Thailand, FDI stocks in manufacturing were still rather small as late as 1985 – only US$0.8 billion – but they grew rapidly in the following years to reach US$4.7 billion in 1991 and US$7.3 billion in 1996 (Table 1.2). Relative to the size of Thai manufacturing, the first increase was particularly large as the ratio of FDI stocks to manufacturing GDP almost doubled, reaching 17 per cent in 1991. Slower growth of FDI and high growth of manufacturing GDP then led to a decline in this ratio, to 14 per cent in 1996. After the crisis, there was another very large boom in FDI and by 2000, FDI stocks had risen to US$14 billion or 38 per cent of manufacturing GDP. As in the Indonesian case, exchange rate depreciation led to a fall in the US dollar value of GDP after the 1997–98 crisis, and this contributed to the rise in the ratio of FDI stocks to GDP.

The only production-related indicator available for a reasonably long period of time in Thailand is an estimate of sales by large manufacturing MNCs from Ramstetter (2003a), which reveals rather different trends than the FDI stock data (Table 1.2). The US dollar value of large MNCs' sales nearly doubled between 1991 and 1996, to reach US$56 billion in the latter year, then declined sharply to US$41 billion in 1998 and rebounded to US$51 billion in 2000. The ratio of large MNC sales to manufacturing GDP was remarkably stable in 1991, 1996 and 1998, but then increased sharply in 2000. The most comprehensive estimates of MNC production come from large samples of MNC plants

Table 1.2   Manufacturing MNC activities in Thailand 1985–2000 (US$ millions, except per cent as noted)

Country, variable, industry	1985	1991	1996	1998	2000
Manufacturing, FDI stocks	780	4,690	7,300	11,329	14,410
% of manufacturing GDP	8.98	16.75	13.64	29.10	37.70
Food	57	327	544	844	1,031
Textiles	142	370	541	708	757
Chemicals	94	618	1,195	1,583	1,974
Petroleum products	106	193	–269	70	108
Non-metallic mineral products, metals	66	471	883	1,441	1,797
Electric machiney	209	1,643	2,554	3,422	4,145
General & transportation machinery	64	324	695	1,752	2,813
Manufacturing, MNCs' value added	–	–	17,241	6,900	2,568
% of manufacturing GDP	–	–	32.22	17.72	6.72
Food, beverages, tobacco	–	–	1,509	1,020	538
Food	–	–	963	514	213
Textiles, apparel, leather, footwear	–	–	1,154	511	129
Textiles	–	–	792	278	99
Wood, furniture	–	–	231	32	26
Paper, printing	–	–	771	88	37
Chemicals, rubber, plastics	–	–	2,428	829	260
Chemicals	–	–	1,203	426	121
Non-metallic mineral products	–	–	377	583	86
Basic metals	–	–	285	106	22
Metal products, machinery	–	–	10,144	3,499	1,397
Metal products	–	–	677	173	98
General machinery	–	–	951	833	212
Electric & precision machinery	–	–	3,905	1,557	899
Office & computing machinery	–	–	939	395	306
Electric machinery	–	–	2,573	1,100	556
Transportation machinery	–	–	4,611	936	188
Motor vehicles	–	–	4,517	909	170
Miscellaneous manufacturing	–	–	343	231	72
Jewellery	–	–	160	25	35
Manufacturing, MNCs' output-a	–	–	64,919	23,320	18,090
Manufacturing, large MNCs' sales	–	28,949	55,656	40,715	50,673
% of manufacturing GDP	–	103	104	105	133

Note: FDI stocks are the cumulative value of FDI inflows from 1970 forward.
Sources: Bank of Thailand (2005); National Economic and Social Development Board (various years); Ramstetter (2003a: Table 1; 2003b: Appendix Tables 2a–2c).

covered in the industrial census of 1996 data. These estimates suggest that the sales of large MNCs amounted to about 86 per cent of the gross output of all manufacturing MNCs and that the value added of manufacturing MNCs was about 32 per cent of manufacturing GDP in that year.

The FDI stock data show that electric machinery was the largest industry of MNC activity in 1996, followed distantly by chemicals, non-metallic minerals and metals, and then general and transportation machinery (Table 1.2). Electric machinery remained the largest industry in 2000, though its share fell slightly. In contrast, the share of general and transportation machinery rose markedly between 1996 and 2000, reflecting the rapid expansion of MNCs in motor vehicles (Chapters 6 and 8). However, according to the value added data from the industrial census, motor vehicles was already the largest industry in 1996, accounting for a little over one-quarter of the total. Electric and precision machinery (including office and computing machinery) was also large, accounting for just under one-quarter of the total. These two industries were followed distantly by chemicals, food, general machinery and textiles.

In order to examine the extent of MNC presence relative to the size of the local industry, it is necessary to use samples from the Indonesian industrial surveys, the Thai industrial census for 1996, and smaller samples from Thai industrial surveys for 1998 and 2000. These samples, which are identical or very similar to the samples used for the micro analyses in the following chapters, have three important characteristics. First, they exclude smaller plants with nineteen employees or less. Second, although sample coverage is not comprehensive, the samples are thought to cover large plants, and especially MNC plants, relatively well. In other words, the ratios of MNCs' value added to GDP for Indonesia in Table 1.1 and for Thailand in 1996 in Table 1.2 are probably relatively good estimates of MNC presence in the manufacturing sector overall. Likewise, MNCs' shares of the value added of sample plants are larger than shares of total manufacturing mainly because these samples exclude many local plants, especially the smaller ones (Table 1.3). Although this is not a large problem in most of the analyses in the following chapters, it does mean that MNCs' shares of sample plants overestimate actual MNC presence. Third, the coverage of the Indonesian surveys has apparently improved over time, which means that the extent of overestimation is probably larger in earlier years.[12] On the other hand, samples from the Thai industrial surveys for 1998 and 2000

Table 1.3   MNCs' shares of value added in sample plants (per cent)

Industry	Indonesia					Thailand		
	1975–85	*1986–91*	*1992–96*	*1997–99*	*2000–01*	*1996*	*1998*	*2000*
Manufacturing	27	22	28	36	36	52	59	47
Food, beverages, tobacco	24	16	19	25	21	20	37	27
Food	15	13	15	24	19	25	31	30
Textiles, apparel, leather, footwear	29	22	26	37	34	45	41	34
Textiles	30	24	20	33	27	57	45	40
Wood, furniture	18	13	15	14	11	24	13	19
Paper, printing	12	25	29	23	31	36	24	14
Chemicals, rubber, plastics	35	30	40	49	37	45	54	49
Chemicals	37	35	47	57	40	58	57	49
Non-metallic mineral products	46	21	29	34	34	24	60	30
Basic metals	30	30	33	44	31	46	37	33
Metal products, machinery	37	40	41	56	65	84	89	85
Metal products	43	42	50	53	44	60	50	56
General machinery	44	32	39	62	55	72	92	85
Electric & precision machinery	55	39	48	74	75	90	93	89
Office & computing machinery	–	–	–	–	–	100	99	99
Electric machinery	56	39	48	74	76	86	93	87
Transportation machinery	18	41	34	39	64	87	92	86
Motor vehicles	–	–	–	–	–	89	93	91
Miscellaneous manufacturing	13	5	8	14	9	52	74	61
Jewellery	–	–	–	–	–	50	44	73

Notes: samples include plants reporting positive employment and value added; for Indonesia, office and computing machinery is included in general machinery, but the office and computing machinery industry is very small in the Indonesian case.
Sources: Takii and Ramstetter (2004: Appendix Tables 3d, 3e); Ramstetter (2003b: Appendix Table 2a).

are much smaller than the 1996 census sample and the differences in coverage are so large as to make it impossible to use these data to analyse changes over time. This is why the Thai chapters in this book focus primarily on analysis of 1996 data.[13]

In both countries, MNC shares tend to be larger in electric and precision machinery than in other industries, reaching three-quarters in Indonesia in 1997–2001 and 90 per cent in Thailand in 1996 (Table 1.3). MNCs literally dominate this industry in Southeast Asia and in most countries worldwide, largely because costs related to the development of firm-specific assets are relatively large and production technologies allow for the production process to be broken up into distinct stages with different factor requirements. In Indonesia and Thailand, MNCs are primarily engaged in labour-intensive assembly operations, for example. MNC presence is also relatively large in general machinery and transportation machinery (primarily motor vehicles) in Thailand, and in chemicals, metal products, general machinery, and less frequently in transportation machinery in Indonesia.[14] On the other hand, MNC presence was always relatively small in food as well as wood and furniture in both countries. This was also true less frequently in paper and printing in both countries, as well as in non-metallic mineral products and basic metals in Thailand.[15] Here again the relative importance of costs related to the development of firm-specific assets is an important reason for the variation in the importance of MNCs across industries, but it is certainly not the only reason.

1.3.2 Economic policies and manufacturing multinationals

Economic policies are also related to the variation of foreign presence across industries and over time.[16] For example, high import tariffs and non-tariff trade barriers have kept imports of motor vehicles very low and encouraged MNCs to produce for the local market in both countries (James and Ramstetter 2005). Indeed, several of the MNCs now operating in Indonesia and Thailand set up operations years ago, when both countries encouraged import substitution with high levels of import protection and subsidies to firms in targeted industries such as motor vehicles. On the other hand, relatively low levels of import protection or exemptions on import duties for imported inputs encouraged MNCs in export-oriented processing industries such as electric and precision machinery. Moreover, a trend towards lower levels of import protection encouraged export-oriented MNCs in both countries and was an important reason why export-oriented MNCs grew rapidly in the late 1980s and early-to-mid-1990s.

The shift to export promotion was particularly abrupt and far-reaching in Indonesia during the mid-1980s. For example, in 1986, the Indonesian government relaxed a large number of import licensing restrictions, replaced a large number of non-tariff barriers with tariffs, and lowered tariffs markedly. This was one of the first major steps in what became a highly successful campaign to increase non-oil exports from only one-fifth of the total in 1985 to over three-fifths in 1993–96 and just under two-thirds in 1999–2000 (Ramstetter and Takii 2005: Table 1).[17] In 1989, further liberalization of import licences, as well as further reductions in tariffs and non-tariff barriers, followed.

Thailand began its shift away from emphasis on import substitution towards export promotion earlier in the 1970s and gradually reduced tariffs and non-tariff barriers thereafter. As a result of these changes, as well as the lack of substantial natural resources to export, non-oil exports already accounted for over two-fifths of the total in 1973 (Ramstetter 1997: 111). The share subsequently increased to three-fifths in 1980 and then four-fifths in 1990 .[18] There was also a marked reduction in tariffs in the early 1990s, although this change was far less significant than the Indonesian reduction that began a few years earlier. In addition, many MNCs were able to get exemptions on import duties for intermediate goods and some capital goods through the Thai Board of Investment (BOI).

Both countries have also tried to encourage FDI with incentives, while at the same time restricting the operations of MNCs in various respects. Restrictions on MNCs were related to nationalism in both countries. Negative sentiment towards MNCs has a particularly long tradition in Indonesia and was most conspicuous during the 1950s when several MNCs were nationalized. Negative sentiment was also evident in both countries in the early 1970s, when there was a particularly strong backlash against MNCs. This reaction was targeted mainly at Japanese MNCs, which had grown rapidly in the previous years, and involved sizeable demonstrations in Bangkok and Jakarta. Recently, there are also signs of a new wave of economic nationalism in the wake of the 1997–98 crisis, which is partly a reaction to the liberalization that followed the crisis. The Thaksin government has been quick to espouse nationalist sentiment in Thailand, at times resisting efforts to restructure the debts of Thai firms when the restructuring might benefit foreign parties. There have also been several recent cases where foreign takeovers of domestically owned firms have been blocked or delayed by various Indonesian authorities (Athukorala 2002). However, recent nationalism has yet to result in substantial new restrictions on MNCs or a reversal of trends towards more open policies.

The policy effects of nationalism are perhaps most obvious in the closing of certain industries (e.g. some agricultural activities) to FDI and restrictions on foreign ownership shares in industries where FDI was allowed. Both countries have employed such policies in the past, and

Indonesia has also imposed divestment requirements. In Indonesia, foreign ownership restrictions and divestment requirements were first relaxed for export-oriented projects in 1985–86. Foreign investors were allowed to own 100 per cent of the equity in certain projects in 1992 and the list of eligible projects was expanded in 1993. Then in 1994, divestment requirements were abolished for all but a few projects, most ownership restrictions were eliminated, and the list of industries closed to FDI was reduced as a part of a sweeping liberalization of FDI policy.[19]

Thailand also had foreign ownership restrictions, which were enshrined in its Alien Business Law of 1972, and formally limited foreign shares to 49 per cent until the promulgation of the Foreign Business Act of 1999, which removed most of these restrictions. On the other hand, the Thai BOI, which was established by the Investment Promotion Act of 1977, had wide discretion to offer various incentives, including exemptions to foreign ownership limits. Other incentives included tax reduction, exemptions to limits on the hiring of foreign workers, as well as exemptions on import duties for intermediate and some capital goods. These incentives were offered to MNCs that met criteria such as investing a large amount of capital, using sophisticated technology, creating a large number of jobs, exporting a large percentage of output, and locating plants in priority regions outside the Greater Bangkok area. Although most FDI in Thailand went through the BOI in order to obtain one or more of the aforementioned incentives, MNCs were not required to get BOI approval to invest if they did not want to apply for incentives. US MNCs in particular tended to shy away from the BOI because a bilateral treaty between the United States and Thailand made them exempt from foreign ownership requirements and a few of the other constraints facing MNCs from other countries.

In contrast, all FDI in Indonesia's non-oil manufacturing industries required the approval of the Indonesian Investment Coordinating Board (BKPM). The BKPM also offered incentives to some MNCs, including some generous fiscal incentives, but was generally less flexible than the Thai BOI, especially with respect to ownership and divestment requirements before the early 1990s.

Macroeconomic fluctuations were also related to changes in the policies affecting MNCs, especially in the Indonesian case. Following the installation of former President Soeharto's 'new order' government, Indonesia imposed very few restrictions on MNCs for a brief period in the late 1960s and early 1970s, primarily because the economy was struggling to recover from some severe macroeconomic imbalances and badly needed investment of any type.[20] However, a subsequent increase in oil revenues allowed President Soeharto to appease the nationalist sentiments and impose new restrictions on MNCs in the mid-1970s. Conversely, in the early 1980s, falling oil revenues were a major factor in the decision to promote non-oil exports with the liberalization of imports and FDI. The severe economic crisis starting in 1997 also led to further liberalization and deregulation in both Indonesia and Thailand. This included the effective suspension of foreign ownership require-ments by the Thai BOI in 1998 and the eventual elimination of most formal ownership restrictions in 1999.

The effects of these policies are readily apparent from the data. For example, MNC shares tend to be larger in Thailand than in Indonesia (Tables 1.1, 1.2, 1.3), partly because Thai policies have generally been more consistent and favourable towards inward FDI than Indonesian policies. The rapid increase in FDI in Thailand after the crisis was also related to the suspension and subsequent removal of ownership restric-tions, which made it easy for MNCs to increase equity in joint ventures, many of which ran into financial difficulties after the crisis.[21] Similar problems also affected many joint ventures in Indonesia where the earlier removal of most ownership restrictions also gave MNCs the option of increasing equity in struggling affiliates.

The effects of liberalizing foreign ownership restrictions and the economic crisis are also apparent from trends in the share of heavily-foreign MNCs (MNCs with foreign ownership shares of 90 per cent or more) in the value added of sample plants in Indonesia (Table 1.4). In overall manufacturing, the shares rose from a low of 2 per cent in 1986–91 to 5 per cent in 1992–96, and then to 13–15 per cent in subse-quent years. In Thailand, the share of wholly-foreign MNCs was already 11 per cent in 1996, which was nearly twice the corresponding share of heavily-foreign MNCs in Indonesia (5.9 per cent, Takii and Ramstetter 2004: Appendix Tables 3c, 3e). This suggests that the Thai ownership restrictions were not particularly strict in practice and/or that the effects of the 1994 liberalization were yet to be realized in Indonesia.

The relatively large importance of electric and precision machinery in Thailand is another reason why the overall Thai share is larger, because shares of heavily- or wholly-foreign MNCs tend to be relatively large in this industry in both countries (Table 1.4). The observation of high shares in this industry is also suggestive of policy effects, because the industry was targeted for early removal of ownership restrictions in Indonesia and for the promotion of export-oriented investments in Thailand. Shares were also relatively high in general machinery after 1997. Part of the reason for the observation of high shares for heavily-foreign or

Table 1.4 Heavily-foreign (Indonesia) or wholly-foreign MNCs' (Thailand) shares of value added in sample plants (per cent)

Industry	Indonesia					Thailand, 1996
	1975–85	1986–91	1992–96	1997–99	2000–01	
Manufacturing	4	2	5	13	15	11
Food, beverages, tobacco	4	1	3	8	7	1
Food	3	1	2	7	5	2
Textiles, apparel, leather, footwear	4	4	6	14	16	3
Textiles	3	3	3	11	11	5
Wood, furniture	0	1	1	5	7	1
Paper, printing	0	0	2	7	1	0
Chemicals, rubber, plastics	9	3	5	13	14	6
Chemicals	10	2	4	13	15	11
Non-metallic mineral products	0	0	0	1	4	1
Basic metals	0	4	2	8	11	1
Metal products, machinery	5	0	8	28	31	24
Metal products	3	1	3	13	11	8
General machinery	2	0	4	22	23	33
Electric & precision machinery	16	1	23	57	60	54
Office & computing machinery	–	–	–	–	–	76
Electric machinery	16	1	23	59	60	43
Transportation machinery	0	0	2	5	10	1
Motor vehicles	–	–	–	–	–	1
Miscellaneous manufacturing	3	1	3	6	3	13
Jewellery	–	–	–	–	–	16

Notes: samples include plants reporting positive employment and value added; for Indonesia, office and computing machinery is included in general machinery, but the office and computing machinery industry is very small in the Indonesian case.
Sources: Takii and Ramstetter (2004: Appendix Tables 3c, 3e); Ramstetter (2003b: Appendix Table 2a).

wholly-foreign MNCs in these machinery industries is also technical. In other words, MNCs in these industries are probably more concerned with preventing the leakage of firm-specific assets to competitors than are MNCs in other industries, which tend to use more standardized technologies and export less of their output.

1.4   Multinationals, wages, productivity and exports

Changes in MNC presence and related economic policies have important implications for the relationships studied in this book. In particular, analyses of Indonesia prior in the 1970s and most of the 1980s must take account of numerous policy distortions that became far less severe in subsequent years. Conversely, analysis of Thailand is probably less affected by policy distortions, even though several rather strict, formal restrictions remained in effect in 1996, the year on which the analyses in this book focus. Second, primarily because the Indonesian data cover a longer period, greater attention to cyclical considerations is required. The effects of the economic crisis in 1997–98 were particularly large and mandate caution when interpreting results that span the crisis years. Similar caution is also required when interpreting results from the small Thai samples for 1998 and 2000. Keeping these factors in mind the remainder of this section summarizes some of the major results of the chapters to follow.

1.4.1   Manufacturing multinationals and wages

Simple compilations in Chapter 2 reveal rather large wage differentials in Indonesia, which have tended to decline over time. In all manufacturing, blue-collar workers in foreign plants earned 180 per cent more per worker in 1975 than in local plants and this wage differential then fell rather steadily to 127 per cent in 1985 and 44 per cent in 1999. Wage differentials for white-collar workers were much larger in 1975 – 211 per cent – but declined very rapidly to 81 per cent in 1985, and then more slowly to 68 per cent in 1999. In the nine industries for which wage differentials were calculated, negative differentials were rare and positive differentials exceeding 10 per cent were common.

Similar calculations for Thailand in 1996 in Chapter 3 suggest wage differentials were smaller in Thailand – 36 per cent for all workers in a sample of 10,494 plants. Calculations from a somewhat smaller sample of 8432 manufacturing plants revealed differentials of 25 per cent for blue-collar workers and 53 per cent for white-collar workers. As in Indonesia, negative wage differentials were rare and positive differentials exceeding 10 per cent were common in these samples. Wage differentials were somewhat smaller in samples of large plants: 21 per cent for all workers, 5 per cent for blue-collar workers, and 23 per cent for white-collar workers. Negative differentials were more common and positive differentials exceeding

10 per cent were rarer in the samples of large plants, especially for blue-collar workers.

This discussion highlights how other factors such as plant size might be related to wage differentials. Correspondingly, Chapter 2 reviews calculations for all Indonesian manufacturing plants, which indicate that wage levels for both white-collar and blue-collar workers in 1996 were positively and significantly related to worker educational achievement, energy input per worker, intermediate input per worker, and plant size. However, wage differentials remained positive and statistically significant for both blue-collar and white-collar workers even after accounting for these factors.

Chapter 3 analyses similar calculations showing that wage differentials in Thailand tended to be positively related to labour productivity, export propensities and import propensities, for both blue-collar and white-collar workers in Thailand, but that the correlation with size differed depending on the type of labour: negative for blue-collar workers and positive for white-collar workers. Here again, wage differentials between MNCs and local plants remained statistically significant after accounting for these factors, as well as the effect of industry affiliation and location in Greater Bangkok on intercepts in the wage equations.

Chapter 3 also relaxes the assumption that correlations between wage levels and foreign ownership were identical in all industries by estimating wage equations at the industry level. Results are somewhat weaker, with positive and statistically significant wage differentials remaining in less than one-half the industries examined. Other results also indicate that significantly positive differentials are slightly more common at the industry level if MNCs are distinguished by country of ownership or foreign ownership share. MNCs from Europe, Japan and the United States generally paid relatively high wages. Relatively large overall wage differentials were also observed for majority- and wholly-foreign plants in some industries, as well as for white-collar wages in majority-foreign plants. However, results distinguishing labour types also suggested relatively low (blue-collar) or insignificant (white-collar) wage differentials for wholly-foreign plants and relatively large differentials for wages paid to blue-collar workers by minority-foreign plants.

Both Chapters 2 and 3 also summarize evidence suggesting that foreign MNC presence in an industry is positively and significantly correlated with the wages of local plants in that industry. In other words, there is evidence of positive wage spillovers. For Indonesia, this finding is further reinforced by Chapter 2's findings from a panel for

1975–99 that MNCs did not select high-wage plants to take over and that foreign takeovers, not takeovers in general, led to relatively large wage increases and high wages.

1.4.2 Multinationals and productivity

Perhaps the simplest and most common measure of productivity is value added per worker or average labour productivity. In the context of this project, this measure of productivity is also one of the most important because labour productivity is an important determinant of wage levels. In short, one reason MNCs may pay higher wages is because they are generally expected to have a higher labour productivity. Productivity differentials between MNCs and local plants are also expected to be largest for wholly-foreign or heavily-foreign MNCs and smallest for minority-foreign MNCs, as explained above.

The results summarized in Chapters 4 and 5 suggest that the evidence on this latter hypothesis is mixed for Indonesia and not very consistent for Thailand. Calculations of average labour productivity for all manufacturing industries in Indonesia indicate that majority-foreign MNCs generally had the highest average labour productivity, while minority-foreign MNCs had the highest level in a few cases examined and heavily-foreign MNCs had the lowest labour productivity in a number of cases. However, the Indonesian evidence is consistent with the first hypothesis, as all foreign ownership groups generally had markedly higher labour productivity than local plants in all years.

In Thai manufacturing in 1996, labour productivity was highest on average in majority-foreign MNCs, followed by minority-foreign MNCs and wholly-foreign MNCs, but productivity differentials were generally much smaller than corresponding differentials in Indonesia. Majority-foreign MNCs had the highest labour productivity in most industries, while minority-foreign MNCs had the highest labour productivity in most of the remaining industries. In Thailand there were also a few industries in which MNCs had lower labour productivity than local plants.

As with wage differentials, productivity differentials may result from other characteristics of the plants involved. Correspondingly, Chapters 4 and 5 first examine labour productivity differentials after removing the influences of factor intensities, plant size and plant vintage on those differentials. For Indonesia in 1986–2001, the results suggest that statistically significant differences were most common in chemicals and electric and precision machinery, and least common in apparel, footwear and transportation machinery. Significant differences were most common between majority-foreign MNCs and local plants. Similar calculations for Thailand in 1996 suggest a weak tendency for wholly-foreign MNCs to have relatively high productivity in the few cases significant productivity differentials were observed, but these results and those of numerous previous studies suggest that MNCs did not have significantly higher labour productivity than local plants in most of the cases examined.

One reason that differences in labour productivity were not statistically significant could be the use of unduly restrictive assumptions about technology. Thus, Chapters 4 and 5 also made comparisons using general assumptions about technology for Indonesia in 1995 and Thailand in 1996, respectively.

Assuming the relationship between technology and foreign ownership (and other control variables) is the same in all industries (i.e. using results from samples of all manufacturing plants combined), results for Indonesia suggest that foreign-owned plants had higher productivity levels than locally-owned plants, and wholly-foreign plants tended to have higher productivity levels than other foreign-owned plants if plant vintage is accounted for. Relatively new foreign-owned plants tended to have relatively low productivity levels. However, if the relationship between productivity and foreign ownership is allowed to vary across industries (i.e. results from individual industry samples are used), productivity differentials between all MNCs and local plants are usually positive, though there is wide variation across industries and differences among MNC ownership groups are not statistically significant.

All results for Thailand assume the relationship between productivity and foreign ownership varies across industries (an assumption supported by large variation in results across industries), focusing on tests of whether production functions differ between MNCs and local plants at the industry level. Although this approach generates a few more statistically significant differences between MNCs and local plants than previous studies using more restrictive assumptions (e.g. those comparing labour productivity), results are consistent in suggesting that differences in technology in MNCs and local plants are statistically insignificant in most of the cases examined.

Chapter 6 provides a detailed industry-level study of automobile plants in Thailand in 1996 and Indonesia in 1990–99. For Thailand, simple comparisons suggested relatively high labour productivity in MNCs but that after differences in capital intensity and other control variables are accounted for, differences between MNCs and local plants become statistically insignificant. Comparisons of total factor productivity (TFP) levels in foreign and local plants also reveal no evidence that foreign plants have relatively high TFP in Thailand after accounting for the effects of other control variables. At a more disaggregate level, MNCs in Thailand tended to have relatively low capital productivity in the motor vehicle bodies and trailers and the motor vehicle parts and accessories industries, while MNCs in the motor vehicle assembly industry had relatively high labour productivity, capital productivity and TFP.

Results for Indonesia suggest that labour productivity was relatively high in MNCs but there were no statistically significant differences in TFP levels between MNCs and local plants. In Indonesia, both foreign and local plants exhibited increasing returns to scale and capital utilization was extremely inefficient in MNCs. The largest portion of TFP growth in Indonesia is explained by changes in scale and capacity utilization, while the technological change effect was negligible both for foreign and local plants. The chapter thus concludes that the small size of the Indonesian and Thai automobile markets prevented both MNCs and local plants from exploiting scale economies.

Chapter 4 examines productivity spillovers in Indonesia, using panel data for 1990–95.[22] Similar to other results, these results suggest the existence of positive productivity spillovers. However, these results differ from others by suggesting that the magnitude of spillovers tended to be smaller in industries where the share of majority-foreign plants was relatively large or in industries where technological gaps between foreign- and locally-owned plants were relatively large. Chapter 5 also indicates that productivity spillovers were positive for Thailand in 1996, and examines the possibility that the existence of extremely rapid spillovers might be one reason for the lack of significant productivity differentials in Thailand.

1.4.3   Multinationals and exports

Chapters 7 and 8 first emphasize that MNCs in Indonesia and Thailand (and other Southeast Asian economies) have made perhaps their largest direct contributions to these host economies in terms of exports. This is reflected in relatively high average export propensities among MNCs in Indonesian manufacturing and a much higher frequency of high export propensities in Thai manufacturing. In Indonesia, the average export propensity of MNCs in manufacturing rose from 28 per cent in the early 1990s to 40 per cent in the mid-1990s, and then fell back to 26 per cent in the crisis period before recovering to 36 per cent in 2000. These export propensities were always more than three times larger than corresponding levels in local plants. Export propensities were particularly high among MNCs in textiles, apparel, footwear and leather as well as wood and furniture and then other manufacturing. In Thailand, the percentage of local plants that exported half or more of their output was only 15 per cent for all manufacturing in 1996, which was much lower than for MNCs. Moreover, among MNCs, this percentage was relatively low for minority-foreign plants – 41 per cent – and much higher for majority- or wholly-foreign plants – 70 per cent and 81 per cent respectively. Similar patterns were observed in most industries.

Chapter 7 then examines the determinants of export propensities in a panel of all manufacturing for 1990–99, focusing on the role of foreign ownership and the import of intermediate products as avenues into exporting networks. After controlling for the effects of related plant characteristics such as previous exporting experience, electric power consumption, skill intensity, size, labour productivity, and the effect of industry affiliation on intercepts, the findings suggest that MNCs had significantly higher export propensities than local plants, but that imports of intermediate products have no impact on export propensities. They find no difference between export propensities in majority- or wholly-foreign plants and minority-foreign plants. In contrast, results for Thailand in Chapter 8 (1996) emphasize that there is positive correlation at the industry level between foreign ownership shares and the probability that plants will export or have relatively high export propensities, after controlling for differences in factor intensity, size, vintage, and BOI-promotion.

1.5 Conclusion

The results summarized in this book first suggest that there are important differences in wages, productivity and trade propensities between MNCs and local plants. Wage and productivity differentials are largest and most pervasive in Indonesia and these differentials remained large and statistically significant after removing the effects of relevant control variables. The evidence also suggests that MNCs do not appear to target high wage industries or plants for takeovers in Indonesia, and foreign takeovers, not takeovers in general, increase wages in target plants. Wage differentials were smaller in Thailand, though they were usually positive and statistically significant. However, productivity differentials were usually statistically insignificant in Thailand after accounting for the effects of relevant control variables. There is also evidence of both wage and productivity spillovers to local plants in both Indonesia and Thailand. Finally, there was strong evidence that MNCs had significantly higher export propensities for both countries. In short, MNCs are an important avenue through which both Indonesia and Thailand access export markets.

These findings suggest that MNCs have imparted important positive effects on economic performance in these two developing economies. Moreover, these positive effects have generated important benefits for the Indonesian and Thai economies in the form of higher wages, higher productivity, and exposure to export markets. Of course, these are not the only aspects of foreign MNC involvement that need to be studied. However, the relationships studied in this book are important and the evidence generated provides little or no support for the idea that MNCs exploit their workers in these important developing economies. On the contrary, the evidence strongly suggests that Indonesian and Thai workers, as well as their host economies, would have been substantially worse off in important respects without the presence of the MNCs.

Notes

1. In this book, the term MNC refers to foreign-owned MNCs as opposed to local firms that are also MNC parents. Note that there were relatively few locally-owned MNC parents in Indonesia and Thailand during the period under study.
2. See Barro and Sala-i-Martin (1995: 277–9); Borensztein, De Gregario and Lee (1998) and Carkovic and Levine (2005).
3. Articles from this project include Ito (2004a, 2004b), Lipsey and Sjöholm (2002, 2004a, 2004b), Matsuoka (2001a, 2001b, 2001c), Ramstetter (2002a, 2002b, 2003b, 2004), Takii (2004, 2005), Takii and Ramstetter (2000, 2003, 2004, 2005) and Sjöholm and Takii (2003).
4. Location advantages are the final determinant in Dunning's OLI (ownership, location, internalisation) framework.
5. It is important to note that the possession of firm-specific assets means that MNCs have at least some market power and therefore do not operate in perfectly competitive markets. Correspondingly, one cannot rigorously prove that the *Stolper-Samuelson Theorem* holds in markets where MNCs operate. However, although not perfectly competitive, many of these markets have highly competitive structures (either monopolistic competition or competitive oligopoly) and it is logical to expect a similar mechanism to be relevant in many cases.
6. For example, Moran (2001) suggests that closely controlled MNC affiliates will be more closely integrated with the parent and its network and thus be in a better position to access information about advanced technologies, marketing networks and other intangible assets. See Chao and Yu (1996); Caves (1996: chs 3, 7, 9); Dunning (1993: chs 7–9, 11) for similar arguments.
7. Similar evidence is also available for Indonesia (Ramstetter 1999b; Ramstetter and Takii 2005) and Vietnam (Phan and Ramstetter 2004).

8. This is implied by Dunning's (1988: ch. 5) investment development cycle that relates a country's net FDI position to the level of development. Kojima's (1978, 1990) assertion that Japanese MNCs were more trade-oriented than US or European MNCs in the 1970s and 1980s was perhaps the most famous specific argument regarding nationality-related differences, but it is not well-grounded in standard theories of the MNC and the empirical evidence suggests this assertion was incorrect in most cases examined (Hill and Johns 1985; Naya and Ramstetter 1992; Ramstetter 1994, 1999a, 2004).

9. Compilations of the industrial survey data for MNCs are not published by the Indonesian authorities, however. The most comprehensive compilations of these data that we know of come from appendices to some of the working papers underlying Chapter 4 in this volume and related research (Takii and Ramstetter 2000, 2003, 2004; Ramstetter and Takii 2005).

10. Indonesia does not compile more commonly cited data on FDI inflows in manufacturing using standard balance of payments' definitions. It is possible to obtain some data on realized FDI in manufacturing from the Investment Coordinating Board (BKPM; Ramstetter 2000: 36–8), but these data do not account for FDI withdrawals and exclude investment in the oil and finance sectors.

11. Figures are reported in current US dollars to facilitate comparison with Thai figures below and to remove the effects of exchange rate fluctuations.

12. For example, the ratio of value added in all sample plants to manufacturing GDP rose from 41 per cent in 1975–85 to 55 per cent in 1986–91, 68 per cent in 1992–96, 62 per cent in 1997–99 and 75 per cent in 2000–01 (Tables 1.1, 1.3).

13. The ratio of value added in all sample plants to manufacturing GDP was 62 per cent for the 1996 sample but only 30 per cent in 1998 and 16 per cent in 2000 (Tables 1.2, 1.3).

14. These are industries where MNC shares are 1.3 times the manufacturing average or more.

15. These are industries where MNC shares are 0.7 times the manufacturing average or less.

16. The discussion in this section draws heavily on Hill (1988: 29–33, 134–54) and Pangestu (1996, 2002) for Indonesia and Board of Investment (various years), Sibunruang and Tambunlertchai (1986) and Tangkitvanich et al. (2004) for Thailand. See these sources for further details.

17. These shares refer to a broad definition of non-oil manufactures designed to be consistent with definitions used in the industrial statistics described above.

18. These shares also refer to the broad definition of non-oil manufactures.

19. This liberalization also included the streamlining of investment procedures, reduction of minimum investment requirements, and the elimination of reinvestment requirements.

20. These imbalances were far more severe than those that preceded or followed the 1997–98 crisis. For example, consumer price inflation exceeded 100 per cent for every year from 1962 to 1968 and peaked at over 1000 per cent in 1966; in contrast it never exceeded 12 per cent in 1982–97 or 2000–04, and peaked at 58 per cent in 1998 (International Monetary Fund 2005).

21. In many cases, joint ventures and the local partners involved in the joint ventures ran into financial difficulties simultaneously. In extreme cases,

MNC parents faced a choice between increasing equity to save the joint venture or see it go bankrupt.
22. The use of panel data is another way of reducing the chance that results will reflect a foreign MNC preference for investing in high-productivity industries.

References

Athukorala, Prema-chandra (2002) 'Survey of Recent Developments', *Bulletin of Indonesian Economic Studies*, 38: 141–62.

Bank of Thailand (2005) Data from the 'Economic Data' section of the Bank of Thailand website, downloaded in May 2005. Bangkok: Bank of Thailand (http://www.bot.or.th/bothomepage/databank/EconData/EconData _e.htm).

Barro, Robert J. and Xavier Sala-i-Martin (1995) *Economic Growth*, New York: McGraw-Hill.

Bernard, Andrew B. and Fredrik Sjöholm (2003) 'Foreign Owners and Plant Survival', NBER Working Paper No. 10039.

Bhagwati, Jagdish (2004) *In Defense of Globalization*, New York: Oxford University Press.

Board of Investment (various years) *A Guide to Investing in Thailand*, January 1990, March 1991 and September 1993 issues, Bangkok: Board of Investment.

Borensztein, Eduardo, Jose De Gregario and Jong-Wha Lee (1998) 'How Does Foreign Direct Investment Affect Growth?' *Journal of International Economics*, 45: 115–72.

BPS-Statistics (various years) Data on GDP by expenditure and industry provided on diskette and downloaded from the BPS website (www.bps.go.id).

Brown, Andrew (2001) 'After the Kader Fire: Labour Organising for Health and Safety Standards in Thailand', in Jane Hutchison and Andrew Brown, eds, *Organizing Labour in Globalizing Asia*, London: Routledge, pp. 127–46.

Budd, John W., Josef Konings and Matthew J. Slaughter (2005) 'International Rent Sharing in Multinational Firms', *Review of Economics and Statistics*, 87, 1: 73–84.

Carkovic, Maria and Ross Levine (2005) 'Does Foreign Direct Investment Accelerate Growth?' in Theodore H. Moran, Edward M. Graham and Magnus Blomström, eds, *Does Foreign Direct Investment Help Promote Economic Development?*, Washington, DC: Institute for International Economics, pp. 195–220.

Casson, Mark (1987) *The Firm and the Market: Studies on the Multinational and the Scope of the Firm*, Cambridge, MA: MIT Press.

Caves, Richard E. (1996) *Multinational Enterprise and Economic Analysis*, second edition, Cambridge: Cambridge University Press.

Chao, C.-C. and Eden Yu (1996) 'Are Wholly Foreign-owned Enterprises Better than Joint Ventures?' *Journal of International Economics*, 40, 1/2: 225–37.

Dobson, Wendy and Chia Siow Yue, eds (1997) *Multinationals and East Asian Integration*, Toronto: International Development Research Centre and Singapore: Institute of Southeast Asian Studies.

Dunning, John H. (1988) *Multinationals, Technology and Competitiveness*, London: Allen & Unwin.

Dunning, John H. (1993) *Multinational Enterprises and the Global Economy*, Workingham, UK: Addison-Wesley Publishing Co.

Fabri, Francesca, Jonathan E. Haskel and Matthew J. Slaughter (2003) 'Does Nationality of Ownership Matter for Labor Demands?', *Journal of the European Economic Association*, Papers and Proceedings, Vol. 1: 698–707.

Hill, Hal (1988) *Foreign Investment and Industrialization in Indonesia*, Singapore: Oxford University Press.

Hill, Hal and Brian Johns (1985) 'The Role of Foreign Investment in Developing East Asian Countries', *Weltwirtschaftliches Archiv*, 121: 355–81.

International Monetary Fund (2005) *International Financial Statistics*, January CD-ROM, Washington, DC: International Monetary Fund.

Ito, Keiko (2004a) 'Foreign Ownership and Plant Productivity in the Thai Automobile Industry in 1996 and 1998: a Conditional Quantile Analysis', *Journal of Asian Economics*, 15: 321–53.

Ito, Keiko (2004b) 'Foreign Ownership and Productivity in the Indonesian Automobile Industry: Evidence from Establishment Data for 1990–1999', in Takatoshi Ito and Andrew K. Rose, eds, *Growth and Productivity in East Asia*, Chicago: University of Chicago Press, pp. 229–70.

James, William E. and Eric D. Ramstetter (2005) 'Trade, Foreign Firms, and Economic Policy in Indonesian and Thai Manufacturing', Working Paper 2005–01, Kitakyushu: International Centre for the Study of East Asian Development.

Koike, Kazuo and Takenori Inoki, eds (1990) *Skill Formation in Japan and Southeast Asia*, Tokyo: University of Tokyo Press.

Kojima, Kiyoshi (1978) *Direct Foreign Investment: a Japanese Model of Multinational Business Operations*, London: Croom Helm; New York: Praeger; Tokyo: Tuttle.

Kojima, Kiyoshi (1990) *Japanese Direct Investment Abroad*, Mitaka, Tokyo: International Christian University, Social Science Research Institute, Monograph Series 1.

Lipsey, Robert E. and Fredrik Sjöholm (2002) 'Foreign Firms and Indonesian Manufacturing Wages: an Analysis with Panel Data', NBER Working Paper 9417, December.

Lipsey, Robert E. and Fredrik Sjöholm (2004a) 'Foreign Direct Investment, Education, and Wages in Indonesian Manufacturing', *Journal of Development Economics*, 73: 415–22.

Lipsey, Robert E., and Fredrik Sjöholm (2004b) 'FDI and Wage Spillovers in Indonesian Manufacturing', *Review of World Economics*, 40: 321–32.

Markusen, James R. (1991) 'The Theory of the Multinational Enterprise: a Common Analytical Framework', in Eric D. Ramstetter, ed., *Direct Foreign Investment in Asia's Developing Economies and Structural Change in the Asia-Pacific Region*, Boulder, CO: Westview Press, pp. 11–32.

Matsuoka, Atsuko (2001a) 'Wages, Foreign Multinationals, and Local Plants in Thai Manufacturing', Working Paper 2001–15, Kitakyushu: International Centre for the Study of East Asian Development.

Matsuoka, Atsuko (2001b) 'Wage Differentials among Local Plants and Foreign Multinationals by Foreign Ownership Share and Nationality in Thai Manufacturing', Working Paper 2001–25, Kitakyushu: International Centre for the Study of East Asian Development.

Matsuoka, Atsuko (2001c) 'Wage Differentials between Local Plants and Foreign Multinationals in Thai Manufacturing: Industry-level Analysis', Working Paper 2001–26, Kitakyushu: International Centre for the Study of East Asian Development.

Moran, Theodore (2001) *Parental Supervision: the New Paradigm for Foreign Direct Investment and Development*, Washington, DC: Institute for International Economics.

Moran, Theodore, Edward M. Graham and Magnus Blomström (2005) *Does Foreign Direct Investment Promote Development?*, Washington, DC: Institute for International Economics.

National Economic and Social Development Board (various years) *National Income of Thailand*, 1997–2003 issues, Bangkok: National Economic and Social Development Board (downloaded from www.nesdb.go.th).

Naya, Seiji and Eric D. Ramstetter (1992) 'United States Direct Foreign Investment in Asia's Developing Economies', in United Nations, Economic and Social Commission for Asia and the Pacific (ESCAP), ed., *Foreign Investment and Industrial Comparative Advantage in East Asia and the Pacific*, Bangkok: ESCAP (document no. E/ESCAP/1015), pp. 51–111.

Pangestu, Mari (1996) *Economic Reform, Deregulation and Privatization: the Indonesian Experience*, Jakarta: Centre for Strategic and International Studies.

Pangestu, Mari (2002) 'Foreign Investment Policy: Evolution and Characteristics', in Farrukh Iqbal and William E. James, eds, *Deregulation and Development in Indonesia*, Westport, CT: Praeger, pp. 45–60.

Phan, Minh Ngoc and Eric D. Ramstetter (2004) 'Foreign Ownership Shares and Exports of Multinational Firms in Vietnamese Manufacturing', Working Paper 2004–32, Kitakyushu: International Centre for the Study of East Asian Development.

Ramstetter, Eric D. (1994) 'Comparisons of Japanese Multinationals and Other Firms in Thailand's Non-oil Manufacturing Industries', *ASEAN Economic Bulletin*, 11: 36–58.

Ramstetter, Eric D. (1997) 'International Trade, Multinational Firms, and Regional Integration in Thailand', in Wendy Dobson and Chia Siow Yue, eds, *Multinationals and East Asian Integration*, Toronto: International Development Research Centre and Singapore: Institute of Southeast Asian Studies, pp. 107–30.

Ramstetter, Eric D. (1999a) 'Comparisons of Foreign Multinationals and Local Firms in Asian Manufacturing Over Time', *Asian Economic Journal*, 13: 163–203.

Ramstetter, Eric D. (1999b) 'Trade Propensities and Foreign Ownership Shares in Indonesian Manufacturing in the Early 1990s', *Bulletin of Indonesian Economic Studies*, 35: 43–66.

Ramstetter, Eric D. (2000) 'Survey of Recent Developments', *Bulletin of Indonesian Economic Studies*, 36: 3–45.

Ramstetter, Eric D. (2002a) 'Does Technology Differ in Local Plants and Foreign Multinationals in Thai Manufacturing? Evidence from Translog Production Functions for 1996 and 1998', Working Paper 2002–04, Kitakyushu: International Centre for the Study of East Asian Development.

Ramstetter, Eric D. (2002b) 'Trade Propensities and Foreign Ownership Shares in Thai Manufacturing, 1996', Working Paper 2002–03, Kitakyushu: International Centre for the Study of East Asian Development.

Ramstetter, Eric D. (2003a) 'Foreign Multinationals in Thailand After the Crisis: the Challenge of Measuring and Interpreting Recent Trends', in Mitsuru Toida and Jinichi Uemura, eds, *Ajia Kogyoken no Keizai Tenbo 2003 [Projections for Asian Industrializing Region 2003]*, Tokyo: Institute of Developing Economies, pp. 83–170.

Ramstetter, Eric D. (2003b) 'Labor Productivity, Wages, Nationality and Foreign Ownership Shares in Thai Manufacturing, 1996–2000', Working Paper 2003–15, Kitakyushu: International Centre for the Study of East Asian Development.

Ramstetter, Eric D. (2004) 'Labor Productivity, Wages, Nationality and Foreign Ownership Shares in Thai Manufacturing, 1996–2000', *Journal of Asian Economies*, 14: 861–84.

Ramstetter, Eric D. and Sadayuki Takii (2005) 'Exporting and Foreign Ownership in Indonesian Manufacturing 1990–2000', Working Paper 2005–15, Kitakyushu: International Centre for the Study of East Asian Development.

Rugman, Alan M. (1980) 'Internalization as a General Theory of Foreign Direct Investment: a Re-appraisal of the Literature', *Weltwirtschaftliches Archiv*, 116: 365–79.

Rugman, Alan M. (1985) 'Internalization is Still a General Theory of Foreign Direct Investment', *Weltwirtschaftliches Archiv*, 121: 570–5.

Sibunruang, Atchaka and Somsak Tambunlertchai (1986) 'Foreign Direct Investment in Thailand: a Background Paper', paper presented at 'A Seminar on the Role of Transnational Corporations in Thailand', 29–30 August, Pattaya, Thailand.

Sjöholm, Fredrik and Sadayuki Takii (2003) 'Foreign Networks and Exports: Results from Indonesian Panel Data', Working Paper 2003–33, Kitakyushu: International Centre for the Study of East Asian Development.

Stiglitz, Joseph (2003) *Globalization and Its Discontents*, New York: W. W. Norton & Co.

Takii, Sadayuki (2004) 'Productivity Differentials between Local and Foreign Plants in Indonesian Manufacturing, 1995', *World Development*, 32: 1957–69.

Takii, Sadayuki, (2005) 'Indonesia', *East Asian Economic Perspectives [Recent Trends and Prospects for Major Asian Economies]*, 16, 1: 101–18.

Takii Sadayuki and Eric D. Ramstetter (2000) 'Foreign Multinationals in Indonesian Manufacturing 1985–1998: Shares and Relative Labor Productivity', Working Paper 2000–18. Kitakyushu: International Centre for the Study of East Asian Development.

Takii Sadayuki and Eric D. Ramstetter (2003) 'Employment, Production, Labor Productivity, and Foreign Multinationals in Indonesian Manufacturing, 1975–2000', Working Paper 2003–25, Kitakyushu: International Centre for the Study of East Asian Development.

Takii Sadayuki and Eric D. Ramstetter (2004) 'Multinational Presence and Labor Productivity Differentials in Indonesian Manufacturing, 1975–2001', Working Paper 2004–15, Kitakyushu: International Centre for the Study of East Asian Development.

Takii, Sadayuki and Eric D. Ramstetter (2005) 'Multinational Presence and Labor Productivity Differentials in Indonesian Manufacturing, 1975–2001', *Bulletin of Indonesian Economic Studies*, 41: 181–202.

Tangkitvanich, Somkiat, Deunden Nikomborirak and Busaba Krairksh (2004) 'Thailand', in Douglas H. Brooks and Hal Hill, eds, *Managing FDI in a Globalizing Economy*, Basingstoke: Palgrave Macmillan, pp. 239–80.

United Nations Conference on Trade and Development (1994) *World Investment Report 1994: Transnational Corporation, Employment and the Workforce*, Geneva: United Nations Conference on Trade and Development.

World Bank (1993) *The East Asian Miracle: Economic Growth and Public Policy*, New York: Oxford University Press.

Yamashita, Shoichi, ed. (1991) *Transfer of Japanese Technology and Management to the ASEAN Countries*, Tokyo: University of Tokyo Press.

Part II

Wage Differentials and Spillovers

2
Foreign MNCs and Wages in Indonesia

Robert E. Lipsey and Fredrik Sjöholm

2.1 Introduction

Most studies of the impact of inward foreign direct investment (FDI) by foreign-owned multinational corporations (MNCs) focus on its role in bringing new capital and, even more, superior technology and access to foreign markets to the host country. An issue that has been studied much less, although it is prominent in popular discussion, is the impact on host country labour markets.

The addition of capital to an economy, whether from direct investment or in other forms, would raise the marginal productivity of labour and, on that account, raise average wages. Since inward investment is usually small relative to a host country's capital formation, the effect is difficult to detect. Inward direct investment not only raises the host country's capital stock, but may change the production function, raising the productivity of the existing capital stock. Its impact, related to the technology it brings, might be stronger in the industries and regions where the FDI is concentrated, or stronger in the foreign-owned firms themselves than in locally-owned firms, or might be concentrated on particular types of labour if labour markets are not very competitive. It is these aspects of labour markets that we have examined in this chapter. These impacts are of interest in themselves, because of their relation to host country welfare through the level of wages and the distribution of host country income. They are of interest also because they reflect the productivity effects of FDI, drawing on different types of data from those used for most productivity studies.

We have divided these issues into several different questions. The first is whether foreign-owned establishments in Indonesia pay higher wages than domestically-owned ones. If they do, are the higher wages explained by the industry or geographical location of the foreign-owned firms, or are they higher within their industries and regions? If they are higher within their industries and locations, are they higher because the foreign-owned establishments hire more educated workers, or do the foreign establishments pay a higher price for labour, in the sense that they pay higher wages for workers of given education levels? Does the technology of the foreign firms, if it enables them to pay higher wages, affect only their operations, or do the higher wages, and possibly the technology too, spread to domestically-owned establishments?

2.2   The level of wages

It has long been recognized that inward FDI has the potential to bring economic benefits to the host economy in the forms of capital, new technology, organizational and management skills, and access to foreign markets. Such considerations seem to have been shaping Indonesian policies towards FDI: a generally sceptical view of foreign firms has given way to more liberal attitudes where domestic capacity for industrial expansion and export is lacking (Winters 1996). An additional benefit of inflows of FDI, but which has been lacking in the Indonesian policy debate, is that foreign-owned firms and plants may pay higher wages than domestically-owned ones. There are a few possible explanations as to why foreign firms would choose to pay higher wages than domestic ones (Lipsey and Sjöholm 2004a). It could be the case that foreign firms with little knowledge of the local labour market have to pay a wage premium to attract suitable workers. It could also be the case that foreign firms pay higher wages to try to prevent technology leakages to domestic competitors by minimizing labour turnover. Hill (1988: 121–3) reports that turnover in Indonesia is relatively high in domestically-owned firms and relatively low in foreign-owned firms, a fact that supports the turnover reduction motivation. Other possible explanations of high wages in foreign-owned firms include goodwill reasons and the need to satisfy critical opinions in the host or home countries. However, it has also been suggested that FDI changes the bargaining positions between employers and employees, in a way that lowers wages in foreign-owned firms. The reason is that foreign owners can credibly threaten to move the operation to another country if the wages are too high (Huizinga 1990).

There is substantial empirical evidence in many countries of relatively high wages in foreign-owned firms. That is true not only in developing countries, but also in high-income countries, such as the United States and the United Kingdom (Lipsey 2004). Part of the gap in average wages can be explained by industry composition. Foreign multinationals tend to operate in relatively high-wage industry sectors. However, the gap exists within industries as well; in most industries, in almost all countries, foreign-owned firms or establishments pay higher wages than domestically-owned ones.

The apparent existence of wage gaps between foreign-owned and domestically-owned establishments in a country raises two related questions about foreign MNCs and wages. One is about the operation of labour markets in a host country and one is about host country policy towards inward investment. The labour market question is whether foreign-owned operations face a higher price of labour, in the sense that they pay more for labour of a given quality, at least as measured by education and broad skill categories. The policy question is whether the wage level of an industry, a region, or a whole country will be raised if the host country reduces the barriers to foreign firms or actively encourages them. Such an increase in wages could result from foreign firms paying a higher price for labour than domestic firms, as described above, but there could be impacts on wages even if foreign and domestic firms of similar characteristics paid the same price for labour within any industry or region. The inflow of foreign firms might increase wages simply by raising the demand for labour. In addition, foreign firms might introduce new high-wage industries to a country or expand a country's high-wage, high-skill, sector. Foreign firms might, by introducing new or more advanced technology, cause the upgrading of average skill levels within industries. Foreign firms might shift the composition of establishment sizes in the industries in which they operate towards larger-scale, higher-wage operations.

In this chapter, we try to shed light on both of these questions as they relate to the Indonesian manufacturing sector. We examine wages in the Indonesian manufacturing sector on the BPS plant level data set (BPS-Statistics, various years), which includes all plants with at least twenty employees. The wage ratios between foreign-owned and private, domestically-owned plants are shown in Table 2.1. In 1975, wages were about three times as high in foreign-owned plants than in private domestic plants. The wage differences have gradually decreased over time and by 1999 were about 44 per cent for blue-collar workers and 68 per cent for white-collar workers. The finding that wages in foreign establishments were relatively high agrees with previous studies by Hill (1990) and Manning (1998: ch. 6).[1] The foreign wage premium in Indonesia seems substantially higher than the difference reported for most other countries: the wage differentials between domestically- and foreign-owned firms ranges from about 10 per cent in the US (Lipsey 1994), to about 70 per cent in Morocco (Haddad and Harrison 1993), and the bulk of studies find a wage difference of about 15–20 per cent.[2] In addition,

Table 2.1 Ratios of average wages in foreign-owned and private, domestically-owned plants between 1975 and 1999 at a 2-digit level of ISIC

Sector	1975		1985		1990		1999	
	Blue-collar	*White-collar*	*Blue-collar*	*White-collar*	*Blue-collar*	*White-collar*	*Blue-collar*	*White-collar*
Total Manufacturing	2.80	3.11	2.27	1.81	1.67	1.70	1.44	1.68
31 = Food, beverages, tobacco	4.10	4.64	3.55	1.98	1.94	1.70	1.70	2.11
32 = Textiles, apparel, leather, footwear	2.21	3.15	1.46	1.55	1.13	1.28	1.31	1.69
33 = Wood products, furniture	1.24	1.24	1.18	1.27	1.23	1.53	1.12	1.49
34 = Paper products, printing & publishing	2.56	4.44	1.74	2.42	1.80	1.18	1.79	1.22
35 = Chemicals, rubber, plastics	3.98	2.81	2.98	1.96	1.97	2.24	1.79	1.41
36 = Non-metallic mineral products	4.69	4.75	2.66	2.02	2.63	2.06	2.19	1.71
37 = Basic metals	0.86	1.30	1.45	0.69	1.31	1.28	1.04	0.80
38 = Metal products, machinery	1.58	1.48	1.85	1.73	1.49	1.54	1.29	1.96
39 = Miscellaneous manufacturing	0.76	1.00	1.61	2.28	1.45	2.16	1.16	2.08

Note: Average wages for domestic-private and foreign plants have been calculated at a 3-digit level of ISIC and aggregated up to a 2-digit level of ISIC using shares of total blue-collar and white-collar employees as weights.
Source: Lipsey and Sjöholm (2002: Table 2).

other types of labour compensation in Indonesia, such as bonuses, gifts, social security, insurance and pensions, are typically higher in foreign firms. If all such forms of labour compensation are included, foreign plants pay about 60 per cent higher total labour compensation than private domestically-owned plants (not shown).[3]

Some of the explanation for the higher wages in foreign plants shown in Table 2.1 is evident in Tables 2.2 and 2.3, which give the distributions of blue-collar and white-collar employees by educational attainment in 1996.[4] Among blue-collar employees, over 5 per cent of those in private and government domestic plants, but only 2 per cent in foreign-owned plants, had less than a primary education. More than 30 per cent of the workers in domestically-owned plants, but only 17 per cent in foreign-owned plants, had completed only primary education. At the other end of the distribution, about one-third of the employees in domestic plants, but more than half the employees of foreign-owned firms, had completed high school, and only between 1 and 2.5 per cent of employees in domestically-owned plants, but 3 per cent in foreign-owned plants, had completed university education.

The difference in education between workers in foreign-owned and those in domestically-owned plants, among white-collar employees, is mainly in the elementary school and university levels. Domestically-owned plants had a high proportion of workers with only an elementary education – 14 per cent for private plants and 23 per cent for government plants – but that was the case for only 10 per cent in foreign-owned plants. Only 13 per cent of workers in private plants and 11 per cent in government plants had completed university education, as compared to 19 per cent in foreign-owned plants.

Thus, for both blue-collar and white-collar workers, the labour force in foreign-owned plants was tilted towards workers with a higher level of education than that in domestically-owned plants. That difference in labour quality explains some of the higher level of wages in the foreign-owned plants.

Foreign-owned and domestically-owned plants differ also in some other characteristics, as described in Table 2.4. Foreign-owned plants used more energy per worker and more of other current inputs per worker, by about the same margin. They were also much larger in terms of average employment: almost five times as large, on average, as domestically-owned plants. Finally, foreign plants have the highest proportion of female workers and government-owned plants the lowest. If there is wage discrimination against female employees, we would expect this to have a negative effect on overall relative wages in foreign plants.

Table 2.2 Educational level of blue-collar workers in 1996 at a 2-digit level of ISIC (per cent of total employees)

ISIC	Private-domestic establishments				Government-domestic establishments				Foreign establishments			
	Primary	*Junior high school*	*Senior high school*	*University*	*Primary*	*Junior high school*	*Senior high school*	*University*	*Primary*	*Junior high school*	*Senior high school*	*University*
Total	31.7	28.7	32.2	1.2	30.7	25.9	35.6	2.5	16.6	25.4	53.0	3.0
31	43.9	22.7	17.9	1.0	39.6	15.6	32.2	1.5	22.3	23.0	48.9	2.8
32	30.7	34.1	31.7	0.7	25.6	37.0	34.8	1.6	16.9	35.5	45.8	1.4
33	28.1	29.2	36.4	0.8	31.7	25.9	34.9	0.6	20.8	25.0	50.0	1.0
34	20.0	27.6	47.2	2.8	22.8	14.6	57.3	5.1	7.1	14.8	67.2	10.4
35	30.8	30.1	31.7	1.3	35.9	24.6	25.0	2.9	14.4	21.0	55.9	4.0
36	43.9	19.6	22.8	1.4	58.7	13.8	22.2	1.9	20.9	23.6	49.4	1.9
37	14.6	27.8	53.4	3.3	14.7	22.0	57.8	3.6	13.4	23.5	59.3	3.8
38	19.6	26.8	49.6	2.2	13.4	26.6	50.0	8.1	4.3	13.0	75.3	7.3
39	35.3	35.2	24.6	0.7	36.1	24.1	38.6	1.2	17.6	31.7	47.6	0.5

Note: Sector names are found in Table 2.1. The groups do not add up to 100 per cent since some employees have not finished primary school. Educational level for different ownership groups have been calculated at a 3-digit level of ISIC and aggregated up to a 2-digit level of ISIC using shares of total blue-collar employees as weights.

Source: Lipsey and Sjöholm (2001: Table 3).

Table 2.3   Educational level of white-collar workers in 1996 at a 2-digit level of ISIC (per cent of total employees)

ISIC	Private-domestic establishments				Government-domestic establishments				Foreign establishments			
	Primary	Junior high school	Senior high school	University	Primary	Junior high school	Senior high school	University	Primary	Junior high school	Senior high school	University
Total	13.7	16.5	53.4	13.3	22.6	17.4	42.1	10.9	10.3	13.8	51.1	19.4
31	22.6	17.4	45.4	8.8	40.5	19.7	25.9	2.9	14.3	13.8	42.5	17.4
32	8.9	17.5	60.0	12.9	12.9	24.3	51.4	10.8	8.4	14.6	62.4	14.3
33	11.8	17.8	58.5	10.3	17.6	15.1	52.5	11.1	10.3	17.9	59.9	10.8
34	8.6	12.2	57.2	20.8	18.4	14.4	51.7	15.4	6.7	11.8	57.4	23.4
35	14.2	16.2	49.1	15.5	20.8	10.0	41.5	8.6	11.9	12.1	40.4	25.2
36	11.6	21.2	51.8	12.8	19.1	18.5	45.1	16.5	8.7	12.7	46.7	30.6
37	5.9	11.9	63.2	18.6	5.3	6.8	59.1	28.8	7.1	12.2	60.5	19.8
38	5.7	13.6	59.9	20.2	8.1	18.0	48.5	25.3	4.5	12.1	57.6	25.7
39	7.3	11.8	63.2	16.4	15.8	10.5	52.6	21.1	6.0	15.5	60.2	18.0

Note: Sector names are found in Table 2.1. The groups do not add up to 100 per cent since some employees have not finished primary school. Educational level for different ownership groups have been calculated at a 3-digit level of ISIC and aggregated up to a 2-digit level of ISIC using shares of total white-collar employees as weights.

Source: Lipsey and Sjöholm (2002: Table 4).

Table 2.4 Inputs per employee (1,000 rupiah), size and the female share of the labour force in 1996 at a 2-digit level of ISIC

ISIC	Average inputs per employee, size, and female share					Ratio between government-domestic and private-domestic establishments					Ratio between foreign and private-domestic establishments				
	Size	Energy per employee	Inputs per employee	Female share – blue-collar (%)	Female share – white-collar (%)	Size	Energy	Inputs	Female share – blue-collar	Female share – white-collar	Size	Energy	Inputs	Female share – blue-collar	Female share – white-collar
Total	164	913	27,984	55	27	1.96	1.07	0.84	0.40	0.65	4.86	1.92	1.93	1.15	1.07
31	123	547	31,188	53	24	4.04	1.00	0.38	0.30	0.71	3.27	1.92	1.97	1.00	1.34
32	228	490	17,901	65	38	1.83	0.32	1.00	0.54	0.50	12.24	2.12	1.37	1.17	1.01
33	175	622	20,548	38	22	0.49	0.48	0.79	0.38	0.77	1.69	1.15	2.15	0.82	0.90
34	143	2,331	39,585	27	25	4.47	3.65	1.48	0.52	0.52	4.83	5.01	1.24	0.64	0.63
35	179	996	39,632	47	29	2.19	1.72	0.71	0.39	0.81	1.70	1.21	2.12	0.65	0.78
36	79	5,180	20,379	31	15	1.82	1.34	1.73	0.13	0.39	2.62	1.90	2.42	0.58	0.78
37	292	5,351	98,539	3	20	1.26	0.33	1.19	0.19	0.44	1.27	1.43	1.25	2.26	0.72
38	179	394	41,919	31	22	3.71	0.34	1.18	0.19	0.58	3.88	1.37	2.45	1.63	0.93
39	144	119	12,514	68	40	0.48	0.15	0.54	0.57	0.38	4.62	1.55	1.23	1.10	0.88

Note: Sector names are found in Table 2.1. Size is measured as average number of employees; energy- and inputs per employee are in 1,000 rupiah per employee; female share is the share of females in the labour force. The figures have been calculated at a 3-digit level of ISIC and aggregated up to a 2-digit level of ISIC using shares of total employees as weights.
Source: Authors' compilations from BPS-Statistics (various years).

Since foreign-owned and domestically-owned plants differ in so many respects, judging whether foreign ownership or plant characteristics account for wage differences requires an econometric approach. Lipsey and Sjöholm (2004a) examined wages in foreign- and domestically-owned Indonesian plants after controlling for the educational level of the workforce and for various plant characteristics. Wages were higher in foreign-owned plants even for workers of a given educational level. The margin was about a quarter for blue-collar workers and over a half for white-collar workers (ibid.: 13). Hence, foreign-owned plants were paying a much higher price for labour of a given quality than were domestically-owned plants.

Some of those differences in the price paid for labour were associated with the characteristics of foreign-owned plants. They were in different industries and different regions from those of domestically-owned plants, and they were larger and used more inputs per worker. Taking all these factors into account, it was still found that a foreign-owned plant of a given size, in a given industry and in a given region, paid more for a worker of a given level of education than a corresponding domestic plant. The margin was about 12 per cent for blue-collar workers and 20 per cent for white-collar workers.

2.3   Foreign takeovers and Indonesian wages

The existence of higher wages in foreign-owned plants is unequivocally clear, and the differences cannot be accounted for by the educational composition of the labour force or the characteristics of the individual plants. It is still conceivable that the differentials may not be caused by foreign ownership itself. It has been suggested that they arise because of what is referred to as selectivity or 'cherry-picking'. That is, foreign firms may tend to acquire domestic plants that already pay above-average wages, because of unmeasured characteristics of the labour force or other unobserved plant characteristics. If foreign firms tended to take over Indonesian plants with the highest average wage, either nationally, within industries, within regions, or within industries within regions, a cross-section analysis would find that foreign-owned establishments paid higher wages than domestically-owned establishments. However, higher foreign shares or increases in foreign shares would have no effect on average wages and would be associated with lower wages or decreases in wages in domestically-owned plants.

Fortunately, the Indonesian data permit us to observe the takeovers themselves to judge both whether they involve plants of substantially higher pre-takeover wage levels and whether and how the new foreign owners change wage levels. We first observe wage levels in target plants before takeovers to learn whether it is the selection of domestic firms for takeover that produces the higher wages observed in foreign-owned plants. We then calculate the changes in wage levels that followed takeovers, relative to wage changes in domestically-owned Indonesian manufacturing plants, to see whether differential wage changes could account for the higher wages in foreign-owned plants.

Table 2.5 shows the number of domestic takeovers of foreign plants and the number of foreign takeovers of domestic plants from 1975 to 1999. Fewer than 1 per cent of the total number of plants changed ownership from domestic to foreign or from foreign to domestic in each year. However, the number increased over time, especially foreign takeovers. They grew from an average of 23 per year between 1975 and 1989

Table 2.5 The number of takeovers in the Indonesian manufacturing sector 1975–99

Sector	Number of takeovers		Average size			
	Domestic	Foreign	Takeovers		Existing plants	
			Foreign	Domestic	Foreign	Domestic
1975–1989						
Total	408	326	250	210	358	103
31	116	92	219	160	303	105
32	96	80	265	243	732	105
33	50	37	290	230	368	136
34	15	6	42	79	263	78
35	47	45	297	309	230	113
36	28	19	192	264	423	54
37	4	1	61	401	477	248
38	48	39	283	150	318	110
39	4	7	124	98	241	69
1990–1999						
Total	637	917	426	418	539	153
31	95	127	316	226	358	119
32	177	226	681	701	1054	210
33	85	92	367	363	471	188
34	16	23	285	795	633	134
35	90	150	281	233	283	158
36	33	44	385	357	447	75
37	8	13	177	224	292	221
38	106	205	379	310	453	135
39	27	37	481	339	568	120

Note: Size is the average number of total employees. Domestic takeovers refer only to takeovers of foreign plants. See Table 2.1 for sector names.
Source: Lipsey and Sjoholm (2002: Table 3).

to 90 per year between 1990 and 1999. The sharp increase in foreign takeovers was primarily caused by the liberalization of the FDI regime that has taken place in Indonesia since the mid-1980s. Domestic take-overs of foreign plants also increased, but not as much, from 29 per year in the first period to 64 per year in the 1990s.

Takeovers in both directions, foreign of domestic plants and domestic of foreign plants, were of plants that were larger, on average, than existing domestic plants, overall and in almost every industry group in each period. However, takeovers in both directions were considerably smaller than existing foreign plants. Foreign takeovers were, on average, larger than domestic takeovers, but the margin was small overall and not consistent among industry groups. Thus, with respect to size, take-overs were not a random selection among domestic plants or foreign plants. Foreign takeovers were biased towards the larger domestic plants and domestic takeovers towards the smaller foreign plants.

Table 2.6 answers the question as to whether foreign firms pay high wages on average simply because they took over high-wage local firms. The table shows the wages one year and two years before a foreign takeover of a private, domestically-owned plant relative to wages in private, domesti-cally-owned plants. It also shows the same information for foreign-owned plants that were taken over by domestic owners.

Plants taken over by foreigners paid blue-collar wages somewhat above the average in all privately-owned plants. The differentials were in the range of 10–20 per cent, far below the differential in Table 2.1. For white-collar employees, the contrast was even more striking. While existing foreign plants paid 60–70 per cent more to such employees, the target firms, before takeover, had been paying them about average wages for privately-owned plants. Thus there is no evidence that the differentials in existing plants resulted from selective acquisition of high-wage domestic plants.

The evidence for selectivity relative to domestic wage levels (but not foreign-owned plant wage levels) is stronger for domestic takeovers of foreign-owned plants. White-collar wages in domestic takeovers were at about average for domestically-owned plants, but blue-collar wages were about 30 per cent higher. However, although domestic firms were acquiring foreign-owned plants with blue-collar wage levels well above average domestic levels, they were not as much above as in the average foreign plant. Thus, domestic takeovers of foreign-owned plants were of plants that paid relatively low wages for foreign-owned plants, particu-larly relatively low white-collar wages.

Taken together, the two sets of averages suggest, first, that the tendency of foreign takeovers of domestic plants to be biased towards

Table 2.6 Wages in target establishments relative to all private establishments

Industry, labour type	Foreign takeovers of private-domestic plants		Private-domestic takeovers of foreign plants	
	2 years before takeover	*1 year before takeover*	*2 years before takeover*	*1 year before takeover*
Unweighted				
Total, blue-collar	1.18	1.22	1.30	1.31
Total, white-collar	0.95	0.99	0.98	0.98
Weighted by sector of employment				
Total, blue-collar	1.09	1.06	1.43	1.38
Total, white-collar	0.87	0.91	1.35	1.32
By sector				
31, blue-collar	0.99	1.03	2.12	2.08
31, white-collar	0.73	0.72	1.70	1.52
32, blue-collar	1.16	1.12	1.13	1.21
32, white-collar	1.15	1.38	1.40	1.41
33, blue-collar	1.17	0.90	1.05	0.81
33, white-collar	0.75	0.74	1.29	1.19
35, blue-collar	1.22	1.21	1.84	1.52
35, white-collar	1.01	0.82	0.98	1.05
38, blue-collar	0.88	0.94	1.09	1.07
38, white-collar	0.65	0.82	1.16	1.24

Note: See Table 2.1 for industry names.
Source: Lipsey and Sjöholm (2002: Table 4).

high-wage domestic plants did not account for most of the differentials found in existing plants between foreign and domestic owners. Second, the bias of domestic takeovers of foreign-owned plants towards plants with higher wages than existing domestic plants tended to reduce the wage differential between foreign-owned and domestically-owned plants.

Given the starting point for foreign takeovers described in Table 2.6, we can observe the events that followed for the target plants in Table 2.7. For manufacturing as a whole, domestic plants taken over by foreign firms enjoyed large wage increases relative to existing domestically-owned plants. Blue-collar wages, weighted by sector employment, which had been about 5–10 per cent above average before takeover, were 64 per cent higher two years after takeover. White-collar wage levels, weighted by sector employment, had been close to average before takeover. They rose even faster after takeover than did blue-collar wages. After two years of

Table 2.7 Changes and levels after takeover in the ratio of wages in target establishments to wages in all privately-owned establishments

Industry, labour type	Foreign takeovers of private-domestic plants		Private-domestic takeovers of foreign plants	
	Changes between 1 year before and 2 years after	Levels 2 years after takeover	Changes 1 year before and 2 years after	Levels 2 years after takeover
Unweighted				
Total, blue-collar	0.26	1.48	–0.16	1.15
Total, white-collar	0.82	1.81	0.17	1.15
Weighted by sector of employment				
Total, blue-collar	0.58	1.64	–0.23	1.15
Total, white-collar	0.65	1.56	0.00	1.32
By sector				
31, blue-collar	1.04	2.07	0.98	1.10
31, white-collar	0.65	1.37	–0.93	0.59
32, blue-collar	0.44	1.56	–0.27	0.94
32, white-collar	1.02	2.40	0.39	1.80
33, blue-collar	–0.04	0.86	0.39	1.20
33, white-collar	0.27	1.01	–0.17	1.02
35, blue-collar	0.52	1.73	0.64	2.16
35, white-collar	0.58	1.40	1.39	2.44
38, blue-collar	0.95	1.89	–0.11	0.96
38, white-collar	0.50	1.32	–0.47	0.77

Note: See Table 2.1 for industry names.
Source: Lipsey and Sjöholm (2002: Table 5).

foreign ownership, white-collar wages in the target plants, weighted by sector employment, were 56 per cent higher than the average white-collar wages.

The story was very different in plants that passed from foreign to domestic ownership. Blue-collar wages, which had been about 30 per cent above the average in private domestic plants when these plants were foreign-owned, rose more slowly than average and after two years of domestic ownership were only 15 per cent above the average in domestic private plants. White-collar wages remained the same in relative terms according to the weighted calculations. After two years of domestic ownership, they were still somewhat above domestic average wages, but by nowhere near as much as the wages in the plants moving into foreign ownership or the plants in foreign ownership throughout our period.

One reason for comparing foreign takeovers with takeovers by domestic firms is to test whether the wage increases we see in the former group are the result simply of takeovers, regardless of ownership. The results indicate that change of ownership itself is not the source of the wage increases. It is the change to foreign ownership that produced rapid wage growth and high wage levels.

2.4   Foreign takeovers and employment

This finding that average wages rose after takeovers does not necessarily imply that individual workers' wages increase with foreign ownership. An increase in the average wage might come, for example, through the dismissal of low-wage workers. We therefore examined changes in employment after takeovers. There were major changes in employment after takeovers, and the changes were strikingly different for blue- and white-collar employees, as seen in Table 2.8. While the number of

Table 2.8   Employment of blue- and white-collar workers before and after takeovers (average workers per plant, growth rates in per cent)

Industry, labour type	*Foreign takeovers of private-domestic plants*			*Private-domestic takeovers of foreign plants*		
	1 year before takeover	*2 years after takeover*	*Growth (%)*	*1 year before takeover*	*2 years after takeover*	*Growth (%)*
Unweighted						
Total, blue-collar	327	452	38.4	243	243	0.1
Total, white-collar	61	44	−27.4	66	45	−32.1
Weighted by sector of employment						
Total, blue-collar	380	573	50.8	336	355	5.6
Total, white-collar	64	46	−28.7	70	45	−36.1
By sector						
31, blue-collar	167	247	47.9	90	108	21.2
31, white-collar	97	74	−23.5	86	28	−67.2
32, blue-collar	595	1002	68.3	670	737	10.0
32, white-collar	67	37	−45.4	66	78	18.2
33, blue-collar	431	524	21.4	140	112	−19.9
33, white-collar	84	73	−13.4	46	40	−12.8
35, blue-collar	216	223	3.1	91	99	9.0
35, white-collar	29	19	−33.6	73	25	−65.2
38, blue-collar	223	264	18.3	224	159	−29.1
38, white-collar	29	19	−33.6	61	53	−12.4

Note: See Table 2.1 for industry names.
Source: Lipsey and Sjöholm (2002: Table 9).

blue-collar workers increased by 38 per cent after foreign takeovers, the number of white-collar employees decreased by 28 per cent. The decrease in white-collar employees was even larger after a domestic takeover of a foreign plant – 32 per cent. Domestic takeovers had almost no effect on the number of blue-collar workers.

The figures at a sector level confirm that foreign takeovers consistently raised the number of blue-collar workers and reduced the number of white-collar workers. Domestic takeovers of foreign-owned plants had a consistent negative effect on the number of white-collar workers and a more uncertain effect on the number of blue-collar workers. Hence, it seems that there were changes in the number of employees that could have had an impact on average wages.

Lipsey and Sjöholm (2002) included a variable for changes in the number of employees in the firm after a foreign takeover. The variable was statistically significant with a negative sign. Hence, an increase in employment has a negative effect on average wages, implying that new blue-collar employees had, on average, lower wages than existing employees. By the same argument, the decrease in white-collar workers found in Table 2.8, in combination with the increase in average wages shown in Table 2.7, implies that those removed were lower-paid than the average. However, including growth in employment in the regressions had only a marginal effect on the wage effect of foreign takeovers and no effect on the wage effect of domestic takeovers. The implication is that the change in employment is not the major explanation for the change in wages following a takeover by foreign firms.

2.5   Wage spillovers to domestic firms

It seems well established from the analyses above that foreign-owned plants pay higher wages than domestically-owned ones. The impact of foreign direct investment on overall wages depends not only on how high the foreign firms' wages are, but also on their effect, if any, on wages in locally-owned firms. The direction of the effect on local firms' wages is uncertain. For instance, foreign firms might raise the demand for labour or increase competition in labour markets, and thereby, in relatively competitive labour markets, force domestic plants to increase wages. Moreover, technological externalities – spillovers – from FDI may increase productivity and, possibly, wages in domestic plants. On the other hand, foreign firms might recruit the best, presumably high-wage, workers from domestic firms, or acquire high-wage local firms. Inflows of foreign firms might also lead to a lower scale of production and lower productivity in domestic firms (Aitken and Harrison 1999). Either one of these effects could result in lower wages, on average, in domestic firms. The impact on overall average wage levels is therefore also uncertain.

Whereas the literature on wage comparisons between foreign- and domestically-owned firms is large, there are relatively few studies that examine the effect of FDI on wages in domestically-owned firms. Görg and Greenaway (2004) list six studies on wage spillovers, and report that of those with conclusions, three panel studies found negative spillovers and two cross-section studies found positive ones. Other studies, some published after the summary above, have reported signs of wage spillovers. Figlio and Blonigen (2000) concluded that the effect of a large new foreign investment in South Carolina on aggregate wage levels was so large that it could not have been the result only of the high wages in the foreign-owned plants but must have involved spillovers to domestically-owned plants. Their study differed from most others in that it concentrated on geographical effects, not on effects within the industry of the investment.

Lipsey and Sjöholm (2004b) made a variety of calculations of spillovers in Indonesian manufacturing in a cross-section of manufacturing establishments in which the quality of the labour force, as measured by education, could be accounted for – the only wage-spillover study we know of where that was done. Assuming national labour markets within broad industry groups, they found significant spillovers to wages in domestically-owned plants. Narrower industry groups, still measured assuming national labour markets, revealed significant spillovers, but smaller ones, and assuming that an industry within an individual province represented a labour market, still revealed spillovers to domestically-owned plants. The combination of higher wages in foreign-owned plants and spillovers to domestically-owned plants implies that foreign ownership results in higher overall wages.

The appropriate definition of the relevant labour market is rarely examined. Most studies define a labour market as an industry, at whatever level of detail industry is reported. Some define the market as an industry within the narrowest geographical area at which industry data are available. That may be appropriate for some countries or industries, but there may also be national labour markets within an industry, or local labour markets that straddle many industries, or national labour markets that do so.

The question is of the range of a labour market within which wages tend to be equalized, or at least within which one firm's wages influence those in other firms. Again, the answers might be different in different countries, or industries, or at different times. A test of the effect of different definitions of a labour market is to use different industry and geographic classifications to examine the sensitivity of the results. This was

Table 2.9   Coefficients for impact of FDI on wages in Indonesian manufacturing

FDI variables	Blue-collar wages	White-collar wages
FDI-2digit-national	1.07 (21.83)***	1.04 (16.42)***
FDI-3digit-national	0.28 (6.20)***	0.34 (5.43)***
FDI-5digit-national	0.16 (7.48)***	0.35 (11.46)***
FDI-all sectors-province	1.05 (32.81)***	1.22 (28.27)***
FDI-2digit-province	0.47 (13.85)***	0.53 (12.26)***
FDI-3digit-province	0.39 (12.93)***	0.44 (12.12)***
FDI-5digit-province	0.24 (11.34)***	0.38 (13.12)***

Note: t-statistics within brackets; *** = significant at the 1 per cent level.
Source: Lipsey and Sjöholm (2004b: Tables 2–3).

done by Lipsey and Sjöholm (2004b), where foreign ownership measures at 2-, 3- and 5-digit industry levels, and at both national and province level, were constructed to examine the effect of foreign presence on the wages in locally-owned plants. The results for these various definitions of a labour market are shown in Table 2.9. The coefficients vary substantially, but they remain statistically significant in all specifications.[5] The largest coefficients are for definitions of the relevant market as either national, at the 2-digit industry level, or at the province level, for all manufacturing industries combined. The worry about these coefficients is that they may represent the tendency of foreign firms to move into high-wage geographical locations or to move into high-wage industries. Those possible biases are reduced by moving to a finer geographical breakdown, by province, and to successively greater industry detail, culminating in breakdowns by 5-digit industry and province. The coefficients are greatly reduced in size, but remain strongly significant, showing margins of a quarter for blue-collar and over a third for white-collar workers. The most detailed breakdown is not necessarily the truth, however. It may miss the effect of higher wages and increased employment in foreign-owned establishments in one industry or province on wages in other industries and provinces, possibly a more important effect than any within the same industry and province. Even the more aggregate measures may understate the wage effect because they are confined to manufacturing, ignoring any impacts on agriculture, services and trade.

2.6   Concluding remarks

For Indonesia, there is strong evidence that foreign-owned plants pay higher wages than domestically-owned plants. They pay higher wages because they use more educated employees, but they also pay higher wages for given levels of education. They also pay higher wages because they are relatively large and use more purchased materials but they also pay high wages for plants of their size and other characteristics. Their higher wages come not from their selection of high-wage firms to take over, but from their raising the wage levels within acquired plants after takeover.

The effect of foreign firm presence appears to be to raise wage levels in Indonesian-owned plants. That influence on wages in domestically-owned plants, combined with the higher wages in the foreign-owned plants themselves, must be to raise Indonesian manufacturing plant wages in general.

There may be broader effects of the spread of the foreign-owned manufacturing sector. The fact that foreign-owned plants tend to hire more educated workers may encourage the local population to seek higher education levels, an effect that would be stronger if the foreign-owned plants not only hired more educated workers but also paid a larger premium for higher education than did locally-owned firms.

Notes

1. There are exceptions. For instance, affiliates of firms from the Asian NIEs in the 1990s did not always pay high wages (Manning 1993).
2. See Lipsey (2004) for a survey on FDI and wages.
3. The figures on types of labour compensation other than wages have to be treated with caution, since many plants do not release this information. Therefore, our further analysis will mainly be restricted to differences in wages rather than differences in total labour compensation.
4. Information on education is available for only a few years in the 1990s.
5. See Lipsey and Sjöholm (2004b) for the complete empirical specifications and results.

References

Aitken, Brian J. and Ann E. Harrison (1999) 'Do Domestic Firms Benefit from Direct Foreign Investment? Evidence from Venezuela', *American Economic Review*, 89: 605–18.

BPS-Statistics (various years) Unpublished plant-level data underlying *Statistik Industri: Besar Dan Sedang* (Industrial Statistics: Large and Medium Manufacturing Statistics), 1975–99 issues. Jakarta: BPS-Statistics.

Figlio, David N. and Bruce A. Blonigen (2000) 'The Effects of Foreign Direct Investment on Local Communities', *Journal of Urban Economics*, 48: 338–63.

Görg, Holger and David Greenaway (2004) 'Much Ado about Nothing? Do Domestic Firms Really Benefit from Foreign Direct Investment?', *The World Bank Research Observer*, 19: 171–97.

Haddad, Mona and Ann Harrison (1993) 'Are There Positive Spillovers from Direct Foreign Investment?', *Journal of Development Economics*, 42: 51–74.

Hill, Hal (1988) *Foreign Investment and Industrialization in Indonesia*, Oxford: Oxford University Press.

Hill, Hal (1990) 'Indonesia's Industrial Transformation Part II', *Bulletin of Indonesian Economic Studies*, 26: 75–109.

Huizinga, H. (1990) 'Unions, Taxes and the Structure of Multinational Enterprises', *Economic Letters*, 34: 73–5.

Lipsey, Robert E. (1994) 'Foreign-Owned Firms and US Wages', NBER Working Paper No. 4927.

Lipsey, Robert E. (2004) 'Home- and Host-Country Effects of Foreign Direct Investment', in Robert E. Baldwin and L. Alan Winters, eds, *Challenges to Globalization*, Chicago, IL: University of Chicago Press, pp. 333–79.

Lipsey, Robert E. and Fredrik Sjöholm (2001) 'Foreign Direct Investment and Wages in Indonesian Manufacturing', NBER Working Paper 8299, May.

Lipsey, Robert E. and Fredrik Sjöholm (2002) 'Foreign Firms and Indonesian Manufacturing Wages: an Analysis with Panel Data', NBER Working Paper 9417, December.

Lipsey, Robert E. and Fredrik Sjöholm (2004a) 'Foreign Direct Investment, Education, and Wages in Indonesian Manufacturing', *Journal of Development Economics*, 73: 415–22.

Lipsey, Robert E. and Fredrik Sjöholm (2004b) 'FDI and Wage Spillovers in Indonesian Manufacturing', *Review of World Economics*, 40: 321–32.

Manning, Chris (1993) 'Industrial Relations and Structural Change During the Suharto Period: an Approaching Crisis?', *Bulletin of Indonesian Economic Studies*, 29: 51–95.

Manning, Chris (1998) *Indonesian Labour in Transition: an East Asian Success Story?* Cambridge: Cambridge University Press.

Winters, J. (1996) *Power in Motion: Capital Mobility and the Indonesian State*, Ithaca: Cornell University Press.

3
Multinational Corporations and Wages in Thai Manufacturing

Oleksandr Movshuk and Atsuko Matsuoka-Movshuk

3.1   Introduction

It is common to observe wage differentials among different types of firms. A notable example is that large firms tend to pay higher wages than smaller ones. There is also some evidence that foreign multinational corporations (MNCs) are likely to pay higher wages compared to local plants in host economies. This chapter examines available evidence about the magnitude of such wage differentials between MNCs and local plants in Thai manufacturing. We focus on analysis of micro data from the industrial census for 1996, and compare more limited results from smaller survey samples in 1998 and 2000 and a firm-level sample for 1990 as relevant. In addition, the chapter reviews available evidence as to whether the presence of MNC plants has any effect on wage levels in local plants that operate in the same industry.

Section 3.2 first reviews the theoretical literature on possible causes of wage differentials between MNCs and local plants, emphasizing how standard theories might explain why MNCs tend to pay relatively high wages compared with local plants. Section 3.3 examines descriptive statistics on wage differentials and related indicators. These comparisons indicate that MNCs tended to pay higher wages than local plants, with substantial variation in wage differentials across industries, and between production and non-production workers. Section 3.4 is the most important section in this chapter, and provides evidence that these wage differentials remained statistically significant after controlling for other plant-level characteristics such as factor intensities or labour productivity, size and location. Moreover, wage differentials tended to be larger for non-production workers than for production workers, smaller for large plants than for small plants, and relatively large in plants that imported a majority of their raw materials and parts. Wage differentials were generally positive for both majority- and minority-foreign MNCs, but tended to be smaller and statistically insignificant with greater frequency for wholly-foreign MNCs. Wage differentials were also relatively large for MNCs from Japan, Europe and the United States compared to MNCs from three of Asia's newly-industrialized economies (NIEs).[1] Finally, we report evidence on positive wage spillovers in Thai manufacturing, as wages in local plants were positively correlated with the degree of MNC presence in an industry. Thus, as in Indonesia (see Chapter 2), MNCs appear to raise the general wage level in Thai manufacturing, not only by paying relatively high wages to their own workers, but also by exerting a positive influence on wages in local plants. Finally, section 3.5 concludes by providing a list of stylized facts that emerge from this chapter.

3.2   Literature survey

This section surveys the features of various wage differentials and how these features can result in wage differentials between MNCs and local firms, as well as some of the related empirical evidence.

3.2.1   The major features of wage differentials

Wage differentials can be traced to either demand-side or supply-side differences in the labour market. Based on this distinction, there are two major types of wage differentials. Wage differentials that reflect demand-side differences usually result from different labour requirements for specific tasks. On the other hand, wage differentials that result from supply-side causes usually reflect differences in labour services that workers can provide.[2] Davis and Haltiwanger (1991) illustrated wage differentials resulting from supply-side differences, focusing on various institutional peculiarities and policy distortions in labour markets. They pointed out that different plants may demand different skill mixes, resulting in what they call 'sorting by ability'. In this case, wage differentials may arise even if markets for each type of labour are perfectly competitive, because the skill level of each type of labour cannot be distinguished exactly.

These differences in required labour skills depend on two factors: firstly, technological heterogeneity among plants, and secondly, differences in demand for final goods produced.[3] For example, more capital-intensive or more technology-intensive plants are likely to demand more skilled labour. Similarly, demand for skilled labour is likely to be higher in plants that face greater demand for technology-intensive products.[4]

International trade may also be an important factor in creating wage differentials. Plants that export a sizeable share of their output may face greater demand for skill-intensive products, and results from Bernard and Jensen (1997) indicate that exports are indeed the major cause of wage gaps for skilled and unskilled labour. In a related analysis, Feenstra and Hanson (1996a, 1996b) emphasized how outsourced production lines are typically intensive in unskilled labour, which in turn affects the structure of labour demand and wage gaps between skilled and unskilled labour in developed countries. As for developing countries, the structure of their labour demand (and wage gaps) may be also affected by imports of intermediate goods or capital goods from developed countries, because these goods often embody the latest technology in developed countries and may become an important source of technology transfer.[5]

3.2.2 Causes of wage differentials between MNCs and local plants

The classification of wage differentials from the preceding section can be applied to explaining wage differentials between MNCs and local plants. MNCs are often claimed to operate in output markets and factor markets that are imperfectly competitive (e.g. Casson 1987; Caves 1996; Dunning 1988, 1993). Moreover, the possession of superior production technology is often thought of as a necessary condition to become an MNC (e.g. Dunning 1988, 1993). These particular features of MNCs increase the likelihood that MNCs are skill- or technology-intensive plants with high demand for skilled labour. This view is supported by a large body of empirical evidence that MNCs have relatively high expenditures on research and development (R&D) and advertising, and possess a relatively large number of patents.

Finally, another possibly important factor behind wage differentials is the segmentation of labour markets, with MNC plants facing different labour markets than local plants do. Lipsey and Sjöholm (2001) suggested three reasons why this segmentation may occur. First, regulations in host countries might affect the ability of MNCs to employ certain types of labour. Second, workers may prefer to be employed by either locally-owned plants, or by foreign-owned plants. Third, foreign-owned firms may pay high wages to minimize employee turnover, because these plants typically make more investments in training compared with locally-owned ones. Finally, if certain labour skills (such as the combination of good engineering skills and the proficiency in foreign languages) are in very short supply and MNC presence is relatively large, the high demand for such exceptional skills from MNCs could result in the domination of MNCs in such labour markets.

3.2.3 Empirical evidence on wage differentials

Aitken, Harrison and Lipsey (1996) examined wage differentials in Venezuela and Mexico, and concluded that MNCs paid higher wages than local plants. Similarly, there is now substantial evidence that MNCs paid higher wages than local plants in Indonesia, and the gap remained after controlling for various plant characteristics and the educational attainment of workers (see Chapter 2). The first study that estimated wage differentials in a sample of Thai firms was done by Ramstetter (1994) who found that MNCs paid higher wages than local firms, but the corresponding differences in labour productivity turned out statistically insignificant. This is a perplexing result, because wages are expected to be positively correlated with the average revenue product of labour across plants. Chapter 5 discusses productivity differentials more thoroughly, while the paper by Ramstetter will be reviewed in more detail in section 3.4.

3.3 Indicators of wage differentials in Thai manufacturing

Starting from the late 1980s, Thailand experienced an unprecedented economic boom, which included a particularly rapid expansion of the manufacturing sector. As a result, in 1996 manufacturing accounted for 28 per cent of GDP and 13 per cent of employment, up from 24 per cent and 8 per cent, respectively, a decade earlier (Table 3.1 and its sources).

There are several ways to measure wages per employee in Thailand. In principle, the most comprehensive measure is the ratio of total compensation (taken from national accounts statistics) to total employment (available in labour force surveys). Such calculations suggest that during 1986–96, nominal compensation per employee rose 21 per cent per annum, reaching 9369 baht per month in 1996, as shown in the second column of Table 3.1. However, this figure is likely to be an overestimate, because Thai labour force surveys probably underestimate manufacturing employment and the Thai national accounts statistics may overestimate compensation in manufacturing (for details, see Ramstetter 1997: 167–9).

Labour force surveys provide an alternative estimate of compensation per employee, but they cover only a small sample of employees who reported wages. These estimates suggest a much lower figure for 1996 – 6245 baht – and a much lower growth rate during 1986–96 – 9 per cent annually – as shown in the third column of Table 3.1. However, this sample of employees may not be representative, since it contains only 3.2 million workers, while the total employment in manufacturing was

Table 3.1 Economic indicators for Thai manufacturing in 1996 and 1986–96 (units as noted)

Indicator	NESDB, National Accounts, or NSO, Labour Force Surveys, samples of all employees	NSO, Labour Force Surveys, samples of employees reporting wages	NSO, 1987 industrial survey or 1997 industrial census, published estimates	NSO, 1997 industrial census, small samples
1996				
Value added, million current baht	1,303,417	na	998,144	748,255
Total workers, number	4,334,200	3,206,500	2,431,584	1,444,827
Monthly compensation per employee, current baht	9,369	6,245	8,108	8,415
Value added, % of all industries	28.20	na	na	na
Total workers, % of all industries	13.45	33.16	na	na
1986–96 (average annual percentage changes)				
Value added, 1988 baht	12.79	na	na	na
Value added, current baht	17.02	na	17.23	na
Total workers, number	7.68	9.14	10.32	na
Monthly compensation per employee, current baht	21.45	9.23	na	na
GDP deflator for all industries, index	5.10	na	na	na
GDP deflator for manufacturing, index	3.75	na	na	na

Notes: For labour force data, compensation includes bonuses, overtime, other income, cash benefits and payments in kind (e.g. food, clothing, housing, transportation); for industrial census data in 1996, compensation includes wages, overtime, bonuses, cash benefits and payments in kind; na = not available.

Sources: National Economic and Social Development Board (1999); National Statistical Office (1999, various years).

estimated at 4.3 million employees in the labour force surveys. In this chapter, we analyse an even smaller sample of employees from plant-level data that were taken from the industrial census for 1996 (National Statistical Office 1999). Published figures from this census covered 2.4 million employees in 23,677 plants and compensation per employee was 8108 baht per month in this sample, as shown in the fourth column of Table 3.1.

The original sample of plants from the 1996 industrial census data had to be cleaned up in three respects to make comparison of plant wages more meaningful. First, this plant-level data set contains a large number of duplicate records, typically because plants that belonged to multi-plant firms reported the same firm-wide data. Thus, to avoid double counting, all duplicate records or all but one record in each set of duplicates must be removed from the sample.[6] This study uses the former approach to create a sample of all plants (small sample (A)) as well as a sample of large plants (small sample (L3)), and the latter approach to create two alternate samples of large plants (small samples (L1), (L2)). Second, the data set contains a lot of small plants and plants that report implausibly small values for many variables. Because comparisons of MNCs are not thought to be meaningful in samples including very small plants, we also eliminated plants reporting less than twenty employees from the sample. Third, we dropped data for plants that reported less than 1000 baht in sales of goods produced, beginning- or end-of-year total fixed assets, and beginning-of-year machinery fixed assets. Such low values are thought to be unrealistic and accurate estimates of these variables are required for some analyses.

If all duplicates are dropped, these adjustments generate what we call small sample (A). It consists of 8432 plants with 1.4 million employees, whose compensation averaged 8415 baht per month (Table 3.1, last column). Note that this sample is even smaller than similarly defined small samples in Chapters 5 and 8, because all duplicates are eliminated and stricter conditions are imposed on some fixed assets' measures.[7] Though this sample covers only 33 per cent of total manufacturing employment that was reported in the labour force survey, it still accounts for a markedly large portion of value added reported in the national accounts – 57 per cent. Coverage rates for the industrial census (published figures and all samples) vary greatly across industries, however (see Table 5.1), and the same can be said for this sample.

Table 3.2 reports the share of foreign MNCs in employment, in value added, and in output by industry. For all manufacturing, foreign MNCs accounted for 43 per cent of all employment, 54 per cent of all value

Table 3.2 Shares of MNC plants by industry and size group, small sample A, 1996

Industry	Number of plants		Value added (million baht)		Output (million baht)		Total workers	
	All plants	MNC plants	All plants	MNC share (%)	All plants	MNC share (%)	All plants	MNC share (%)
BY INDUSTRY								
Manufacturing	8,432	1,444	748,255	53.5	2,388,891	58.4	1,444,827	42.9
Food	470	82	49,507	24.0	162,480	30.3	144,174	35.4
Textiles	548	102	27,415	63.1	111,935	65.8	115,252	43.7
Apparel	607	82	17,162	35.6	58,051	38.0	115,360	32.4
Leather & footwear	216	30	8,081	20.9	21,669	27.5	41,030	28.7
Chemicals & products	402	108	38,244	71.4	115,464	59.0	51,807	33.5
Rubber & plastics	690	153	45,965	44.7	165,054	42.8	115,401	39.6
Non-metallic mineral products	824	51	27,042	28.6	78,478	40.0	76,280	22.7
Metal products	653	94	25,141	61.4	89,456	60.9	72,842	37.6
General machinery	379	87	29,629	75.2	114,978	75.6	81,136	66.1
Electric machinery	421	216	99,065	90.3	336,515	90.3	181,987	83.6
Motor vehicles	375	72	124,991	91.4	402,366	91.5	68,117	64.2
BY SIZE								
Small plants (30 workers or less)	2,415	92	15,516	4.7	40,227	6.2	56,498	4.0
Small-medium plants (31–60 workers)	2,214	210	25,312	14.5	87,119	19.0	95,998	9.7
Medium-large plants (61–150 workers)	1,812	386	65,053	41.9	194,856	37.3	174,768	22.3
Large plants (more than 150 workers)	1,991	756	642,374	57.3	2,066,689	63.1	1,117,563	50.9

Source: Compilations from plant-level data underlying National Statistical Office (1999).

added, and 58 per cent of all output.[8] However, there is a very large variation of these shares across industries. Shares were very large in electric machinery and transportation machinery, where MNCs dominate overwhelmingly, followed by general machinery and textiles. In contrast, shares were much smaller in food, leather and footwear, and non-metallic mineral products.

Table 3.2 also shows the same shares for all manufacturing plants divided into four groups by plant size, where plant size is measured as the number of total workers (i.e. the sum of non-production workers and production workers) per plant. Large plants (plants with more than 150 workers) accounted for 86 per cent of all value added and 87 per cent of output of all the plants in this sample. It is noteworthy that 57 per cent of the value added and 63 per cent of the output of these large plants originated in MNC plants, but MNC shares were smaller in groups of smaller firms. The share of large plants in total workers (77 per cent) and the MNC share of total workers in large plants (51 per cent) are both smaller than corresponding shares for value added and output.

Table 3.3 first calculates hourly wages for both non-production workers and production workers by industry and owner. In this table and in the analysis below, hourly wages are broadly defined to include all employee compensation except social security payments.[9] In all manufacturing, the mean of hourly wages for non-production workers was 75 baht in MNC plants and 49 baht in local plants. In other words, the average wage differential between MNCs and local plants for non-production workers was 53 per cent. These differentials were highest in motor vehicles (94 per cent) and chemicals (59 per cent), and smallest in leather and footwear (3 per cent), textiles (9 per cent), metal products (17 per cent), general machinery (20 per cent), apparel (32 per cent), electric machinery (36 per cent), and rubber and plastics (38 per cent). Mean wages for production workers were lower than for non-production workers, reflecting the relatively low skill levels of the former. The differential between wages for production workers in MNCs (31 baht) and in local plants (24 baht) was also smaller than for non-production workers, only 25 per cent in all manufacturing. Wage differentials for production workers were largest in non-metallic mineral products (61 per cent), motor vehicles (48 per cent), chemicals (34 per cent), and lowest in food (–3 per cent), rubber and plastics (–2 per cent), leather and footwear (0 per cent), and textiles and apparel (5 per cent each).

Table 3.3 reports that by industry, MNCs paid the highest wages to production workers in chemicals and motor vehicles, followed by

Table 3.3 Hourly wages by owner and industry, plant size or trade status, small sample A, 1996

Industry	Non-production workers				Production workers			
	Local plants		MNC plants		Local plants		MNC plants	
	Mean	S.D.	Mean	S.D.	Mean	S.D.	Mean	S.D.
BY INDUSTRY								
Manufacturing	49	69	75	115	24	28	31	37
Food	42	46	61	76	20	19	19	12
Textiles	43	54	46	51	19	13	20	16
Apparel	57	102	75	76	25	26	26	11
Leather & footwear	78	211	81	77	27	17	27	17
Chemicals & products	63	80	101	173	32	30	43	37
Rubber & plastics	40	38	55	88	19	14	19	20
Non-metallic mineral products	44	61	63	62	22	44	36	34
Metal products	55	51	64	56	27	19	34	27
General machinery	64	110	76	68	31	24	37	27
Electric machinery	55	43	74	97	32	26	35	73
Motor vehicles	46	45	88	86	29	16	43	32
BY SIZE (by number of workers)								
Small plants (30 or less)	42	75	73	74	23	18	33	20
Small-medium plants (31–60)	46	44	74	77	25	22	31	24
Medium-large plants (61–150)	55	85	80	115	25	34	35	58
Large plants (more than 150)	56	69	72	127	26	40	28	26
BY EXPORT PROPENSITY								
Export propensity <50%	47	65	76	118	24	26	36	49
Export propensity ≥50%	59	87	74	113	25	36	26	22
BY IMPORT PROPENSITY								
Import propensity <50%	46	65	65	76	24	27	29	25
Import propensity ≥50%	60	85	85	146	29	30	32	46

Note: S.D. = standard deviation; sample sizes by trade status were 6,669 for export propensity <50%; 1,763 for export propensity ≥50%; 6,603 for import propensity <50%; 1,829 for import propensity ≥50%; for other sample sizes see Table 3.2.
Source: Compilations from plant-level data underlying National Statistical Office (1999).

general machinery, non-metallic mineral products, electric machinery and metal products. As for non-production workers, MNCs paid the highest wages (once again) in chemicals and motor vehicles, followed by leather and footwear. In the case of local plants, production workers were paid the highest wages in chemicals, electric machinery, general machinery and motor vehicles. For non-production workers, wages were the highest in leather and footwear, general machinery and chemicals. Thus, there is some weak evidence of a wage premium in industries like chemicals and motor vehicles for both types of labour in both ownership groups, and it is likely that this premium reflects, at least in part, differences in skill mixes that are not captured by the simple distinction between production and non-production workers.

Table 3.3 also reports mean wages for MNCs and local plants in all manufacturing, as differentiated by plant size and ownership. For local plants, mean wages for production workers were slightly higher for large plants than for small plants, or for two intermediate size groups. Differences were somewhat larger for non-production workers in local plants. Production worker wages in medium-large and large plants both greatly exceeded corresponding levels in small and small-medium plants. For MNC plants, mean wages for both types of labour were highest among medium-large plants. For production workers, wage levels in medium-large MNC plants were followed by small plants, small-medium plants, and finally by large plants. For non-production workers, wage levels in other size classes were similar and lower than in medium-large MNC plants. The most important point here is that for each combination of size class and type of labour, wages in MNCs were once again higher than for local plants. These differentials (measured in percentage terms) were smaller for large plants compared with groups of smaller plants, and were also smaller for production workers than for non-production workers.

A similar pattern is observed when wages are classified by trade propensity and ownership (Table 3.3). It is noteworthy that for each trade propensity class and for each type of labour in all manufacturing, mean wages of MNC plants were higher than in local plants. Moreover, the percentage differential was larger for non-production workers than for production workers in all comparisons as well. Mean wages were also higher for both ownership groups and for both types of labour in plants importing the majority (50 per cent or more) of their raw materials and parts, as compared with plants importing only half or less of their raw materials and parts. These differentials were much larger for non-production workers than for production workers. Wages are also higher for non-production workers in local plants that export a majority of their output, but this differential was very small for production workers. MNC plants that exported the majority of their output paid lower wages than MNC plants that exported less than half of their output, with the gap being largest for production workers.

3.4 Econometric evidence on wage differentials in Thai manufacturing

This section summarizes econometric evidence on wage differentials between MNCs and local plants in Thailand. In contrast to calculations of wage differentials from simple descriptive statistics that were reported in the previous section, the estimation of econometric models allows one to examine wage differentials between MNCs and local plants after controlling for other factors thought to affect the wages paid by a plant, including plant-level variation in labour productivity or capital intensity, location, size, international trade status, and industry affiliation. In addition, it would be very helpful to control for worker skills or educational attainment as was done for Indonesia in Chapter 2, but unfortunately the Thai data do not contain such information. Nonetheless, this analysis gives one a better idea if the wage differentials observed in the previous section are indeed related to foreign ownership or if they are explained by other, systematic differences between MNCs and local plants (e.g. the fact that MNCs tend to be relatively large and capital-intensive).

The plant-level data set underlying the 1996 industrial census as well as more limited samples from the 1998 industrial survey and the 2000 manufacturing survey make it possible to examine wage differentials in greater detail than previously possible for Thailand. Since the 1998 and 2000 data are much more limited, and 1998 was a very peculiar year in which the Thai economy contracted sharply after the Asian financial crisis, the discussion focuses on results for 1996. Moreover, the emphasis is on summarizing major results emerging from analysis of the small samples summarized in section 3.3 because these results are the most detailed available in many respects. Results from simpler analyses of the large samples described in Chapter 5, and results from studies of more limited samples for other years (1990, 1998, 2000) are also compared as relevant.

3.4.1 Wage differentials between MNCs and local plants: general results

Six alternative estimates of wage differentials between all MNCs and local plants are summarized for production workers and non-production workers in Table 3.4. These results differ somewhat because the alternative specifications were used to estimate wage differentials in three different samples.[10] In the most basic specification (1a) used for small sample (A) of all plants, controls were average labour productivity, location in the

Table 3.4 Wage differentials between all MNCs and local plants 1996: estimates for all plants pooled in various small samples

Sample characteristics, specification (number)	Non-production workers	Production workers
SAMPLE (A); SPECIFICATIONS (1a)–(1d) (all plants; outliers = 1/32 of observations) (basic controls = labour productivity, location in Greater Bangkok industry affiliation)		
(1a) Basic controls only	0.26	0.08
(1b) Basic controls + size	0.21	0.11
(1c) Basic controls + exporters + importers	0.15	0.06
(1d) Basic controls + size + exporters + importers	0.14	0.08
Sample size (identical for 1a, 1b, 1c, 1d)	6,924	8,170
SAMPLE (L1), SPECIFICATION (2) (large plants with output ≥25 million baht, outliers = 1/128 of observations)		
(2) Controls = labour productivity, location in Greater Bangkok, industry affiliation, duplicate record tag	0.20	0.08
Sample size	5,122	5,122
SAMPLE (L2), SPECIFICATION (3) (large plants with output ≥25 million baht; outliers = 1/32 of observations)		
(3) Controls = capital intensity, location in Greater Bangkok, industry affiliation, duplicate record tag	0.17	0.06
Sample size	4,377	4,377

Notes: The table reports coefficients on a dummy variable identifying all MNCs from estimates using the controls identified in the table as additional independent variables and the log of hourly wages as the dependent variable; the control for size is the log of total employment and controls for exporters and importers are dummy variables identifying plants that export outputs or import inputs; all coefficients are significant at the 5 per cent level; tests of statistical significance use heteroscedasticity-consistent standard errors; sample A excludes all duplicate records; samples L1 and L2 include one record from each set of duplicate records; all samples exclude a portion of extreme observations as outliers.
Sources: Matsuoka (2001a: Tables 7–8; 2001b: Table 6; 2001c: Appendix Tables B1–B2).

Greater Bangkok area, and dummies for industry affiliation. A dummy variable for MNCs was then added and its coefficient estimate measures the difference in the mean of the dependent variable (i.e. the log of hourly wages) between MNCs and local plants after accounting for the influences of the controls included.

In the basic specification (1a) described above, estimated wage differentials were 26 per cent for non-production workers and 8 per cent for production workers after accounting for plant-level variation in average labour productivity, location and industry affiliation. Estimates including an additional control for size (specification (1b)) suggested smaller wage differentials for non-production workers (21 per cent), but larger ones for production workers (11 per cent). An alternative specification (1c) added a control for plants that engage in international trade and those that do not, and yielded wage differentials that were even smaller for both non-production and production workers, 15 and 6 per cent respectively. Finally, if the influences of both size and trade status are accounted for, wage differentials were 14 and 8 per cent, respectively. Thus, estimates of wage differentials appear particularly sensitive to the inclusion of international trade status as a control, but somewhat less sensitive to the inclusion of size.

Alternative estimates were also made for two more limited samples of large plants (L1, L2), where large plants were defined as those with output of 25 million baht or more (a little under US$1 million, International Monetary Fund 2005). Estimates of wage differentials are generally thought to be more meaningful in samples of large plants because they exclude a large number of small, predominantly local plants, which are not easily compared to generally large, MNC plants. The two samples of large plants differ in that the first sample (L1) excludes only 1/128 of possible observations as outliers, while the second sample (L2), as well as the samples of all plants (A) mentioned above, excludes 1/32 of possible observations (Table 3.4).

The set of controls used to estimate wage differentials in the first sample of large plants (L1) included a tag for duplicate plants and the same basic controls as in the analyses described above (specification (2)). These estimates indicated that the wage differential was 20 per cent for non-production workers, or somewhat smaller than the estimate for the sample of all plants, and 8 per cent for production workers, or identical to the estimate for the sample of all plants. In other words, limiting the sample to large plants reduced wage differentials for non-production workers but did not affect wage differentials for production workers. In the second sample of large plants (L2), the labour productivity control was replaced with a capital intensity control, but other controls were identical to those used in the first large sample (specification (3)). The combination of a smaller sample and the alternative specification yielded somewhat smaller wage differentials: 17 per cent for non-production workers and 6 per cent for production workers.

Although the estimates of wage differentials vary somewhat, they all share two important characteristics. First, all estimates of wage differentials were positive and statistically significant. This implies that MNCs paid both non-production and production workers more than local plants, after controlling for numerous other influences thought to affect wages. However, it remains possible that part of the wage differentials observed resulted in part from differences in worker skills and/or educational background in MNCs and local plants because these differences could not be controlled for using this data set. Second, wage differentials were much smaller for production workers than for non-production workers in all samples and specifications. This finding can be attributed to a greater similarity in the skill mix of production workers and/or a greater segmentation of labour markets for non-production workers compared to production workers. Importantly, these two characteristics are also shared by estimates from more limited samples for 1998.[11]

3.4.2   Wage differentials between MNCs and local plants: sorted samples

In order to further examine the relationships among wage differentials and other factors thought to affect wages, the samples were sorted by plant size, trade status and the type of capital used, and differentials were estimated in samples with different characteristics. For example, to further examine the relationship between size and wage differentials, samples of all plants (A) were sorted into four different size groups (small, small-medium, medium-large, and large) by number of employees and differentials were estimated using the full set of controls in specification (1d). These estimates revealed an inverse relationship between plant size and wage differentials for non-production workers: 27 per cent for small plants, 23 per cent for small-medium plants, 17 per cent for medium-large plants and 8 per cent for large plants (Table 3.5). On the other hand, wage differentials did not differ much among most size groups for production workers. Differentials were 11–13 per cent for all groups except large plants, where this differential was not significant statistically. Wage differentials for non-production workers were also higher than for production workers in all size groups, suggesting that this result was not affected by a closer consideration of the influence of size.

A similar approach was used to examine the relationship between wage differentials and trade status in two groups of large plants sorted by trade propensities. In this case, sample plants were separated into those that exported half or more of their output or those that exported less than half of output, as well as into plants that imported half or more of their inputs or those that imported less than half their input. Two sets of equations were then estimated. The first set used samples of large employers with 60 or more employees (L3) and the specification (1d)

Table 3.5 Wage differentials by size, capital usage and trade status 1996: estimates for all plants pooled in various small samples

Sample characteristics, specification	Non-production workers	Production workers
SAMPLE (A), SORTED BY NUMBER OF EMPLOYEES, SPECIFICATION (1d)		
Small plants (30 or less)	0.27	0.13
Small-medium plants (31–60)	0.23	0.11
Medium-large plants (61–150)	0.17	0.13
Large plants (151 or more)	0.08	ns
Total sample sizes (plants of all sizes)	6,928	8,172
SAMPLE (L3), SORTED BY TRADE PROPENSITY, SPECIFICATION (1d)		
(large plants with employment ≥60, outliers = 1/32 of observations)		
Export propensity <50% of output	0.12	0.09
Export propensity ≥50% of output	0.14	0.07
Total sample sizes (plants of all export propensities)	3,467	3,685
Import propensity <50% of raw materials & parts	0.12	0.06
Import propensity ≥50% of raw materials & parts	0.21	0.13
Total sample sizes (plants of all import propensities)	3,469	3,687
SAMPLE (L2), SORTED BY TRADE PROPENSITY, SPECIFICATION (3)		
Export propensity <50% of output	0.22	0.07
Export propensity ≥50% of output	ns	ns
Import propensity <50% of raw materials & parts	0.15	0.06
Import propensity ≥50% of raw materials & parts	0.15	ns
Total sample sizes (plants of all trade propensities)	4,377	4,377
SAMPLE (L2), SORTED BY FIXED CAPITAL SHARES, SPECIFICATION (3)		
Plants with small machinery share	0.28	0.08
Plants with large machinery share	0.10	ns
Plants with small office equipment share	0.18	ns
Plants with large office equipment share	0.14	0.07
Total sample sizes (plants of all fixed capital shares)	4,377	4,377

Notes: The table reports coefficients on a dummy variable identifying all MNCs from estimates using the controls identified in Table 3.4 as additional independent variables and the log of hourly wages as the dependent variable; see Table 3.4 for details on samples and specifications; ns = insignificant at the 5 per cent level; tests of statistical significance use heteroscedasticity-consistent standard errors.

Source: Matsuoka (2001a: Tables 9–12; 2001c: Appendix Tables B1–B2).

described above. The second set used the second sample of large producers with output of 25 million baht or more (L2) and the specification (3) described above. Differences in sampling resulted in large differences in sample size and probably affected the results slightly, despite the fact that the two samples most likely overlapped a great deal. Moreover, if the results from specifications (1a)–(1d) in Table 3.4 are any indication, the differences between specifications (1d) and (3) probably had important effects on the results.

Correspondingly, it is not surprising that the results are contradictory in some respects. For example, when the samples consist of large employers (L3) and a relatively large number of controls are used (specification (1d)), plants with high import propensities appear to have larger wage differentials for both types of labour than plants with low import propensities, but corresponding differences are much smaller and not consistent for both types of labour when samples are sorted by export propensity (Table 3.5). On the other hand, when samples consist of large producers (L2) and relatively few controls are used (specification (3)), wage differentials between MNCs and local plants are generally insignificant in large exporters and importers (the exception being non-production workers in large importers), but positive and significant for smaller exporters and importers. All significant wage differentials were again larger for non-production workers than for production workers.

The sample of plants with large output (L2) was also sorted into groups of plants by the type of fixed capital used, namely the shares of machinery and office equipment in total fixed capital, in order to examine the hypothesis that wage differentials might be related to the nature of the capital goods a plant uses. Plants were then separated into groups that used relatively large or small amounts of each type of capital and specification (3) was estimated in each of these four samples. The results suggest that wage differentials were insignificant for production workers in plants with large machinery shares and small office equipment shares (Table 3.5). In contrast, wage differentials were positive and significant (at about 7–8 per cent) in plants with small machinery shares and large office equipment shares. Wage differentials were also larger for non-production workers in plants with small machinery shares (28 per cent versus 10 per cent), but wage differentials were marginally higher in plants with large office equipment shares (18 per cent versus 14 per cent). Thus, although MNC plants with small machinery shares appear to pay a higher wage premium for all workers compared to plants with high machinery shares, the relationship between the wage premium and the use of office equipment is not as strong. The small differentials observed in the sample sorted by office equipment might be explained by the fact that in practice it included not only computers (for which wage premiums are likely to be substantial), but also other office equipment (like photocopiers) for which skill requirements are not so high.

Using the second sample of plants with large output (L2), estimates for trade propensity- and fixed capital groups were also performed for thirteen individual industries. Estimates by individual industry are particularly helpful when slope coefficients such as the coefficient on the foreign ownership dummy used to measure wage differentials here, differ across industries. For example, estimates for all plants in each industry (the 'All' columns in Table 3.6) suggest that wage differentials varied markedly across industries, between 0 per cent (i.e. insignificant estimated coefficients on MNC dummies) in seven of twelve industries, and 34 per cent (plastics) for non-production workers. Similarly, for production workers, the variation was between –25 per cent (rubber) and 57 per cent (motor vehicles). However, here again positive wage differentials appeared to be more common and larger for non-production workers than for production workers.[12]

When samples were sorted by trade propensity or fixed capital share, some of the industry-level estimates are affected by problems related to small sample size, which are not present in regressions for all manufacturing combined. These problems are particularly common in samples of large exporters and large importers, because such plants were uncommon in some Thai industries in 1996.[13] For production workers, positive and significant wage differentials were rather rare in the industry-level regressions, never being observed in more than three of the twelve industries for which estimates were made. Negative differentials were also observed for some samples in food, rubber and general machinery, but were not particularly common in any one group of plants. On the other hand, positive and significant wage differentials were much more common for non-production workers, and most common in plants which had small machinery shares (seven of twelve), small office equipment shares (six of twelve), and small export shares (six of twelve). The result for non-production workers in plants with small office equipment shares contrasts with the result for all manufacturing combined, suggesting that the previous finding of no significant wage differential for all manufacturing may mask important industry-level differences.

Table 3.6 Wage differentials by trade propensity and capital type by industry 1996: industry-level estimates in small samples of large producers

Industry	Non-production workers									Production workers								
	All	EX ≥ 50%	EX < 50%	IM ≥ 50%	IM < 50%	KM ≥ 50%	KM < 50%	KO ≥ 50%	KO < 50%	All	EX ≥ 50%	EX < 50%	IM ≥ 50%	IM < 50%	KM ≥ 50%	KM < 50%	KO ≥ 50%	KO < 50%
SAMPLE (L2), SPECIFICATION (3)																		
Food	ns	ns	ns	ns	ns	ns	ns	ns	0.33	ns	ns	−0.41	ns	ns	ns	ns	ns	ns
Textiles	0.29	ns	0.28	ns	ns	ns	0.53	ns	0.29	ns	ns	ns	ns	0.37	ns	ns	ns	ns
Apparel	0.27	0.30	ns	0.44	ns	ns	0.25	ns	0.48	0.17	0.20	ns	ns	0.16	0.25	0.15	0.14	0.26
Leather & footwear	ns	ns	0.52	ns	ns	ns	0.51	ns	ns	0.25	0.28	0.44	0.33	ns	ns	0.38	ns	ns
Chemicals & products	0.26	ns	0.37	ns	0.42	ns	0.51	ns	ns	ns	ns	0.25	ns	ns	ns	0.27	ns	ns
Rubber products	ns	ns	−0.37	ns	ns	−0.39	ns	ns	ns	−0.25	−0.26	ns	ns	−0.28	−0.34	ns	−0.32	ns
Plastics & products	0.34	0.47	0.30	0.38	0.35	0.31	0.49	0.33	0.33	ns	ns	ns	ns	ns	ns	ns	ns	ns
Non-metallic mineral products	ns	ns	ns	ns	ns	ns	ns	ns	ns	ns	ns	ns	ns	ns	ns	ns	ns	ns
Metal products	ns	ns	ns	ns	ns	ns	ns	ns	ns	ns	ns	ns	ns	ns	ns	ns	ns	ns
General machinery	ns	ns	0.49	ns	ns	ns	0.45	ns	ns	ns	ns	ns	−0.32	ns	ns	ns	−0.22	ns
Electric machinery	ns	ns	ns	ns	0.40	ns	ns	ns	ns	ns	ns	ns	ns	ns	ns	ns	ns	ns
Motor vehicles	0.31	1.50	ns	ns	ns	ns	0.46	ns	0.43	ns	0.57	ns	ns	ns	ns	ns	ns	ns

Notes: The table reports coefficients on a dummy variable identifying all MNCs from estimates of equations using sample (L2), the controls in specification (3) as additional independent variables, and the log of hourly wages as the dependent variable (see Table 3.4 for details on the sample and specification); ns = insignificant at the 5 per cent level; tests of statistical significance use heteroscedasticity-consistent standard errors; EX = exports as a percentage of output; IM = imports as a percentage of inputs (raw materials and parts); KM = machinery as a percentage of all fixed assets; KO = office equipment as percentage of all fixed assets.
Source: Matsuoka (2001c: Tables 3, 4.1, 4.2).

3.4.3   Wage differentials between ownership and nationality groups of MNCs and local plants

One of the earliest comparisons of wage differentials between MNCs and local firms in Thailand used data on non-oil manufacturing firms in 1990 to compare wage levels in alternative nationality groups of MNCs. Data from a sample of 732 non-oil manufacturing firms promoted by the Thai Board of Investment (BOI), suggest that the average annual wage cost per employee was 57 per cent higher in Japanese firms than in local firms, 52 per cent higher in firms from other developed economies, but only 0.9 per cent higher in MNCs from developing countries (Ramstetter 1994: 44–6). If this sample is limited to 385 medium-large firms, and other influences on wages are controlled for, the differentials were smaller: 18 per cent for Japanese MNCs and 21 per cent for MNCs from other developed economies.[14] Both of these wage differentials were highly significant statistically (at the 1 per cent level), but the wage differential between MNCs from developing economies was statistically insignificant (in addition to being very small). The results for MNCs from developed countries are similar to those obtained for non-production workers in 1996, as previously reported in Tables 3.3 and 3.4.

More recent papers by Matsuoka (2001b) and Ramstetter (2004) include more detailed analyses of how foreign ownership shares or nationality affect wage differentials in MNCs using the 1996 census data, as well as more limited survey data for 1998 and 2000. As discussed in Chapter 1, and other studies in this volume, MNCs may hesitate to transfer technologies to affiliates that they do not control, and may thus transfer more technology to foreign subsidiaries in which they hold larger ownership shares. This could result in higher skill requirements for labour, and consequently, higher wages for MNCs. Similar differences might also be observed in plants of different nationality if, for instance, MNCs from developed countries have more sophisticated technology than MNCs from developing countries, driving up labour productivity, as well as wages, in MNCs from developed countries.

To examine the variation in wage differentials by nationality and ownership, specification (2) was first estimated in the first sample of large producers (L1), which excluded relatively few outliers (Table 3.4). For all manufacturing plants combined, the variation in wage differentials among foreign ownership groups was then investigated by replacing the dummy for all MNCs with several dummies that identified various ownership or nationality groups. Results from these regressions are summarized in Table 3.7. They suggest that European and US plants paid the highest wages for non-production workers in 1996 (34 per cent more than local plants), followed by Japanese plants (23 per cent), and

Table 3.7 Wage differentials by foreign ownership share and nationality 1996: estimates for all plants pooled in small samples of large producers

Sample characteristics, specification, MNC group	Non-production workers	Production workers
SAMPLE (L1), SPECIFICATION (2)		
Differences by foreign ownership share		
Wholly-owned MNCs	ns	0.10
Majority-foreign MNCs	0.27	0.16
Minority-foreign MNCs	0.21	0.27
Sample size	5,122	5,122
Differences by parent company nationality		
Europe+US	0.34	ns
Japan	0.23	0.14
Asian NIEs (Korea, Singapore or Taiwan)	0.12	0.07
Other	0.17	ns
Sample size	5,122	5,122

Notes: The table reports coefficients on a dummy variable identifying each group of MNCs from estimates using sample (L1), the controls in specification (2) as additional independent variables, and the log of hourly wages as the dependent variable (see Table 3.4 for details on the sample and specification); ns = insignificant at the 5 per cent level; tests of statistical significance use heteroscedasticity-consistent standard errors.
Source: Matsuoka (2001b: Tables 7–8).

more distantly by plants from the Asian NIEs or other owners (12 and 17 per cent, respectively). These results also indicate that Japanese firms paid the highest wages to production workers (14 per cent more than local plants), followed by plants from the Asian NIEs (7 per cent), but differences between local plants and other MNC groups were not significant statistically for production workers. Thus, these results, as well as similar results from more limited samples for 1998, also suggest that MNCs from developed economies paid somewhat higher wages than firms from developing economies and that all nationality groups tended to pay higher wages than local plants.[15]

Among foreign ownership groups, estimates indicate that minority-foreign plants paid the highest wages for production workers – 27 per cent more than local plants – but wage differentials were much smaller for majority- and wholly-foreign plants – 16 and 10 per cent, respectively (Table 3.7). On the other hand, majority-foreign plants paid the most to non-production workers – 27 per cent more than local plants – with a somewhat smaller differential observed in minority-foreign plants – 21 per cent. However, somewhat surprisingly, the estimated wage differential for wholly-owned MNCs turned out to be statistically insignificant.

Industry level estimates of wage differentials for all (both production and non-production) workers combined generate rather similar results, though there is again wide variation in wage differentials across industries. These estimates were made in large samples of all plants identical to those described in Chapter 5 and more limited samples of large plants (with output of 25 million baht or more) derived from that sample.[16] The results from samples of all plants suggest that the combined wage differential was statistically insignificant in half of the fourteen industries analysed, 14–21 per cent in five industries, and 33 per cent or more in the remaining two industries (Table 3.8). If samples were limited to large plants, positive and significant wage differentials were only observed in three of the fourteen industries (apparel, plastics, non-metallic mineral products; Ramstetter 2004: Table 4).

Variation in wage differentials for all workers by nationality was examined in two ways at the industry level. First MNCs from the so-called Triad, which consists of Europe, Japan and the United States, were compared with MNCs from the three Asian NIEs and MNCs from other countries. Second, comparisons were made among all five of these nationality groups. In samples of all plants, MNCs from the Triad had wage differentials that varied between 18 and 49 per cent in nine of the fourteen industries examined (Table 3.8). If the Triad is disaggregated, positive and significant wage differentials are observed in eight industries for Japanese plants and five industries for European plants, but only one industry each for plants from the United States, the Asian NIEs or other economies. Because the disaggregation of MNCs did not generally improve the fit of the estimated equations, it is not clear that the differences among nationality groups shown in Table 3.8 are particularly meaningful. Moreover, results from more limited samples of large plants in 1996 or for 1998 and 2000 (both samples of all plants and samples of large plants) suggest that differences among nationality groups are much less prevalent in those samples.[17] However, taken together with the estimates presented in Table 3.7, these results do suggest a weak tendency for Japanese and European MNCs to pay relatively high wages in Thai manufacturing in 1996.

Wage differentials between ownership groups of MNCs and local plants also suggest patterns similar to those observed in regressions from all manufacturing above. Namely, positive and significant differentials were most common in groups of minority-foreign and majority-foreign plants, being observed in four of fourteen industries for each group, but less common in wholly-foreign plants, being observed in only two industries. Conversely, negative and significant differentials

Table 3.8 Wage differentials by foreign ownership share and nationality 1996: industry-level estimates for all workers in large samples of all plants

Industry	All MNCs	By ownership share			By nationality, grouped			By nationality, detailed				
		Minority-foreign	Majority-foreign	Wholly-foreign	Europe +US +Japan	Asian NIEs	Other	Europe	US	Japan	Asian NIEs	Other
Food	0.16	0.15	ns	ns	0.18	ns	ns	ns	ns	ns	ns	ns
Textiles	ns	ns	0.39	ns	ns	ns	ns	0.66	ns	ns	ns	ns
Apparel	0.14	ns	ns	0.48	ns	ns	ns	ns	ns	0.21	ns	ns
Leather & footwear	ns	ns	ns	ns	0.31	ns	ns	ns	ns	0.48	ns	ns
Chemicals & products	0.21	ns	0.35	0.39	0.31	ns	ns	ns	ns	0.27	ns	ns
Rubber products	ns	ns	−0.29	−0.34	ns	ns	ns	−0.84	ns	ns	ns	ns
Plastics & products	0.18	ns	0.40	ns	0.29	ns	ns	ns	0.34	0.30	ns	ns
Non-metallic mineral products	0.44	0.39	0.73	ns	0.49	0.46	ns	0.59	ns	0.51	0.46	ns
Metal products	0.14	0.18	ns	ns	0.28	ns	ns	ns	ns	0.29	ns	ns
General machinery	ns	ns	ns	ns	ns	ns	0.58	ns	ns	ns	ns	0.58
Electric & precision machinery	ns	ns	ns	ns	ns	ns	ns	0.64	ns	ns	ns	ns
Motor vehicles	ns	ns	ns	ns	0.30	ns	ns	ns	ns	0.27	ns	ns
Furniture	ns	ns	ns	ns	0.20	ns	ns	0.55	ns	ns	ns	ns
Jewellery	0.33	0.41	ns	ns	0.40	ns	ns	0.33	ns	0.77	ns	ns

Notes: The table reports estimated coefficients on dummy variables identifying various MNC groups from estimates using large samples of all plants at the industry level (see Appendix Table 5.1); controls for capital intensity, non-production labour intensity, BOI promotional status ([dummy], vintage [dummy], and size [dummy]) are additional independent variables and the log of hourly wages is the dependent variable; ns = insignificant at the 5 per cent level; tests of statistical significance use heteroscedasticity-consistent standard errors if the White heteroscedasticity test is significant at the 5 per cent level or less (if the White test cannot be used and the LM heteroscedasticity test is used); Asian NIEs are Korea, Singapore and Taiwan.
Source: Ramstetter (2004: Table 4).

were observed in one industry each for majority- and wholly-foreign plants, but in none for minority-foreign plants. Results are even weaker in samples of large plants.[18] Thus, if anything, it appears that wholly-foreign MNCs tended to pay relatively low wages compared to other MNCs in Thailand in 1996. Like a similar result obtained for productivity differentials (see Chapter 5), this result is perhaps the opposite to what one would expect if MNCs really do transfer superior technology to their affiliates with large foreign ownership shares.

3.4.4   Wage spillovers

Spillover effects on wages occur when the presence of MNCs affects wage levels in local plants of host countries. These spillovers occur through several possible channels, the most obvious being when MNCs increase the demand for labour in a competitive labour market and thereby force local firms to pay higher wages as well. On the other hand, if MNCs drive local plants out of business and reduce competition, the overall demand for labour might fall. In addition, there may be technological spillovers through which MNCs affect the level of productivity in local plants, either positively or negatively, and thus their wage levels. As indicated, either of these effects can be positive or negative, but the existing evidence for Thailand suggests positive productivity spillovers (Chapter 5, section 5.5). This section looks at the corresponding evidence for wages.

The methodology for examining wage spillovers is very similar to that used for Indonesia in Chapter 2, except that the controls differ somewhat, most notably in that the Thai data contain no information on worker skills or educational attainment. The log of hourly wages in local plants was regressed on controls identical to those in specifications (1a)–(1d), as well as the share of MNC plants in the output of each industry. These equations were estimated separately for production workers and non-production workers in samples of all local plants (from sample (A) described above). If the coefficient on the foreign share variable is positive, it suggests that higher wages were paid by local plants in industries where MNC presence was relatively large, and this is often interpreted as a positive wage spillover. However, one needs to be careful with this explanation when interpreting results of spillover estimates from simple cross-sections such as the one used in this case, because MNCs may be attracted to industries with high wages (and productivity).

Coefficients on the MNC share variable from estimates of the equations described above were positive and statistically significant in seven of

Table 3.9 Estimated spillover effects on wages in local plants 1996: estimates for local plants in small samples of all plants

Specification	Non-production workers	Production workers
(1a′) Basic controls only	0.11	0.30
(1b′) Basic controls + size	0.13	0.30
(1c′) Basic controls + exporters + importers	ns	0.28
(1d′) Basic controls + size + exporters + importers	0.10	0.27
Sample size (identical for 1a′, 1b′, 1c′, 1d′)	5,590	6,770

Notes: The table reports estimated coefficients on the share of MNCs in industrial output from estimates using local plants from sample (A), the controls identified in specifications (1a)–(1d) of Table 3.4 as additional independent variables, and the log of hourly wages as the dependent variable. ns = insignificant at the 5 per cent level; tests of statistical significance use heteroscedasticity-consistent standard errors.
Source: Matsuoka (2001a: Tables 13–14).

the eight specifications estimated (Table 3.9). The exception was the specification (1c′) for non-production worker wages. Moreover, significant coefficients were relatively insensitive to changes in the specification, and varied in relatively narrow ranges (0.27–0.30 for production workers and 0.10–0.13 for non-production workers). This is in marked contrast to corresponding estimates of wage differentials which were much more sensitive to alternative specifications (cf. Table 3.4). The fact that MNC share coefficients were also larger for production workers than for non-production worker wages also contrasts with the finding of consistently larger wage differentials for non-production workers. In other words, these findings suggest that MNCs themselves paid a relatively low wage premium to their production workers, but had a relatively large effect on the wages of production workers in local plants. These results are also consistent with the hypothesis that MNCs create positive wage spillovers by stimulating increases in the demand for labour or through positive productivity spillovers. Results for Thailand and Indonesia are thus very similar in this respect.

3.5 Conclusions

This chapter surveyed available evidence about relative wage levels of MNC plants that operate in Thai manufacturing. The evidence suggests the following six stylized facts about wages in MNC plants in Thailand:

1. Simple descriptive statistics suggest that the average wage differential between MNCs and local plants in manufacturing was a little above 50 per cent for non-production workers, and about 25 per cent for production workers.
2. More sophisticated analysis that estimated wage differentials after accounting for the effects of other factors that may influence wages revealed considerable evidence that MNCs paid a positive wage premium in Thailand, and that this premium was consistently larger for non-production workers than for production workers.
3. If the influences of basic controls (labour productivity, location and industry) are accounted for, wage differentials were about one-half and one-third of the non-adjusted size for non-production and production workers, respectively. Furthermore, after accounting for plant size and trade status, wage differentials were even smaller for non-production workers, though these controls had relatively small effects on estimates for production workers.
4. Estimates suggested that wage differentials were particularly large for (a) non-production workers in relatively small plants; (b) non-production and production workers in plants with small machinery shares of fixed capital; (c) non-production workers in majority-foreign MNCs; (d) production workers in minority-foreign MNCs; (e) non-production workers in MNCs from developed economies; and (f) production workers in Japanese MNCs.
5. There was a large variation in wage differentials among industries. Moreover, wage differentials were positive and statistically significant in only about half of the industries examined for production workers and less than one-quarter of these industries for non-production workers.
6. There is limited evidence that wages in local plants were higher in industries where MNC presence is relatively large, indicating the existence of positive wage spillovers.

This chapter has presented a large number of alternative estimates of wage differentials between MNCs and local plants, revealing substantial evidence that MNCs paid relatively high wages in Thai manufacturing and that wage differentials were relatively large for non-production workers. We think that these important results are likely to survive further scrutiny in the future. In the Thai context, the finding of positive wage differentials contrasts markedly with the mounting evidence that labour productivity differentials between MNCs and local plants were generally insignificant statistically (see Chapter 5). The combination of these two findings is of great interest because it implies that wage differentials result from imperfections in output and/or factor markets, not from differences in labour productivity.

Notes

1. The Asian NIEs are defined so as to include Korea (Republic of Korea), Singapore and Taiwan. Hong Kong is excluded because it is impossible to identify Hong Kong-owned plants in the Thai data.
2. For example, worker-specific characteristics are often measured in terms of a worker's sex, race, age, educational attainment, skill-level, occupation and length of their service.
3. Skill-biased technological change and/or international trade are thought to be the main causes of wage differentials between skilled and unskilled labour in developed countries. See Davis and Haltiwanger (1991), Berman, Bound and Griliches (1994), Doms, Dunne and Troske (1997), Hanson and Harrison (1995).
4. See explanations in Hermash (1993), Adams (1999) and Troske (1999) for details about higher wages of larger firms and plants and for details about the substitutability and complementarity between various types of labour and various types of capital, or R&D.
5. See Romer (1993) or Coe, Helpman and Hoffmaister (1997).
6. See Ramstetter (2001: 9–10) for details on how duplicates were identified.
7. In contrast, the large sample used later in this chapter is identical to that in Chapter 5 and differs from the small sample by retaining one observation from each group of duplicates and imposing fewer restrictions on the fixed assets variables.
8. Note that these shares refer to this sample only. Shares for all Thai manufacturing, including plants not covered in the industrial census, are probably much smaller as explained by Ramstetter (2004: 868).
9. Hours worked are calculated as the number of employees times the number of hours a factory is in operation in the year. Hourly wages are the wage bill (including wages and salaries, overtime, bonuses and fringe benefits other than social security) divided by the number of hours worked.
10. See Matsuoka (2001a, 2001b, 2001c) for more details on the samples and specifications used in Tables 3.4, 3.5, 3.6 and 3.7.
11. 1998 estimates are made in the sample (L1) and using specification (2). They revealed wage differentials of 28 per cent for non-production workers and 12 per cent for production workers (Matsuoka 2001b: Table 6).
12. For non-production workers there were positive differentials of 26–34 per cent in five of twelve industries, while for production workers positive differentials of 17 per cent or less were observed in two of twelve industries and there was a –25 per cent differential in one industry.
13. For example, samples were under 40 in food (large importers=27), chemicals (large exporters=38), rubber (large importers=21), non-metallic mineral products (large exporters=30, large importers=28), motor vehicles (large exporters=24) (Matsuoka 2001c, Tables B3–B15).

14. The controls were industry wage levels and industry-level concentration, as well as plant-level variation in labour productivity, the ratio of skilled employees to total employees, vintage and size.
15. The 1998 results suggest that wage differentials were largest for Japanese firms (39 per cent for production workers and 16 per cent for non-production workers), followed by European and US plants (29 and 12 per cent, respectively), Asian NIEs plants (15 and 8 per cent, respectively), and other plants (21 per cent and not significant (0 per cent), respectively). Note that the 1998 sample was much smaller (2407) than the 1996 sample and is not comparable for this reason.
16. See Chapter 5, section 5.3 and Ramstetter (2004) for more details on these samples. These estimates used capital intensity, non-production labour intensity, BOI-promotional status, plant size and vintage as controls.
17. Ramstetter's (2004: 876, 878) results for 1998 and 2000 contrast by suggesting that positive wage differentials were actually more common between all MNCs and local plants than between nationality groups and local plants.
18. In samples of large plants, wages were significantly higher in one industry for minority-foreign plants, three industries for majority-foreign plants, and two industries for wholly-foreign plants (Ramstetter 2004: 878).

References

Adams, J. D. (1999) 'The Structure of Firm R&D, the Factor Intensity of Production, and Skill Bias', *Review of Economics and Statistics*, 81: 499–510.

Aitken, B., A. Harrison and R. E. Lipsey (1996) 'Wages and Foreign Ownership: a Comparative Study of Mexico, Venezuela, and the United States', *Journal of International Economics*, 40: 345–71.

Berman, E., J. Bound and Z. Griliches (1994) 'Changes in the Demand for Skilled Labor within US Manufacturing: Evidence from the Annual Survey of Manufactures', *Quarterly Journal of Economics*, 109: 367–97.

Bernard, A. W. and J. B. Jensen (1997) 'Exporters, Skill Upgrading, and the Wage Gap', *Journal of International Economics*, 42: 3–31.

Casson, M. (1987) *The Firm and the Market*, Cambridge, MA: MIT Press.

Caves, R. E. (1996) *Multinational Enterprise and Economic Analysis*, Cambridge: Cambridge University Press.

Coe, D. T., E. Helpman and A. W. Hoffmaister (1997) 'North–South R&D Spillovers', *Economic Journal*, 107: 134–49.

Davis, S. J. and J. Haltiwanger (1991) 'Wage Dispersion Between and Within US Manufacturing Plants, 1963–86', *Brookings Papers on Economic Activity: Microeconomics*: 115–200.

Doms, M., T. Dunne and K. R. Troske (1997) 'Workers, Wages, and Technology', *Quarterly Journal of Economics*, 112: 253–90.

Dunning, J. H. (1988) *Explaining International Production*, London: Unwin Hyman Ltd.

Dunning, J. H. (1993) *Multinational Enterprises and the Global Economy*, New York: Addison-Wesley Publishing Company Inc.

Feenstra, R. and G. Hanson (1996a) 'Globalization, Outsourcing, and Wage Inequality', *American Economic Review*, 86: 241–5.

Feenstra, R. and G. Hanson (1996b) 'Foreign Investment, Outsourcing, and Relative Wages', in R. C. Feenstra, G. M. Grossman, and D. A. Irwin, eds, *The Political Economy of Trade Policy*, Cambridge, MA: MIT Press, pp. 89–127.

Hanson, G. H. and A. Harrison (1995) 'Trade, Technology, and Wage Inequality', NBER Working Paper, No. 5110, Cambridge, MA: National Bureau of Economic Research.

Hermash, S. D. (1993) *Labor Demand*, Princeton, NJ: Princeton University Press.

International Monetary Fund (2005) *International Financial Statistics*, January 2005 CD-ROM. Washington, DC: International Monetary Fund.

Lipsey, R. E. and F. Sjöholm (2001) 'Foreign Direct Investment and Wages in Indonesian Manufacturing', Working Paper Series Vol. 2001–02, Kitakyushu: International Centre for the Study of East Asian Economic Development.

Matsuoka, A. (2001a) 'Wages, Foreign Multinationals, and Local Plants in Thai Manufacturing', Working Paper Series Vol. 2001–15, Kitakyushu: International Centre for the Study of East Asian Development.

Matsuoka, A. (2001b) 'Wage Differentials among Local Plants and Foreign Multinationals by Foreign Ownership Share and Nationality in Thai Manufacturing', Working Paper Series Vol. 2001–25, Kitakyushu: International Centre for the Study of East Asian Development.

Matsuoka, A. (2001c) 'Wage Differentials between Local Plants and Foreign Multinationals in Thai Manufacturing: Industry-level Analysis', Working Paper Series Vol. 2001–26, Kitakyushu: International Centre for the Study of East Asian Development.

National Economic and Social Development Board (1999) *National Income of Thailand 1980–1996*, Bangkok: National Economic and Social Development Board.

National Statistical Office (1999) *Report of the 1997 Industrial Census: Whole Kingdom*, Bangkok: National Statistical Office and Office of Prime Minister

National Statistical Office (various years) *Report of the Labor Force Survey: Whole Kingdom*, 1986 and 1996, Bangkok: National Statistical Office.

Ramstetter, E. D. (1994) 'Comparisons of Japanese Multinationals and Other Firms in Thailand's Non-oil Manufacturing Industries', *ASEAN Economic Bulletin*, 11: 36–58.

Ramstetter, E. D. (1997) 'The Effect of Foreign Multinational Firms on Production and Trade in Thailand: an Exploratory Macroeconomic Analysis', in Mitsuru Toida and Daisuke Hiratsuka, eds, *Projections for Asian Industrializing Region: Economic Forecasts for 2005*, Tokyo: Institute of Developing Economics, pp. 145–212.

Ramstetter, E. D. (2001) 'Labor Productivity in Local Plants and Foreign Multinationals in Thai Manufacturing, 1996 and 1998', Working Paper Series Vol. 2001–13, Kitakyushu: International Center for the Study of East Asian Economic Development.

Ramstetter, E. D. (2004) 'Labor Productivity, Wages, Nationality, and Foreign Ownership Shares in Thai Manufacturing, 1996–2000', *Journal of Asian Economics*, 14: 861–84.

Romer, P (1993) 'Idea Gaps and Object Gaps in Economic Development', *Journal of Monetary Economics*, 32: 543–73.

Troske, K. R. (1999) 'Evidence on the Employer Size–Wage Premium from Worker-Establishment Matched Data', *Review of Economics and Statistics*, 81: 15–26.

Part III

Productivity Differentials and Spillovers

4

Productivity Differentials and Spillovers in Indonesian Manufacturing

Sadayuki Takii

4.1 Introduction

Traditionally, inflows of foreign direct investment (FDI) were thought to finance additional capital accumulation and thereby increase the marginal product of labour and wage levels in host country labour markets (MacDougall 1960). As explained in Chapter 1, the modern theory of the multinational corporation (MNC) suggests that the transfer of generally intangible, firm-specific assets such as technology and skills is much more important for both MNCs and host economies than the transfer of financial capital through FDI. However, transfers of technology and skills are also thought to increase productivity and wages in the host economy. The results from Chapter 2, for example, are consistent with this story, suggesting that MNCs in Indonesian manufacturing pay higher wages than locally-owned plants even after accounting for differences in workers' education levels and other influences, and that larger foreign presence leads to higher wage levels in locally-owned plants, again after accounting for numerous other factors influencing wage levels.

One reason that MNC affiliates may pay higher wages than local plants is because they have higher productivity. Likewise, positive wage spillovers might result from positive externalities imparted by MNCs that lead to higher productivity levels in locally-owned plants. However, the magnitude of the impacts on productivity levels in a host country depends on various factors. For example, productivity is often expected to be higher in MNCs with large foreign ownership shares than in minority-foreign firms. On the other hand, if the technology transferred from parent MNCs is strictly controlled by MNC affiliates with large foreign ownership shares, and local firms cannot access information about such technologies, the positive impacts on productivity levels in local firms might be limited. These productivity spillovers to local firms can also be limited by the capabilities of local firms to imitate and acquire the technology.

After reviewing major trends of MNC activity in Indonesian manufacturing (section 4.2), this chapter examines these issues in some detail for Indonesian manufacturing plants from 1986 through 2001.[1] Section 4.3 first asks whether MNC affiliates have higher productivity than local Indonesian plants, as expected by economic theory. It also analyses the related question of whether productivity differentials between MNC affiliates and local plants differ depending upon the foreign ownership share in MNC affiliates. If there are positive productivity differentials, this result could be interpreted as an indication that MNC affiliates in Indonesian manufacturing do indeed have more sophisticated technology and skills compared to local firms, and that they thus have the potential to impart externalities that affect productivity levels in local plants, or in other words, create productivity spillovers. Section 4.4 then asks whether productivity levels in local plants are related to the extent of MNC presence in an industry and whether other factors (e.g. the foreign ownership share of the MNCs involved or local plant characteristics) affect the extent of any productivity spillovers. Finally, section 4.5 provides some concluding remarks.

4.2 Foreign MNCs in Indonesian manufacturing

Indonesia's central statistical agency (BPS-Statistics or Badan Pusat Statistik) has compiled relatively comprehensive industrial surveys that include information on a large number of economic indicators, including foreign ownership levels, for large and medium-sized plants with twenty or more employees since 1975. According to compilations from the plant-level data underlying these surveys, employment and value added of MNC affiliates in Indonesian manufacturing increased very rapidly in the 1986–96 period as illustrated in Figures 4.1 and 4.2.[2] Employment more than doubled every five years, rising from 163,457 in 1986 to 350,534 in 1991 and then to 789,899 in 1996. Real value added increased slightly more slowly (1.9 fold) than employment in 1986–91, but much more rapidly (3.0 fold) in 1991–96.

The initial (1986–91) increases were similar to corresponding increases in local plants. As a result, MNCs' share of total manufacturing employment increased rather slowly at first, from 10 per cent in 1986 to 12 per cent in 1991, while the share of value added remained constant at 22 per cent in these two years (Figures 4.1 and 4.2). In other words,

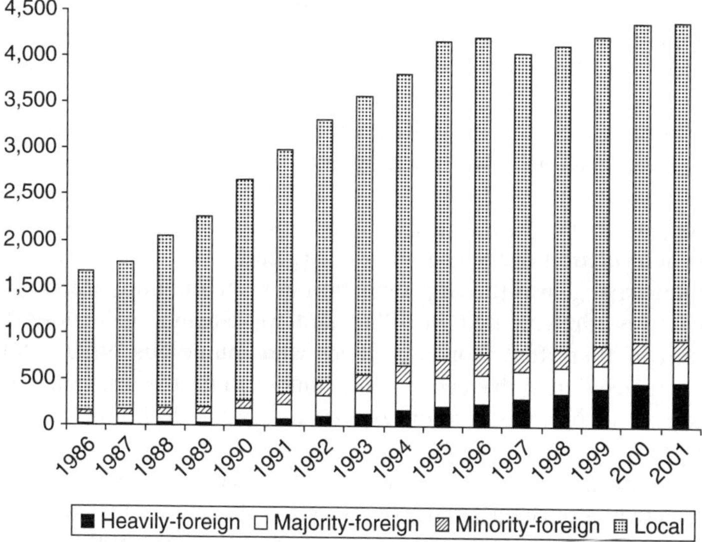

Figure 4.1   Employment in Indonesian manufacturing (thousands)
Source: Takii and Ramstetter (2004: Appendix Tables 2a–2e).

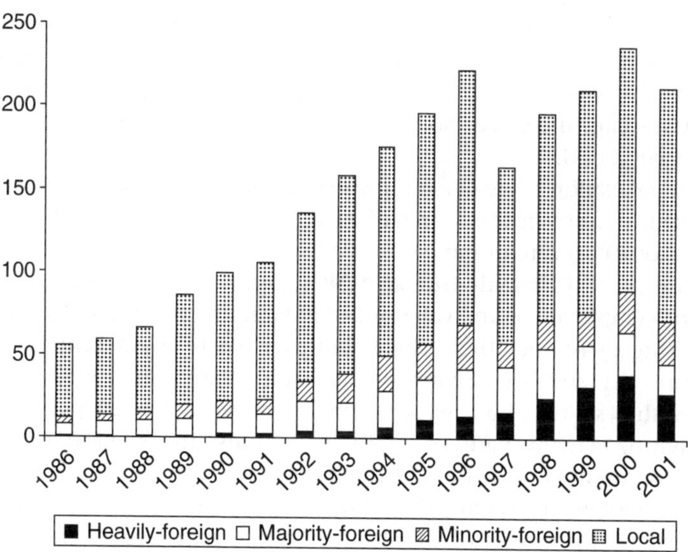

Figure 4.2   Value added in Indonesian manufacturing (billions of 2000 rupiah)
Sources: Calculated from BPS-Statistics (1997); Takii and Ramstetter (2004: Appendix Tables 3a–3e); Takii (2005b).

the entire manufacturing sector expanded rapidly, with both MNCs and local plants expanding. However, MNCs' shares subsequently increased markedly to 19 per cent of employment and 31 per cent of value added in 1996.

The sharp increases in MNC employment and production resulted from several factors. The rapid growth of the Indonesian economy was a key reason why MNCs sought to expand during this period.[3] However, important policy changes played a key role as well. First, there was a large deregulation of the economy in the mid-1980s. Perhaps the most dramatic change was the large reduction in tariff and non-tariff barriers, which was implemented in 1986, and incremental reductions that continued thereafter. However, there were numerous other reforms implemented during this period, when Indonesia for the first time sought in earnest to promote non-oil exports to replace declining oil export revenues.

The gradual relaxation or removal of restrictions on FDI and other MNC activities since the late 1980s was one of the reforms that accelerated in the early-to-mid-1990s and is particularly important in this context. For example, there was a partial deregulation in 1992 that formally allowed 100 per cent foreign ownership for certain types of investments for the first time since the 1970s and relaxed previous divestment requirements. This was followed by a formal, more sweeping deregulation in 1994 that removed restrictions on foreign ownership shares and minimum capital requirements, and further relaxed divestment requirements (Pangestu 1996, 2002). These policy changes explain in part why MNCs' shares increased more rapidly in 1991–96 than in the previous five-year period.

The relaxation of ownership restrictions was also closely related to a marked increase in the shares of MNCs with large foreign ownership shares of 90 per cent or more (referred to as heavily-foreign MNCs below). As late as 1991, heavily-foreign MNCs accounted for only 2 per cent of both employment and value added in large and medium-sized manufacturing plants but these shares both tripled to 6 per cent in 1996 (Figures 4.1 and 4.2). Shares of majority-foreign plants with foreign ownership shares of 50–89 per cent and minority-foreign plants with foreign ownership shares of 10–49 per cent also increased in 1991–96, but less rapidly than shares of heavily-foreign plants.[4]

The Indonesian economy then slowed in 1997 and contracted markedly in 1998 as the effects of the Asian financial crisis set in, the rupiah plummeted, and the thirty-two-year rule of former President Soeharto came to an end. There was a mass exodus of capital as foreigners and many Indonesians moved their funds offshore to avoid the turmoil and asset price deflation. MNCs reacted similarly, with Indonesia's balance of payments statistics suggesting that in net terms, foreign-owned MNCs in all sectors withdrew US$11 billion of FDI in 1998–2001, or an amount equivalent 41 per cent of the FDI they brought into the country in 1986–97 (Takii and Ramstetter 2005: Table 1).

Manufacturing MNCs were also severely affected, but perhaps surprisingly, MNCs' employment and value added continued to grow, albeit at a much reduced pace compared to the previous decade (Figures 4.1 and 4.2). On the other hand, the share of heavily-foreign plants continued to increase conspicuously in 1996–2001, reaching 11 per cent of total employment and 13 per cent of value added in 2001. Meanwhile, corresponding shares for majority-foreign and minority-foreign plants fell or stagnated. This trend resulted in part from the financial distress the crisis caused in local joint venture partners, which left some MNCs with a choice between increasing foreign equity in an affiliate or closing it. Reduced asset prices in Indonesia and a cheap rupiah also made increasing equity a relatively cheap alternative.[5]

Changes in ownership structure among MNCs were also closely related to large changes in the industrial distribution of MNC activity. The most notable change in industrial distribution was the rapid growth of the electric and precision machinery. In 1986–91, MNCs in this industry employed an average of only 12,000 workers and accounted for an average of only 5 per cent of both employment and value added in all manufacturing MNCs (calculated from Tables 4.1 and 4.2). However, the employment of MNCs in this industry increased markedly to 103,000 or 13 per cent of the total in 1995–97 and then to 157,000 or 17 per cent of the total in 2000–01; corresponding shares of the industry in the value added produced by MNCs also increased to 12 per cent and 21 per cent, respectively. Moreover, by the mid-1990s, MNCs came to dominate this industry in Indonesia, much as they do in Thailand and elsewhere in Southeast Asia, accounting for more than half of the employment and value added in the industry. MNC shares then skyrocketed to two-thirds of employment and three-quarters of value added in 2000–01. Shares of heavily-foreign MNCs also increased rapidly to just about one-half of the employment and three-fifths of the value added in this industry in 2000–01. In short, the rapid growth of MNCs in this industry, and particularly of heavily-foreign MNCs, accounts for a large portion of the increase in MNC employment and value added.

Employment also grew extremely rapidly in MNCs in apparel throughout this period and in footwear between 1986–91 and 1995–97

Table 4.1 Employment in MNCs and MNC shares of employment in large and medium-sized plants

Major industry	Employment (1,000's)			MNC shares of employment in all sample plants (per cent)								
	All MNCs			*All MNCs*			*Heavily-foreign*			*Majority-foreign*		
	1986–91	*1995–97*	*2000–01*	*1986–91*	*1995–97*	*2000–01*	*1986–91*	*1995–97*	*2000–01*	*1986–91*	*1995–97*	*2000–01*
Manufacturing	223	777	937	10	19	21	2	6	11	5	7	6
Food	21	49	58	6	9	10	1	2	3	2	3	4
Textiles	44	88	96	12	14	15	2	4	7	8	7	6
Apparel	12	90	123	8	23	25	3	11	17	3	5	3
Footwear	13	141	116	32	48	46	11	14	17	19	24	16
Chemicals	20	40	59	17	22	29	1	4	14	11	12	9
Rubber	18	20	29	15	16	20	6	6	6	5	6	8
Plastics	2	18	25	3	11	14	0	4	8	2	4	3
Metal products	12	38	35	16	25	26	0	4	12	9	13	10
Electric & precision machinery	12	103	157	22	56	65	1	31	48	16	17	11
Transportation machinery	11	30	45	14	24	38	0	4	9	8	12	11

Notes: Figures are annual averages for the periods indicated; foreign ownership shares are 10 per cent or more for all MNCs, 50–89 per cent for majority-foreign MNCs, and 90 per cent or more for heavily-foreign MNCs.

Source: Takii and Ramstetter (2005: Tables 1, 2, 4).

Table 4.2 Value added in MNCs and MNC shares of value added in large and medium-sized plants

| Major industry | Value added (rupiah billions) | | | Shares of value added in sample plants (per cent) | | | | | | | | |
| | All MNCs | | | All MNCs | | | Heavily-foreign | | | Majority-foreign | | |
	1986–91	1995–97	2000–01	1986–91	1995–97	2000–01	1986–91	1995–97	2000–01	1986–91	1995–97	2000–01
Manufacturing	4,060	26,171	90,589	22	32	36	2	7	15	12	14	10
Food	295	1,676	5,687	13	19	19	1	4	5	4	8	10
Textiles	450	2,132	5,442	24	23	27	3	4	11	19	14	12
Apparel	42	1,028	3,024	9	33	34	3	15	23	4	6	4
Footwear	68	1,194	3,302	36	47	56	9	14	24	24	25	15
Chemicals	622	3,813	10,419	35	48	40	2	7	15	22	30	18
Rubber	164	530	1,805	25	34	33	7	7	9	7	24	19
Plastics	35	564	1,074	12	29	22	0	13	13	6	7	6
Metal products	309	1,598	3,763	42	49	44	1	7	11	17	25	26
Electric & precision machinery	210	3,148	19,157	39	53	75	1	31	60	28	15	9
Transportation machinery	495	2,709	16,927	41	39	64	0	3	10	13	11	6

Notes: see notes for Table 4.1.
Source: Takii and Ramstetter (2005: Tables 1, 3, 4).

(Table 4.1). MNC shares of industrial employment were also large in footwear in all years (about one-third or more), though they were not particularly large in apparel (one-quarter or less). On the other hand, shares of heavily-foreign MNCs increased markedly in both of these industries, both in terms of employment and value added (Table 4.2). As a result, heavily-foreign MNCs in three industries – electric and precision machinery, apparel and footwear – combined to account for 26 per cent of all the employment in MNC plants in 2000–01, large increases over only 4 per cent in 1986–91 and 18 per cent in 1995–97. In contrast, MNC employment was largest in textiles in 1986–91, one-fifth of the total, but grew relatively slowly thereafter.

Although MNCs in textiles, apparel and footwear have been large employers at one time or another, they have accounted for much smaller shares of the value added produced by MNCs (Table 4.2). In contrast, especially since the mid-1990s, MNCs in chemicals and transportation machinery have become relatively large, producing between one-third and one-half of the value added in chemicals and about two-fifths to three-fifths of the total in transportation machinery. Shares of heavily-foreign MNCs have also increased rapidly in these two industries, but remain relatively low – 10–15 per cent each in 2000–01. As a result, heavily-foreign MNCs in these two industries and in electric and precision machinery, combined to account for 24 per cent of all MNC value added in 2000–01, compared to only 1 per cent in 1986–91 and 10 per cent in 1995–97.

4.3   Productivity differentials between foreign MNCs and local plants

As explained above, MNCs are thought to make their greatest contributions to host countries by transferring technology and skills, as well as other firm-specific assets, to their affiliates. Indeed the possession of superior firm-specific assets such as technology and skills is a key reason why MNC affiliates can compete successfully in host economy markets, where local competitors have numerous advantages over MNCs (e.g. knowledge of local business practices, language and culture). Conversely, local firms in developing countries cannot easily access information on such technology and skills, especially when they are proprietary assets such as much of the technology and many of the skills controlled by MNCs.[6] Blomström and Kokko (1997) thus suggest that MNC affiliates should be distinguished from local firms in host developing countries. One reason for emphasizing this distinction is that the possession of superior firm-specific assets is generally expected to make MNCs more productive than local plants.

It is also important to recognize that MNCs can choose among several forms of FDI, including various types of joint ventures with local partners or a wholly-owned affiliate. The main merit of a joint venture is that local partners generally have more information about local consumers' preferences, domestic marketing networks, business practices, and other aspects of local markets, which can contribute to the success of business. On the other hand, when establishing a joint venture, the MNC has to share a part of its firm-specific knowledge with the local partner, who may use that knowledge for other purposes. Conversely, MNCs can ensure control of their firm-specific assets by establishing a wholly-foreign firm or a joint venture in which the MNC exercises large owner-ship and/or contractual control over its firm-specific assets. For example, in a majority-owned affiliate, it is usually relatively easy for the parent to control personnel assignments so as to prevent leakage of important knowledge and technology. One the other hand, in a minority-owned affiliate, MNCs may be forced to use personnel the parent would not otherwise hire in important positions such as manage-ment or engineering. And in any case, the local managers and engineers may resign and then use the knowledge obtained while working in an MNC affiliate.

There is thus a growing literature which stresses that MNCs tend to limit the transfer of technology and skills to affiliates which they do not control (e.g. Moran 2001, 2002). If the foreign ownership share is a good proxy for control, this logic suggests that MNCs with high foreign ownership shares are likely to have relatively high productivity. This section reviews the available evidence on this point for Indonesia. The evidence can be divided into two broad types: evidence on labour productivity differentials and more general productivity differentials such as the differences in the production shift factor.

4.3.1   Labour productivity differentials

The data on MNC shares in Tables 4.1 and 4.2 also suggest that MNC shares of value added tended to be much larger than corresponding shares of employment, implying that value added per worker was much higher in MNCs than in local plants. This pattern is also evident from comparisons of labour productivity among ownership groups, which suggests that foreign-owned plants tended to have higher labour productivity compared to locally-owned plants in Indonesian manufac-turing (Table 4.3). As in section 4.2, these comparisons distinguish

Table 4.3 Percentage differences in average labour productivity between MNC ownership groups and local plants, simple calculations from descriptive statistics

Major industry	Heavily-foreign			Majority-foreign			Minority-foreign		
	1986–91	*1995–97*	*2000–01*	*1986–91*	*1995–97*	*2000–01*	*1986–91*	*1995–97*	*2000–01*
Manufacturing	351	375	281	533	501	436	499	745	468
Food	508	448	347	394	441	382	437	283	289
Textiles	156	108	124	474	366	218	139	266	113
Apparel	–10	108	662	58	163	132	–20	134	78
Footwear	80	67	95	245	80	183	26	4	50
Chemicals	270	325	168	271	379	246	392	345	147
Rubber	181	152	178	104	198	193	303	24	–6
Plastics	1	2,076	232	387	221	234	680	322	167
Metal products	344	149	121	402	553	816	280	238	242
Electric & precision machinery	–32	90	109	271	146	41	277	77	44
Transportation machinery	–	450	225	288	281	121	527	360	832

Notes: Annual averages for the periods indicated; foreign ownership shares are 10–49 per cent for minority-foreign MNCs, 50–89 per cent for majority-foreign MNCs, and 90 per cent or more for heavily-foreign MNCs.
Source: Takii and Ramstetter (2005: Table 5).

three groups of MNCs: heavily-foreign, majority-foreign and minority-foreign plants. Labour productivity differentials between these groups and local plants were often very large in Indonesian manufacturing during the three periods considered here (1986–91, 1995–97 and 2000–01).[7] For example, if all manufacturing plants are combined, average labour productivity was between 499 and 745 per cent higher in minority-foreign than in locally-owned plants, 436 to 533 per cent higher in majority-foreign plants, and 281 to 375 per cent larger in heavily-foreign plants. On average, labour productivity in all manufacturing combined was highest in majority-foreign MNCs in 1986–91 and highest in minority-foreign MNCs in 1995–97 and 2000–01, though the differentials were of similar magnitude in these two groups in 1986–91 and 2000–01. In contrast, labour productivity was quite a bit lower in heavily-foreign MNCs than in the other MNC groups during these three periods, though it should be noted that heavily-foreign MNCs had the highest labour productivity of the three groups by this measure in 1975–85 (Takii and Ramstetter, 2005: Table 5).

Comparisons for all manufacturing mask the wide variation of productivity differentials at the industry level, however. Moreover, differentials were generally smaller at the industry level, suggesting that the large differentials observed in the manufacturing total are partly the result of heterogeneity among sample plants, which is reduced at the industry level. However, even at the industry level, large differentials (e.g. 200 per cent or more) were observed in at least two of the three periods in a majority of the industries, namely in food (all MNC groups), textiles (majority-foreign MNCs), chemicals (all MNC groups), plastics (all MNC groups), metal products (majority- and minority-foreign MNCs) and transportation machinery (all MNC groups).[8]

In addition to possessing relatively sophisticated technology and skills, MNCs have several other characteristics that contribute to the large labour productivity differentials. For example, MNCs tend to be more capital-intensive and larger than local plants. In other words, the labour productivity differentials described above, or a large portion of them, might result from differences in factor intensities and plant size, not from differences in ownership *per se*. To investigate this possibility, regression analysis was used to estimate labour productivity differentials between foreign MNCs and local plants after accounting for the influences of electric power per employee (used as a proxy for capital intensity), size and vintage on labour productivity.[9] Not surprisingly, accounting for variation in these other variables greatly reduces the size of productivity differentials between MNCs and local plants. For example, in contrast to the simple comparisons of labour productivity, regression results revealed large differentials of 100 per cent or more in only four of the eighty-nine comparisons shown in Table 4.4. Moreover, at the standard 5 per cent level, a substantial number (twenty-nine) of differentials were statistically insignificant after accounting for the influences of these control variables and a small number (three) were negative. On the other hand, results were consistent with the patterns observed in the simple comparisons of labour productivity in that most (fifty-seven) of the differentials were significantly positive at standard levels and all positive differentials exceeded 20 per cent. Slightly under two-thirds (thirty-six) of the positive differentials were relatively large at 50 per cent or more.[10]

By ownership group, positive and significant labour productivity differentials were most common for majority MNCs, being observed in all three periods for eight of the ten industries examined (Table 4.4). Apparel and footwear were the two exceptions in which all types of MNCs rarely had significantly higher labour productivity than local plants. Positive and significant labour productivity differentials were least common for minority-foreign MNCs in these three periods and were consistently observed in only two industries – chemicals and transportation machinery. Positive and significant differentials were somewhat more common for heavily-foreign MNCs, where they were observed for all three periods in half of the industries (food, textiles, chemicals, rubber and transportation machinery). Majority-foreign MNCs also had higher labour productivity than minority-foreign MNCs in the vast majority of cases (twenty-two of twenty-seven) for which comparisons were possible, but heavily-foreign MNCs had higher labour productivity than minority-foreign MNCs in a somewhat smaller proportion (seventeen of twenty-eight).[11]

The methodology used to do the calculations summarized above is simplistic and was adopted in order to facilitate estimation over a long period for which data availability was limited. In contrast, several other studies have focused on more recent years and employed more sophisticated methodologies. For example, using data for all manufacturing plants in 1991, Blomström and Sjöholm (1999) examined labour productivity differentials after accounting for the influences of capital intensity (measured directly as fixed assets per worker), skill intensity (the ratio of white- to blue-collar workers), capacity utilization, scale, and industry affiliation. These estimates first suggest that the labour productivity differential between all foreign MNCs and local plants was 59 per cent in this year. Alternative estimates then indicated that the

Table 4.4 Percentage differences in average labour productivity between MNC ownership groups and local plants after controlling for factor intensities, size and vintage

Major industry	Heavily-foreign			Majority-foreign			Minority-foreign		
	1986–91	*1995–97*	*2000*	*1986–91*	*1995–97*	*2000*	*1986–91*	*1995–97*	*2000*
Food	40**	34**	44***	64***	23**	44**	31***	3	21
Textiles	33**	21**	71***	61***	64***	80***	14	39**	62***
Apparel	–45***	–5	16	10	–1	14	–65***	11	16
Footwear	–9	12	–13	–23	–10	12	45**	–32**	–36
Chemicals	67***	71***	72***	72***	86***	100***	76***	72***	67***
Rubber	47***	50***	44	41***	60***	78**	55***	13	–27
Plastics	52	46***	88***	94***	38**	78 ***	104***	56***	13
Metal products	50**	27*	46***	66***	50***	89 ***	39***	47***	49*
Electric & precision machinery	18	10	60***	82***	47***	75 ***	73***	–10	29
Transportation machinery	–	–3	77 ***	49***	69***	108***	64 ***	49 ***	120***

Notes: Estimates are calculated from coefficients on an intercept dummy for the relevant MNC from an equation where average labour productivity is estimated as a function of energy consumption per worker, a dummy variable identifying large plants, and a set of dummies identifying a plant's vintage, and a vector of year dummies; '***', '**', and '*' = significant at the 1, 5, and 10 per cent levels, respectively; tests of statistical signficance for coefficients use heteroscedasticity-consistent standard errors; foreign ownership shares as defined in Table 4.3.
Source: Takii and Ramstetter (2004: Appendix Table 5).

labour productivity differential was not different for minority-foreign plants or a group of all majority-foreign plants, defined to include heavily- or wholly-foreign plants as identified above.

4.3.2 General productivity differentials

The focus on labour productivity described in the previous section is limited in a couple of important respects. First, descriptive statistics cannot account for the influences of factor intensities. Second, even if the influences of factor intensities are accounted for, analyses with labour productivity as the dependent variable must usually impose rather strict assumptions about the nature of technology, namely a unitary elasticity of substitution (the percentage change in ratio of two factors (e.g. capital and labour) brought about by a 1 per cent change in the ratio of their prices) and constant returns to scale. As these assumptions are often violated in practice, it is therefore helpful to employ more general assumptions about technology (a variable elasticity of substitution and variable returns to scale) when evaluating productivity differentials.

To facilitate more general estimates of productivity differentials in 1995, translog production functions were estimated both for all manufacturing combined and for selected individual industries. In addition to the standard translog specification of value added as a function of labour and fixed capital inputs, these estimates also controlled for the influences of export propensities, import propensities, the share of production workers in total employment, and plant vintage in local plants and foreign plants separately. Dummy variables were then added for all MNCs in one specification and for three MNC ownership groups, minority-foreign MNCs defined as plants with foreign ownership shares of 10–50 per cent, majority-foreign MNCs defined as plants with foreign ownership shares of 51–99 per cent, and wholly-foreign plants, in another specification to yield estimates of differences in the production shift factor between these MNC groups and local plants.[12] The production shift factor is the constant in an augmented translog production function and measures the production of a plant that cannot be accounted for by variation in factor inputs or other control variables.

In addition to allowing for more general assumptions about technology, the inclusion of separate estimates of the plant vintage's effects for local and MNC plants is another distinguishing characteristic of these estimates. As previously discussed, there was a large increase in MNC activity in the early 1990s, and increases were particularly large for MNCs with relatively high foreign ownership shares. Much of this increase resulted from the start up of new plants. For example, out of the 597 majority-foreign affiliates known to exist in 1995, 295 plants started production after 1991 and 81 started after 1994 (Takii 2004: Table 1). Here it is important to recall that MNCs are generally thought to have less information on various aspects of the local business environment than do locally-owned plants. Moreover, these disadvantages are likely to be relatively large for new MNC affiliates. If this is the case, then even if foreign-owned plants utilize more sophisticated technology than locally-owned plants, statistically significant differences in productivity between foreign- and locally-owned plants may not be observed. In order to account for the possibility that productivity levels of foreign-owned plants depend on vintage, dummy variables for MNC plants established in 1991–93 and 1994–95 are included as controls. Similar dummies are also included for local plants.

The results of estimating this equation without vintage dummies for all MNCs in all manufacturing suggest that the productivity differential between MNCs and local plants was positive (0.32) and that this differential was highly significant statistically (Table 4.5). The addition of dummy variables for plant vintage and distinction minority-, majority- and wholly-foreign plants has a large effect on the results, however. First, estimates of productivity differentials for all groups of MNCs were markedly larger than in the first estimate and all were highly significant statistically. Second, productivity differentials were by far the largest for wholly-foreign plants, followed by majority-foreign plants, and less distantly by minority-foreign plants. However, Wald tests for differences among MNC groups indicate that the difference between wholly-foreign and minority-foreign plants was the only one that was significant at standard significance levels (5 per cent or better). The difference between wholly-foreign and majority-foreign plants was also significant at a somewhat lower level of significance (9 per cent). Third, all newer MNCs had markedly lower productivity differentials than older ones.

These results for all manufacturing plants combined are more in line with the expectations of MNC theory than the previously described results for labour productivity, and suggest that allowing for more general assumptions about technology and more precise accounting for the effects of vintage could be important. However, as mentioned above, there is an extremely large degree of heterogeneity among manufacturing plants, which can be reduced by estimating productivity differentials at the industry level, as was done for the labour productivity estimates in Table 4.4. The specification including vintage dummies was thus estimated for eight industries as summarized in Table 4.5 and these results echo those in Table 4.4 by suggesting a large variation in

Table 4.5 General productivity differentials between MNC ownership groups and local plants, 1995 (except p-values and samples sizes as noted)

MNC group, startup year (foreign ownership share)	Manufacturing	Textiles	Apparel	Footwear	Wood	Industrial chemicals	Metal products	Electric machinery	Transportation machinery
TESTS OF DIFFERENCES BETWEEN ALL MNCS AND LOCAL PLANTS									
All MNCs (10%+)	0.32***	0.27**	0.22*	−0.20*	0.34*	0.60***	0.56***	0.04	0.49**
MNCs, 1991–93 startup	–	0.00	−0.26*	0.24	−0.32	−0.28	−0.69***	0.04	−0.06
MNCs, 1994–95 startup	–	−0.39***	−0.37	0.12	−0.29	−0.68*	−0.95**	−0.25	−0.42
TESTS OF DIFFERENCES BETWEEN OWNERSHIP GROUPS OF MNCS AND LOCAL PLANTS									
Minority-foreign MNCs (10–50%)	0.40***	0.16	0.36*	−0.41	0.37*	0.80***	0.61***	−0.26	0.23
Majority-foreign MNCs (51–99%)	0.46***	0.30*	0.23*	−0.15	0.23	0.54**	0.53***	0.24	0.57**
Wholly-foreign MNCs (100%)	0.59***	0.29	0.00	−0.55**	0.82***	−0.02	0.62	0.36	0.81*
MNCs, 1991–93 startup	−0.28***	0.01	−0.28*	0.29	−0.28	−0.26	−0.69***	−0.10	−0.06
MNCs, 1994–95 startup	−0.43***	−0.37*	−0.27	0.19	−0.43	−0.62	−0.99	−0.40	−0.42
Wald H0: Min = Maj (p-value)	0.35	0.48	0.49	0.23	0.61	0.19	0.69	0.07	0.21
Wald, H0: Maj = Who (p-value)	0.09	0.98	0.26	0.14	0.06	0.25	0.87	0.65	0.54
Wald, H0: Min = Who (p-value)	0.03	0.62	0.12	0.66	0.11	0.08	0.99	0.03	0.15
Sample sizes (same for both)	16,129	1,556	1,318	294	1,395	287	733	334	431

Notes: Estimates are differences in the production shift factor between the group of MNCs identified and local plants; in other words, they are the values of coefficients on intercept dummies identifying MNC groups from estimates of value added as a translogarithmic function of labour and fixed capital augmented with exports as a share of output, imports as a share of materials cost, the share of non-production workers in total employment, and dummy variables identifying newer local plants; '***', '**', and '*' = significant at the 1, 5, and 10 per cent level; tests of statistical signficance for coefficients use heteroscedasticity-consistent standard errors.
Source: Takii (2004: Tables 2, 3).

productivity differentials across industries. For example, in the four industries for which differentials between all MNCs and local plants were positive and statistically significant at standard levels, differentials varied from 0.27 (textiles) to 0.49 (transportation machinery) and 0.56–0.60 (metal products and industrial chemicals). At a somewhat lower level (10 per cent), differentials were significant in apparel and wood, where they were of similar magnitude to the textiles' differential, as well as in footwear, where the differential was negative. As expected, vintage effects were generally negative in the industry-level estimates for all MNCs, but were not significant at standard levels in six of the eight industries (all except textiles and metal products).

When MNCs are distinguished by ownership the results suggest even greater variation among industries. At standard levels, productivity differentials were significantly positive for both minority- and majority-foreign MNCs in industrial chemicals and metal products and of similar magnitude (0.61–0.80 and 0.53–0.54, respectively), but the differentials were not significant for wholly-foreign MNCs. There was also a significant differential of similar magnitude for majority-foreign MNCs in transportation machinery but no other differential is significant. Wholly-foreign MNCs had significantly higher productivity in wood and significantly lower productivity in footwear. There were also some weakly significant positive differentials (at the 10 per cent level) for minority-foreign MNCs in apparel and wood as well as majority-foreign MNCs in textiles and apparel. However, Wald tests suggest that differences among MNC groups were significant at standard levels in only one case – between wholly- and minority-foreign MNCs in electric machinery – but differentials between both of these groups and local plants were not significant at any level. Thus, at the industry level, results combining all MNCs are probably more reliable if the specification including vintage effects is used.

4.4   Productivity spillovers in Indonesian manufacturing

The results of analyses in the previous sections suggest that MNC affiliates have higher productivity than local plants in Indonesian manufacturing and a weak tendency for majority- and wholly-foreign plants to have higher productivity than minority-foreign plants. This section now turns to the question of how MNC entry and presence affect the productivity of local plants in an industry. These effects are called productivity spillovers in the literature (Blomström et al. 2000: 103–6). These spillovers are externalities arising from MNC presence and can occur through several channels. First, local firms can learn how MNC affiliates procure, produce, sell, manage and adapt technology and imitate the behaviour of MNCs, creating a demonstration effect. Second, MNCs may find it profitable to develop local supplier networks and to help improve the performance of these networks by providing information on sophisticated technology, technical assistance, and other services to local suppliers (Moran 2002: 108–9). This creates a backward linkage effect. Third, MNCs may supply similar services to local customers that purchase their products (e.g. for use as inputs), creating a forward linkage effect. Fourth, spillovers can result from the training of workers, who acquire specific knowledge and/or skills and eventually move on to other local plants or share their knowledge with them through some other channel. This mechanism can be extremely important in developing countries where public education systems are weak (Blomström et al. 2000), like Indonesia. Fifth, even if there is no direct contact between MNCs or their workers and local plants, MNCs can increase competition in an industry and motivate local plants to increase productivity in order to protect their market shares and profits.

4.4.1   Evidence on productivity spillovers

Most previous studies of spillovers are based on the assumption that technical innovations are most effectively diffused from MNCs to local plants when there is personal contact between them (Findlay 1978). Accordingly, empirical models often assume that the extent of spillovers in an industry or region is determined by the extent of MNC presence, which is, for example, measured as the foreign share in total employment in the industry or region. If productivity spillovers exist, productivity in local plants is expected to be positively correlated with the extent of MNC presence because larger MNC presence increases the probability that local plants will interact with the MNCs in some respect, making it easier to acquire and adapt technology and knowledge from the MNCs. Therefore, statistical studies of spillovers generally estimate a standard production function (e.g. value added as a function of labour and capital inputs) for samples of local plants, including a measure of MNC presence as an independent variable. Other relevant plant-level controls are often included as well. The coefficient on the MNC presence variable is a measure of the magnitude of spillovers, and if the coefficient is significantly positive, it suggests the existence of positive spillover effects.

Several previous studies have examined productivity spillovers in Indonesian manufacturing (Sjöholm 1999a, 1999b; Blomström and Sjöholm 1999; Todo and Miyamoto 2002; Blalock 2004; Jacob and Meister 2005).[13] In contrast to previous studies for several other developing countries,[14] most of these studies found evidence of positive spillovers. Sjöholm (1999a) examined productivity growth of manufacturing plants during 1980–91 emphasizing regional aspects of spillovers. In this analysis, inter-industry and intra-industry spillovers were distinguished at the provincial or district level. Regression results indicated that inter-industry spillovers were important at the regional level, in turn suggesting the importance of local linkages between local firms and MNC affiliates. Blalock and Gertler (2004) also examined spillovers derived from foreign firms through backward linkages resulting from downstream FDI and intra-industry spillovers resulting from horizontal FDI. Panel estimation results suggested that vertical supply chains are important channels of spillovers but there was no evidence of intra-industry spillovers.

Sjöholm (1999b) examined the determinants of spillovers using data for 1980 and 1991. One of the determinants examined was the extent of technological gaps between MNCs and local plants in an industry, which was measured as the difference in labour productivity between MNCs and local plants. The results suggested that locally-owned plants could benefit more from foreign presence in industries with relatively large technological gaps. One possible interpretation of this result is that pressures for change within the backward firms are positively correlated with the backlog of technological opportunities in the advanced firms (Findlay 1978). However, this finding contrasts with results from another previous study of Mexican manufacturing by Kokko (1994), who argued that the technologies in MNCs may be too advanced for local plants to absorb in developing countries.

Sjöholm (1999b) also examined the possibility that the degree of competition was a determinant of spillovers. Competition was measured as an index depending on the effective rate of protection and the Herfindahl index of concentration. Not surprisingly, the results suggested that spillovers effects were greater in the group of industries with relatively high degrees of competition. Blomström and Sjöholm (1999) also found evidence that productivity spillovers from foreign presence were greater in local plants that did not export than among exporters. This suggests that local exporters did not benefit as much from MNC spillovers, presumably because they already had acquired similar technology and skills by competing internationally.

The results from an industry-level study by Jacob and Meister (2005) contrast with the results from the plant-level studies summarized above by suggesting that there are no positive labour productivity spillovers derived from foreign presence in Indonesian manufacturing. Rather, they conclude that imports from developed countries contributed significantly to labour productivity increases. However, the specification, sampling and estimation techniques used in this study differ greatly from those used in the more standard, plant-level studies described above.

4.4.2 Foreign ownership shares and spillovers

The relationship between the extent of foreign ownership and spillovers is one aspect that has not been well studied for Indonesian manufacturing. In their aforementioned analysis, Blomström and Sjöholm (1999) obtained results suggesting that differences in spillovers derived from minority-foreign MNCs (including 50–50 joint ventures) and from other MNCs were not statistically significant. However, this study analysed spillovers in cross-sections for 1980 and 1991, whereas the results below are obtained from panels covering 1990–95. The use of panel data has two important advantages if individual effects are included. First, one can account for the simultaneity that might arise if MNCs (or MNCs with large foreign ownership shares) tend to prefer investing in industries where local plants have relatively high productivity.[15] Second, one can examine how changes over time affect the level of spillovers, which is impossible in cross-sections. These changes include changes in MNC presence and changes in production structures among local plants. As indicated above, accounting for such changes is important because both MNC presence and Indonesia's production structure changed markedly during the early-to-mid-1990s.

As shown in the previous section, when all manufacturing plants are combined into one sample and vintage is controlled for, productivity levels were higher in majority- and wholly-foreign plants than in minority-foreign plants. This result creates the possibility that the magnitude of spillovers derived from MNCs may also depend on the degree of foreign ownership share in two ways. Namely, the magnitude of spillovers derived from majority- or wholly-foreign plants may be relatively large because these plants are able to transfer more sophisticated technology and/or skills than minority-foreign plants. If this is true and these MNCs seek to foster spillovers in order to improve their own performance, then spillovers are likely to be largest in the case of wholly-foreign affiliates, followed by majority-foreign affiliates, and minority-foreign affiliates. Alternatively, the magnitude of spillovers derived from majority- or wholly-foreign plants may be relatively small because they may be able to limit the spillover of intangible assets such as technology and skills more effectively than minority-foreign plants. If this is possible and the incentive to limit the spillover of intangible assets is strong, then the magnitude of spillovers is likely to be largest for minority-foreign plants, followed by majority-foreign plants, and wholly-foreign plants.

These possibilities are examined by estimating value added in local plants as a function of various measures of MNC presence in an industry and a number of plant- and industry-level control variables. The basic MNC presence variable was the share of all MNCs in the total employment of an industry. In other specifications, shares of wholly-foreign MNCs and majority-foreign MNCs in total MNC employment were added to see if spillovers from these groups differed from spillovers generated by the average MNC. The basic specification includes year dummies and several plant-level control variables, which are capital and labour in local plants (translog specification for generality), exports as a share of output, imports as a share of materials cost, and the share of non-production workers in total employment. In an expanded speci-fication, four industry variables are added as controls: output based Herfindahl indices, average industrial output, import penetration ratios, and the share of new MNCs (plants with positive foreign ownership for two years or less) in industrial employment.[16] These equations were estimated in a panel covering 1990–95, using a technique that allows one to account for time-variant factors captured by the controls mentioned above as well as a set of time-invariant individual effects for each plant.

Results of estimating both the basic and the expanded specification for all MNCs (top two rows of the left column in Table 4.6) suggest that coefficients on the share of all MNCs in industrial employment were positive and highly significant statistically. In other words, these results are consistent with results from numerous other studies in suggesting the existence of positive productivity spillovers in Indonesian manufac-turing. However, not surprisingly, estimated spillovers were about one-quarter smaller when the expanded specification was used.

In alternative specifications including shares of majority- and wholly-foreign plants (middle three columns of Table 4.6), the estimate for the share of all MNCs is again positive and significant, and a bit larger than in the estimates where spillovers are assumed to be the same for all MNCs. Coefficients on the shares of majority- and wholly-foreign plants in total MNC employment were negative, suggesting that spill-overs from these groups of MNCs were positive on average, but relatively small. Thus, these results suggest that the foreign ownership share is an important determinant of spillovers and that the magnitude of spill-overs derived from foreign-owned plants with relatively high foreign ownership shares is smaller than that from other foreign-owned plants.

Table 4.6 Estimates of spillover coefficients, 1990–95 (except p-values and samples sizes as noted)

Sample, measure, specification	Estimates for all MNCs	Estimates by ownership group			Sample size
		All MNCs	Majority-foreign	Wholly-foreign	
ALL LOCAL PLANTS					
Basic specification	0.83***	1.00***	–0.28***	–0.21***	41,274
Expanded specification	0.61***	0.79***	–0.25***	–0.15***	41,274
LOCAL PLANTS SORTED BY INDUSTRY-LEVEL TECHNOLOGICAL GAPS					
14 small gap industries	1.10***	1.08***	–0.13**	0.12	20,082
15 large gap industries	–0.36*	0.47**	–0.29***	–0.25***	21,192
Wald tests: small = large (p-value)	0.00	0.02	0.03	0.00	–
LOCAL PLANTS SORTED BY PLANT SIZE					
Small output	0.66***	0.88***	–0.22***	–0.22***	32,007
Large output	0.43*	0.52**	–0.28**	–0.22	9,267
Wald tests: small = large (p-value)	0.38	0.18	0.53	0.12	–
LOCAL PLANTS SORTED BY PLANT-LEVEL CAPITAL INTENSITY					
Low fixed assets/ employee	0.70***	0.91***	–0.25***	–0.17***	30,490
High fixed assets/ employee	0.31	0.44*	–0.23***	–0.10	10,784
Wald tests: low = high (p-value)	0.13	0.07	0.77	0.36	–
LOCAL PLANTS SORTED BY PLANT-LEVEL WORKER TRAINING EXPENDITURES					
Plants without worker training	0.57***	0.76***	–0.25***	–0.18***	37,222
Plants with worker training	0.80**	0.75**	–0.24**	0.26	4,052
Wald tests: w/o = with (p-value)	0.51	0.98	0.98	0.18	–
LOCAL PLANTS SORTED BY PLANT-LEVEL R&D EXPENDITURES					
Plants without R&D	0.54***	0.74***	–0.27***	–0.16***	37,921
Plants with R&D	1.21***	1.10***	–0.01	0.15	3,353
Wald tests: w/o = with (p-value)	0.07	0.37	0.03	0.43	–

Notes: The estimates refer to coefficients on the MNC share of industrial employment from estimates of value added as a translogarithmic function of labour and fixed capital augmented with exports as a share of output, imports as a share of materials cost, the share of non-production workers in total employment, and year dummies in the basic specification; the expanded specification adds four industry variables as controls, output based Herfindahl indices, average industrial output, import penetration ratios, and the share of new MNCs in industrial employment; all estimates for sorted samples use the expanded specification; '***', '**', and '*' = significant at the 1, 5, and 10 per cent level; tests of statistical signficance for coefficients use heteroscedasticity-consistent standard errors; foreign ownership shares as defined in Table 4.5.
Source: Takii (2005a: Tables 2–5).

4.4.3 Other determinants of spillovers

As previously discussed, the extent of spillovers is thought to be affected by a number of other factors. One factor that has been studied is the relationship between the size of technological gaps between MNCs and local plants on the one hand, and the extent of spillovers on the other. This relationship is re-examined by estimating the expanded specification in the 1990–95 panel data for one group of industries with small technological gaps and another with large gaps. Industry-level data for the initial year (1990) were used to classify industries into low- and high-gap groups as follows. First, industries were sorted in descending order by three gaps between MNCs and local plants: the average wage gap, the average labour productivity gap, and the capital-intensity (fixed asset per worker) gap. Second, industries were sorted by the minimum of the three rankings. Third, if two or more industries shared the same minimum rank, then they were sorted by the sum of the three ranks. The bottom fourteen industries in the resulting ranking were defined as the small-gap group and the other fifteen were defined as the large-gap group.

When spillovers from all MNCs are estimated (Table 4.6, left column), the coefficient on the MNCs is positive and highly significant in the small-gap sample, while the same coefficient is negative and insignificant at standard significance levels for the large-gap group (this coefficient is significant at the 10 per cent level, however). A Wald test was used to test the hypothesis that these two coefficients are equal and this hypothesis was rejected at the 1 per cent significance level. If ownership groups of MNCs are distinguished (Table 4.6, middle three columns), the results change somewhat, however. In the small-gap group, the coefficient on the share of all MNCs is again positive and highly significant. In this case, the coefficient on the share of wholly-foreign MNCs is positive but insignificant, suggesting that spillovers from minority- and wholly-foreign groups were of the same magnitude in this group. However, the coefficient on the share of majority-foreign MNCs is negative and significant, suggesting that spillovers were lower in this group than in other groups. In the large-gap group, the coefficient on the share of all MNCs is again positive and significant, but less than half the size of the corresponding coefficient for the small-gap group. Coefficients on shares of both majority- and wholly-foreign plants were negative and significant, indicating that spillovers were smaller than spillovers from minority-foreign plants in this sample. Here again, results of Wald tests indicate that all of these coefficients were significantly different in the samples of small-gap and large-gap industries. Thus, these results suggest that the extent of spillovers was smaller in industries with relatively large technological gaps in the initial year (1990).[17] They also further highlight the point that spillovers appear to differ among MNC ownership groups in Indonesia.

Relationships between four plant-level characteristics – size, capital intensity, worker training expenditures and research and development (R&D) expenditures – on the one hand, and the extent of spillovers on the other hand, were also examined using similar methodologies. These results were much weaker than the results that distinguished by industry-level technological gaps. In particular, plant size and the existence of worker training expenditures appear to have little relationship to the extent of spillovers as indicated by insignificant (at any level) Wald tests of differences between the groups involved. On the other hand, there were some weak indications that the extent of spillovers was related to capital intensity or the existence of R&D expenditures in local plants.

When sorting by capital intensity, plants with capital intensity below the industry average in 1990 were classified in the low group and the remaining plants were classified in the high group. When spillovers were estimated for all MNCs combined (Table 4.6, left column), differences between these two groups were not significant. However, when spillovers were allowed to differ among ownership groups, there was some indication of a difference as the coefficient on the share of all MNCs was larger in samples with relatively low capital intensity than the corresponding coefficient in sample plants with relatively high capital intensity and this difference was weakly significant (at the 10 per cent level). Thus, there is some weak evidence that spillovers were relatively large in local plants with relatively low capital intensity.

When plants are sorted in groups with positive R&D expenditures and those with no R&D activity, slightly stronger differences emerge. This distinction is thought to be important because plants with R&D activity may have relatively large incentives to increase productivity and may thus be more likely to seek to benefit from spillovers than other local plants.[18] When estimates of spillovers from all MNCs are made (Table 4.6, left column), the coefficient on the foreign share is higher for sub-samples with R&D activity than sub-samples without R&D activity and this difference is weakly significant (at the 10 per cent level). When spillovers are allowed to vary among ownership groups a similar result is obtained in that all coefficients are larger in the group of plants with R&D activity. Differences between the two groups are also highly significant for majority-foreign MNCs, suggesting that spillovers from this group were relatively small in the sample of plants with no R&D activity, but that spillovers were the same for all groups of MNCs in plants with R&D activity. However, differences in other foreign ownership coefficients were not significant between these groups when using this specification. There is thus some weak evidence suggesting that spillovers were larger for locally-owned plants engaged in R&D than for other locally-owned plants regardless of whether MNC ownership groups are distinguished or not.

4.5 Concluding remarks

This chapter has examined how affiliates of multinational corporations affect productivity in Indonesian manufacturing. It began with a brief review of trends in MNC activities, emphasizing that MNCs grew particularly rapidly in the early 1990s and continued to grow even after the 1997–98 crisis. It also showed that MNC shares varied greatly by industry, with MNCs playing by far the largest role in the electric and precision machinery industry after the early 1990s. MNCs also generated large employment in textiles, apparel and footwear, and had relatively large value added in chemicals, metal products and transportation machinery. MNC shares of Indonesian manufacturing activity also tended to be much larger in terms of production than in terms of employment.

Correspondingly, the chapter also highlighted the fact that MNCs tended to have much higher labour productivity than local plants in 1986–2001. When labour productivity differentials were measured with simple descriptive statistics, they were very large, often several hundred per cent. If the influences of factor intensities, size and vintage are accounted for, these differentials become much smaller, however. In general, labour productivity differentials tended to be largest for majority-foreign plants (50–89 per cent foreign ownership), followed by minority-foreign plants (10–49 per cent foreign ownership), and lastly for heavily-foreign plants (90–100 per cent foreign ownership).

When more general estimates of productivity differentials are made at the industry level in 1995, no clear relationship between productivity and differences among ownership groups and productivity emerges. However, results suggest that all MNCs have higher productivity than local plants in at least half of the industries examined and in three-quarters at a slightly lower level of statistical significance. In addition, if all manufacturing plants are combined into one sample, and the lower productivity of relatively new MNCs is accounted for, there is some indication that productivity is highest in wholly-foreign plants, followed by majority-foreign plants (51–99 per cent foreign ownership), and minority-foreign plants (10–50 per cent foreign ownership).

This last result is important because similar specifications are required to examine the extent of productivity spillovers from MNCs in Indonesian manufacturing. The extent of spillovers was estimated using panel data for 1990–95. The results suggest that there is usually a strong and positive relationship between productivity in local plants and MNC presence in an industry. In other words, this basic result is consistent with results from previous studies suggesting the existence of positive productivity spillovers in Indonesian manufacturing.

However, the magnitude of these productivity spillovers depends on the characteristics of the industries, local plants and foreign affiliates involved. For example, these results suggest that spillovers from minority-foreign plants are larger than spillovers from plants with large foreign ownership shares. In other words, the results suggest that MNCs with large foreign ownership shares have higher productivity, but create relatively small spillovers. One possible explanation is that MNCs with large foreign ownership shares can control the leakage of their firm-specific assets more effectively than other MNCs, resulting in relatively high productivity but relatively small spillovers. The extent of techno-logical gaps between MNCs and local plants is another important consideration as spillovers were found to be larger in industries with relatively small technological gaps. Thus, if MNCs with high foreign ownership shares use relatively sophisticated technology, spillovers from these MNCs may be limited by the extent of the technological gaps between these MNCs and local plants.

The results also suggest that the extent of productivity spillovers is related to the characteristics of local plants. For example, results suggesting relatively large spillovers in industries with small technolog-ical gaps further imply that local plants could benefit more from MNC presence by improving their technology and thus narrowing the tech-nological gaps. A similar conclusion is suggested by the result suggesting that spillovers were relatively large for local plants with R&D activity. In other words, the extent of spillovers also depends on whether local plants make efforts to improve their own productivity.

Notes

1. The focus is on the 1986–2001 period primarily because data constraints allow more reliable analyses for this period than for previous years. In addition, Indonesia undertook some very fundamental economic reforms in the mid-1980s that resulted in large structural changes thereafter and so complicate comparisons with earlier periods. For more details on trends before 1986, see Hill (1988), Pangestu (1996) and Takii and Ramstetter (2005).
2. These compilations come from Takii and Ramstetter (2004), which is the most comprehensive of known compilations by ownership.

3. The overall Indonesian economy expanded at a compound annual average rate of 6.9 per cent between 1986 and 1996, while manufacturing grew 11.4 per cent annually (calculated from Takii 2005b: Table 7.1).
4. Majority-foreign plants accounted for 5 per cent of employment in large and medium-sized manufacturing plants in 1991 and 8 per cent in 1996, while corresponding shares for minority-foreign plants increased from 4 per cent to 6 per cent, respectively. Majority-foreign plants' shares of value added increased from 11 per cent to 13 per cent, respectively, while shares of minority-foreign plants increased from 9 per cent to 12 per cent, respectively.
5. These factors are thought to be important reasons why several Japanese auto affiliates increased their holdings in their Indonesian affiliates. For example, there were notable increases in Honda (49 per cent to 51 per cent in 2002), Nissan (35 per cent to 75 per cent in September 2001), Daihatsu (40 per cent to 62 per cent, announced in August 2002), Suzuki (49 per cent to 90 per cent, announced in November 2002), Hino (60 per cent to 90 per cent of its manufacturing firm, announced in January 2003) and Toyota (49 per cent to 95 per cent of its manufacturing firm, announced in February 2003).
6. Local firms in developing countries find it difficult to access more sophisticated technology, partly because markets for such technology are often non-existent because of the asymmetry that exists between potential buyers and sellers of such technology (Markusen 1995).
7. Similarly large differences were also observed in 1975–85, 1992–94 and 1998–99 (Takii and Ramstetter 2005: Table 5).
8. There are also a few very large differentials exceeding 800 per cent for heavily-foreign MNCs in plastics in 1995–97, majority-foreign MNCs in metal products in 2000–01 and minority-foreign MNCs in transportation machinery in 2000–01. These results probably reflect the influence of a few extreme observations, but they also result from plant heterogeneity that persists in these rather broad definitions of industries.
9. See Takii and Ramstetter (2005) for a detailed explanation of the methodology used to make these estimates. Similar comparisons including 2001 were not possible because of data constraints.
10. This pattern is also similar if estimates for 1975–85, 1992–94 and 1998–99 are included (Takii and Ramstetter 2005: Table 5).
11. Some of these results change if estimates for 1975–85, 1992–94 and 1998–99 are included (Takii and Ramstetter 2005: Table 5). First, significant productivity differentials were more common for heavily-foreign MNCs than minority-foreign MNCs. Second, on the other hand, direct comparisons suggested that heavily-foreign MNCs had higher labour productivity in a smaller proportion of cases (28 of 49).
12. Note that the definitions of minority- and majority-foreign plants used in this and the following section differ from those used in sections 4.2 and 4.3.1.
13. Lipsey and Sjöholm (2005) also provide a detailed survey of the evidence on productivity spillovers in Indonesian manufacturing.
14. According to the survey by Görg and Greenaway (2003), of forty studies that investigated the existence of productivity spillovers, only six used panel data and appropriate estimation techniques and none of these studies covered developing countries.

15. On the other hand, a potential simultaneity problem would still be present if MNCs (or MNCs with large foreign ownership shares) choose to invest in industries where local plants have high productivity growth.
16. The inclusion of the share of new MNCs is designed to account for differences in the magnitude of spillovers derived from relatively new plants and others. However, the coefficient on this MNC share was usually insignificant so it is not discussed here. See Takii (2001, 2005a) for more details.
17. The sensitivity of these results was examined using alternative definitions of small- and large-gap industries, but the main results remained unchanged (Takii 2005a).
18. In the 1990–95 sample period, data on R&D expenditures are only available for 1995. Therefore, plants with positive R&D expenditures in 1995 are classified into the group with R&D.

References

Blalock, Garrick and Paul J. Gertler (2004) 'Welfare Gains from Foreign Direct Investment through Technology Transfer to Local Suppliers', Mimeo, Cornell University.

Blomström, Magnus and Ari Kokko (1997) 'How Foreign Investment Affects Host Countries', Working Paper Series No. 1745, World Bank.

Blomström, Magnus, Ari Kokko and Mario Zejan (2000) *Foreign Direct Investment: Firm and Host Country Strategies*, London: Macmillan Press.

Blomström, Magnus and Fredrik Sjöholm (1999) 'Technology Transfer and Spillovers: Does Local Participation with Multinationals Matter?' *European Economic Review*, 43: 915–23.

BPS-Statistics (1997) *Statistics During 50 Years of Independence*, Jakarta: BPS-Statistics.

Findlay, Ronald (1978) 'Relative Backwardness, Direct Investment, and the Transfer of Technology: a Simple Dynamic Model', *Quarterly Journal of Economics*, 92: 1–16.

Görg, Holger and David Greenaway (2003) 'Much Ado About Nothing? Do Domestic Firms Really Benefit from Foreign Direct Investment?' Bonn: IZA Discussion Paper No. 944.

Hill, Hal (1988) *Foreign Investment and Industrialization in Indonesia*, Singapore: Oxford University Press.

Jacob, Jojo and Christoph Meister (2005) 'Productivity Gains, Technology Spillovers, and Trade: Indonesian Manufacturing, 1980–96', *Bulletin of Indonesian Economic Studies*, 41: 37–56.

Kokko, Ari (1994) 'Technology, Market Characteristics, and Spillovers', *Journal of Development Economics*, 43: 279–93.

Lipsey, Robert E. and Fredrik Sjöholm (2005) 'Host Country Impacts of Inward FDI: Why Such Different Answers?', in Theodore H. Moran, Edward M. Graham and Magnus Blomström, eds, *Does Foreign Direct Investment Promote Development?*, Washington, DC: Institute for International Economics, pp. 23–43.

MacDougall, G. D. A. (1960) 'The Benefits and Costs of Private Investment from Abroad: a Theoretical Approach', *Economic Record*, 36: 13–35.

Markusen, James R. (1995) 'The Boundaries of Multinational Enterprises and the Theory of International Trade', *Journal of Economic Perspectives*, 9: 169–89.

Moran, Theodore H. (2001) *Parental Supervision: the New Paradigm for Foreign Direct Investment and Development*, Washington, DC: Institute for International Economics.

Moran, Theodore H. (2002) *Beyond Sweatshops: Foreign Direct Investment and Globalization in Developing Countries*, Washington, DC: Brookings Institution.

Pangestu, Mari (1996) *Economic Reform, Deregulation and Privatization: the Indonesian Experience*, Jakarta: Centre for Strategic and International Studies.

Pangestu, Mari (2002) 'Foreign Investment Policy: Evolution and Characteristics', in Farrukh Iqbal and William E. James, eds, *Deregulation and Development in Indonesia*, Westport, CT: Praeger, pp. 45–60.

Sjöholm, Fredrik (1999a) 'Productivity Growth in Indonesia: the Role of Regional Characteristics and Direct Foreign Investment', *Economic Development and Cultural Change*, 47: 559–84.

Sjöholm, Fredrik (1999b) 'Technology Gap, Competition and Spillovers from Direct Foreign Investment: Evidence from Establishment Data', *Journal of Development Studies*, 36: 53–73.

Takii, Sadayuki (2001) 'Productivity Spillovers and Characteristics of Foreign Multinational Plants in Indonesian Manufacturing 1990–1995', Working Paper 2001–14, Kitakyushu: International Centre for the Study of East Asian Development.

Takii, Sadayuki (2004) 'Productivity Differentials between Local and Foreign Plants in Indonesian Manufacturing, 1995', *World Development*, 32: 1957–69.

Takii, Sadayuki (2005a) 'Productivity Spillovers and Characteristics of Foreign Multinational Plants in Indonesian Manufacturing 1990–1995', *Journal of Development Economics*, 76: 521–42.

Takii, Sadayuki (2005b) 'Indonesia', *East Asian Economic Perspectives [Recent Trends and Prospects for Major Asian Economies]*, 16, 1: 101–18.

Takii, Sadayuki and Eric D. Ramstetter (2004) 'Multinational Presence and Labour Productivity Differentials in Indonesian Manufacturing, 1975–2001', Working Paper 2004–15, Kitakyushu: International Centre for the Study of East Asian Development.

Takii, Sadayuki and Eric D. Ramstetter (2005) 'Multinational Presence and Labour Productivity Differentials in Indonesian Manufacturing, 1975–2001', *Bulletin of Indonesian Economic Studies*, 41: 221–42.

Todo, Yasuyuki and Koji Miyamoto (2002) 'Knowledge Diffusion from Multinational Enterprises: the Role of Domestic and Foreign Knowledge-Enhancing Activities', OECD Technical Paper No. 196, OECD Development Centre.

5
Are Productivity Differentials Important in Thai Manufacturing?

Eric D. Ramstetter

5.1 Introduction

Results of previous studies of foreign multinational corporations (MNCs) in Thai manufacturing present a puzzle for economists.[1] Although they indicate that MNCs have often had higher factor productivity than local plants or firms on average, differences in factor productivity, as well as more general differences in production technology, have not been that pervasive and therefore were statistically insignificant in many of the cases examined.[2] These results contrast markedly with the patterns suggested by theoretical analysis and observed in similar analyses of other countries such as Indonesia.[3] On the other hand, they are more consistent with results from studies of neighbouring Malaysia.[4] The apparent lack of significant differences in labour productivity is also puzzling because other results (e.g. Chapter 3) suggest that MNCs tend to pay relatively high wages and that wage differentials between MNCs and local plants are statistically significant in a number of cases.

The primary purpose of this chapter is to re-examine and add to the evidence regarding productivity differentials in Thailand, while trying to ascertain the robustness of the results obtained, as well as possible explanations for them. The first step is to briefly review analytical principles and the previous literature in the following section. As indicated in note 1, earlier studies for Thailand were based on analysis of rather limited samples of firms promoted by the Board of Investment (BOI), while this chapter focuses on analysis from a relatively comprehensive sample of manufacturing plants from the 1997 industrial census covering 1996 data. Correspondingly, section 5.3 describes the important characteristics of the 1996 data and analyses the patterns

114

observed in descriptive statistics calculated from those data. It also contrasts the patterns observed in the 1996 data with those observed in more limited survey data for 1998 and 2000. Section 5.4 then asks whether productivity differentials were statistically significant in 1996, and compares these results to observations from the 1998 and 2000 data. The analysis focuses on the implications of alternative assumptions regarding technology for productivity differentials between MNCs and local plants. It also considers the implications of accounting for differences among foreign ownership groups and foreign nationality groups. Subsequently, section 5.5 examines the possibility that the failure to observe productivity differentials could be related to the existence of positive productivity spillovers in Thailand, though the ability to analyse spillovers is severely limited by the need to use cross-section data. Finally, section 5.6 offers some concluding remarks.

5.2 Analytical principles and the previous literature

The theoretical literature on MNCs provides a very simple and important rationale for expecting productivity to be higher in MNCs than in non-MNCs in at least some respects. A large body of this literature (e.g. Dunning 1988, 1993; Hymer 1960; Markusen 1991) asserts that the possession of firm-specific assets, especially intangible assets related to production techniques and processes, marketing networks, and/or management ability, is required for a firm to become an MNC. Another body of literature (e.g. Buckley and Casson 1991; Casson 1987; Rugman 1980, 1985) disputes this view by asserting that internalization alone explains the existence of MNCs. However, all theorists agree that MNCs tend to possess the firm-specific assets described above in relatively large amounts. There is also substantial literature documenting the tendency for MNCs to have high expenditures on research and development and advertising, as well as to possess a relatively large number of patents (Caves 1996; Dunning 1993; Markusen 1991).

Because locally-owned firms in host economies like Thailand are predominantly non-MNCs, this logic suggests that affiliates of foreign-owned MNCs will be more efficient than their local counterparts. However, previous evidence on this point is mixed. On the one hand, evidence from industry- or firm-level cross-section studies in Indonesia (see note 2) and Mexico (e.g. Blomström 1990: 28–34) suggests that MNCs tend to use more efficient technology than local firms or plants. Rudimentary evidence from time series in Hong Kong, Indonesia, Malaysia, Singapore and Taiwan (Ramstetter 1999) also suggests that average factor productivity tends to be relatively high in MNCs. On the other hand, previous firm- and plant-level evidence for Thailand, as well as industry-level evidence from Malaysia (see note 1), suggests that productivity differentials between MNCs and local firms are not that prevalent and often statistically insignificant in those host economies.

MNCs are also thought to restrict the access of their foreign affiliates to the MNC's firm-specific assets, depending on the degree of control the parent exercises over the affiliate. More specifically, it is often argued that MNC parents are more reluctant to share their technology-related assets with minority-owned affiliates than with their majority-owned or wholly-owned affiliates (Chao and Yu 1996; Caves 1996: chs 3, 7, 9; Dunning 1993: chs 7–9, 11; Moran 2001). There is also a growing empirical literature suggesting that parents restrict access to exporting networks, which are another important firm-specific asset controlled by MNCs, in affiliates with relatively small foreign ownership shares in Southeast Asia.[5] However, corresponding evidence regarding productivity is more mixed in Indonesia (Chapter 4) and Thailand (Ramstetter 2001a, 2004), where larger foreign ownership shares are not necessarily correlated with higher productivity.

On the other hand, MNC parents may also want to share technology and other firm-specific assets with all affiliates in order to generate high productivity and large profits in those affiliates. The relative importance of competing motives to restrict or share firm-specific assets with minority-owned affiliates in particular is not clear *a priori*. Thus, one could reasonably expect relatively low or similar productivity levels in minority-owned affiliates compared to affiliates with larger foreign ownership shares. It is also important to recognize that preventing the spread of production technology through labour turnover, for example, is especially difficult in countries like Thailand, where many MNC manufacturing operations are labour-intensive and use rather standardized technology. Therefore, even if MNCs actively seek to restrict the transfer of firm-specific assets to minority-foreign affiliates, their efforts may be unsuccessful and productivity differentials between minority-foreign MNCs and other MNCs may be negligible or determined by other factors.

Another important consideration is the potential for technology to spillover from MNCs to local firms or plants. This occurs through several mechanisms including (1) subcontracting and other direct relationships between MNCs and local firms; (2) labour mobility between MNCs and local firms; and (3) increased competition resulting from MNC entry that forces local firms to put more emphasis on improving productivity.

In plant-level samples such as those examined in this chapter, these spillovers are usually hypothesized to lead to relatively high productivity levels in local plants in industries where MNC presence is relatively large. There is now considerable evidence of positive spillovers in Indonesia, for example (Chapter 4).[6] However, Kohpaiboon (2003) is the only known study of this nature for Thailand, suggesting that there were also positive spillovers in Thai manufacturing in 1996, but that spillovers were smaller in industries where protection was high.

5.3   The data, foreign presence and some indicators of productivity differentials

As indicated in the Introduction, this chapter focuses on analysis of data for 1996 from the 1997 industrial census, primarily because this is by far the most comprehensive source available to date.[7] As has been described in more detail elsewhere (Ramstetter 2001a, 2003, 2004), these data have numerous problems that must be addressed before they can be used for meaningful economic analysis. The data set obtained included a total of 32,489 plants of which 23,677 replied to the 1997 census and were included in the final compilation by the National Statistical Office (NSO). However, despite being far more comprehensive than alternative sources, the coverage of the industrial census was apparently rather limited. For example, published census estimates reported only 2.41 million workers or 52 per cent of corresponding estimates from the labour force surveys (Table 5.1). Similarly the value added reported in the census was only 72 per cent of the national accounts' estimate of manufacturing value added. Differences are to be expected because the census included plants with ten or more workers, while alternative estimates are made to cover the entire manufacturing sector. Nonetheless, the differences among the alternatives are probably larger than would be expected in a census year. There are also some particularly large differences at the industry level, with census estimates being much smaller than corresponding national accounts' estimates in apparel, leather and footwear, furniture and jewellery, and substantially larger in plastics, rubber, motor vehicles and chemicals.

In addition to reflecting differences in coverage and how industries are defined, these discrepancies may also be related to several additional problems in the census data. First, the plant-level census data set contains several duplicate or near duplicate records that must be eliminated in order to conduct a meaningful analysis. Almost all of the duplicates that could be identified resulted from plants belonging to one multiplant

Table 5.1 Employment and value added in Thai manufacturing in 1996

Variable, industry	Thai totals	NSO publication	Large sample					Small sample	
			All plants	MNC plants	Minority-foreign	Majority-foreign	Wholly-foreign	All plants	MNC plants
Employment (thousands)	4,644.15	2,413.33	1,772.62	749.13	423.42	141.53	184.18	1,669.50	720.51
Value added (billion baht)	1,385.69	998.11	854.70	441.55	271.17	79.26	91.12	809.58	431.18
Food	107.95	113.56	98.86	24.66	18.81	3.56	2.29	96.73	24.51
Textiles	92.65	46.47	35.32	20.27	16.33	2.20	1.74	32.59	18.06
Apparel	161.44	23.94	19.69	6.75	6.23	0.33	0.19	18.81	6.66
Leather & footwear	44.04	15.75	9.96	2.53	1.34	0.95	0.24	9.64	2.50
Chemicals & products	47.97	58.88	53.29	30.82	11.86	13.32	5.63	53.11	30.82
Rubber products	22.42	36.04	33.33	15.83	5.81	8.69	1.33	32.25	14.86
Plastics & products	14.16	27.04	19.81	7.17	3.97	1.86	1.34	19.12	7.08
Non-metallic mineral products	74.42	65.02	40.60	9.66	7.08	2.27	0.31	34.91	9.66
Metal products	37.88	35.21	28.80	17.33	13.30	1.75	2.28	27.07	16.35
General machinery	55.79	38.51	33.66	24.37	8.68	4.58	11.10	32.49	23.49
Electric & precision machinery	180.04	127.99	111.64	99.99	23.74	16.00	60.25	110.11	98.63
Office & computing machinery	51.64	28.02	24.13	24.04	3.72	1.94	18.38	24.06	23.98
Miscellaneous electric machinery	19.55	40.07	32.76	27.89	11.21	3.42	13.25	32.23	27.49
Radio, TV, communication	92.51	47.98	43.55	38.00	8.38	10.12	19.50	42.67	37.12
Precision machinery	16.34	11.92	11.19	10.07	0.42	0.53	9.12	11.14	10.05
Motor vehicles	104.16	139.67	130.56	115.68	104.47	9.63	1.57	129.40	115.66
Furniture	36.18	14.42	11.41	2.81	1.71	0.81	0.30	10.39	2.50
Jewellery	98.03	9.18	8.15	4.10	1.79	1.02	1.29	8.02	4.09

Note: The large sample includes plants reporting positive value added and workers; the small sample includes plants reporting positive value added, production workers, and non-production workers.
Sources: Ramstetter (2003: Appendix Tables 1a, 2a) for large samples; Ramstetter (2002a: Appendix Tables A2, A3) for small samples.

firm reporting the same firm-level data as plant-level data. The methodology for eliminating duplicate records used in this chapter and in Chapter 8 was to retain one record from each set of duplicates. The approach was probably biased towards leaving a record in the database if there was some doubt as to whether it was a duplicate.[8] In contrast, some of the samples used in Chapter 3 were smaller, partly because they excluded all potential duplicates and eliminated extreme observations. Second, many plants report apparently implausible values for important variables. Plants reporting non-positive values for employment, intermediate consumption or value added were also eliminated from the samples used in this study because non-positive values do not make economic sense in this context. Third, plants with less than twenty employees, which were predominantly local, were also eliminated because they are not thought to be comparable with MNC plants. These three adjustments result in the reduction of the total sample to less than half of the published total or 10,494 plants.[9] This is called the large sample in this chapter. In other analyses it is necessary to limit the sample to plants reporting positive numbers of both production and non-production workers. Imposing this restriction further reduces the sample to 8952 plants, which is called the small sample in this chapter.

Although both of these samples include only a minority of the plants reported in the official publication (National Statistical Office 1999), the plants in these samples accounted for over two-thirds of the employment and more than four-fifths of the value added reported in that publication (Table 5.1). In other words, the plants excluded from these samples were much smaller on average than the plants retained. Moreover, both employment and value added were only 5–6 per cent smaller in the small sample than in the large sample. However, comparisons to economy-wide estimates suggest that the coverage of these samples was less comprehensive: 36–38 per cent of manufacturing employment reported in the labour force surveys and 58–62 per cent of the value added reported in the national accounts.

MNCs in the large sample employed about 749,130 workers or 42 per cent of the large sample total and 16 per cent of the Thai manufacturing total reported in the labour force survey data (Table 5.1). Value added produced by MNCs amounted to 52 per cent of the large sample total and 32 per cent of manufacturing GDP reported in the national accounts. These data also suggest that MNCs accounted for more than half of total Thai value added in motor vehicles, rubber, chemicals, electric and precision machinery, and plastics, though the apparent mismatches between the census and the national accounts data noted above make these very rough estimates at best.[10] Based on the large sample, MNCs accounted for the largest shares in electric and precision machinery and motor vehicles (89–90 per cent), followed by general machinery (72 per cent), and then metal products, chemicals and textiles (57–60 per cent each). In value terms, MNC value added was by far the largest in motor vehicles (116 billion baht) and electric and precision machinery (100 billion baht), followed distantly by chemicals, food, general machinery and textiles (20–31 billion baht each). In short, MNCs accounted for substantial shares of a wide range of Thai manufacturing industries, but MNCs were by far the largest, both absolutely and relative to Thai totals, in motor vehicles as well as electric and precision machinery.

Among MNCs, minority-foreign MNCs accounted for most of the activity, about three-fifths of both employment and value added. Minority-foreign MNCs accounted for particularly large shares of MNC value added (73 per cent or more) in food, textiles, apparel, non-metallic mineral products, metal products and motor vehicles (Table 5.1). Conversely, these shares were low (two-fifths or less) in chemicals, rubber, general machinery, and electric and precision machinery. Majority-foreign MNCs accounted for a little under one-fifth of MNC employment and value added, while wholly-foreign MNCs accounted for one-quarter of MNC employment and a little over one-fifth of MNC value added. Shares of MNC value added were relatively high (30 per cent or more) for majority-foreign MNCs in leather and footwear, chemicals and rubber, and for wholly-foreign MNCs in general machinery, electric and precision machinery, and jewellery. These patterns reflect the fact that Thailand still had some strict foreign ownership restrictions in place in 1996, but that the government often granted exceptions to those restrictions for plants that met specified criteria such as employing a large number of workers, locating outside of the Greater Bangkok area, or exporting a large portion of their output.

Table 5.1 shows that foreign MNC shares of manufacturing value added were slightly higher than corresponding shares of employment in 1996, implying that value added per worker was somewhat higher. Correspondingly, value added per worker hour was an average of 165 baht for MNCs but only 106 baht for local plants, a 56 per cent differential (Table 5.2). Although not directly comparable with the 1996 figures cited above because samples are much smaller, it is also instructive to examine calculations from surveys covering 1998 and 2000, which indicate a similar differential in 2000 (48 per cent) but a somewhat larger one in 1998 (98 per cent).[11] However, all of these differentials were much

Table 5.2 Mean value added per hour worked, large 1996 sample (baht)

Industry	All plants	Local plants	MNC plants	Minority-foreign	Majority-foreign	Wholly-foreign
Manufacturing	116	106	165	166	197	120
Food	136	137	128	124	141	138
Textiles	58	51	86	80	113	82
Apparel	58	57	66	71	43	71
Leather & footwear	73	74	68	54	97	46
Chemicals & products	183	119	341	228	711	301
Rubber products	173	132	285	241	616	31
Plastics & products	64	63	66	72	70	47
Non-metallic mineral products	135	137	109	123	82	23
Metal products	98	83	188	197	148	194
General machinery	104	95	136	147	132	105
Electric & precision machinery	121	99	142	205	87	116
Motor vehicles	151	101	387	394	403	148
Furniture	87	88	78	78	97	53
Jewellery	160	191	116	105	119	137

Source: Ramstetter (2003: Appendix Table 9a).

smaller than corresponding differentials observed in Indonesia, for example (see Chapter 4).

As would generally be expected, Table 5.2 also indicates substantial variation in average labour productivity levels and differentials across industries. The highest productivity levels were observed in MNCs in motor vehicles, chemicals, rubber and metal products. Differentials between MNCs and local plants were also the largest in these industries – over 100 per cent. On the other hand, in five of the fourteen individual industries studied (food, leather and footwear, non-metallic mineral products, furniture and jewellery), MNCs had lower average labour productivity than local plants. The large number of negative differentials is somewhat surprising, but the smaller survey samples for 1998 and 2000 suggest that negative differentials were less common in those years.[12]

Another somewhat surprising pattern is the fact that wholly-foreign MNCs tended to have the lowest average labour productivity (120 baht per hour) of all MNCs in 1996, while majority-foreign MNCs had the highest (197 baht per hour, Table 5.2). Average labour productivity was lower in wholly-foreign MNCs than in minority- or majority-foreign MNCs in ten of fourteen industries for each comparison. It was also lower in wholly-foreign plants than in local plants in six of fourteen industries. Majority-foreign MNCs had higher labour productivity than minority-foreign plants in only slightly more than half (eight of fourteen) of these industries. In other words, among MNC ownership groups, wholly-foreign plants tended to have the lowest average labour productivity, but differences between majority- and minority-foreign plants were not very consistent across industries.

Using calculations made from the small sample, it is possible to distinguish two types of average labour productivity, as well as compile data on average capital productivity and capital intensity (Table 5.3). These calculations suggest that non-production workers produced much more than production workers and that both production workers and non-production workers had higher average productivity in manufacturing MNCs on average.[13] Average productivity differentials for all manufacturing were larger for production workers (251 baht versus

Table 5.3 Average factor productivity and capital intensity, small 1996 sample (baht, except ratio as noted)

Industry	Value added/ production worker hour		Value added/ non-production worker hour		Value added/ fixed capital (ratio)		Fixed capital/ worker hour	
	Local plants	MNC total	Local plants	MNC total	Local plants	MNC total	Local plants	MNC total
Manufacturing	145	251	1,010	1,422	2.453	1.980	436	1,919
Food	207	171	1,183	1,330	2.036	2.111	557	854
Textiles	67	104	592	1,595	1.755	1.479	362	1,120
Apparel	73	72	741	1,209	4.137	2.569	139	163
Leather & footwear	92	80	834	1,333	3.246	3.523	177	254
Chemicals & products	188	709	767	1,162	1.743	2.438	696	2,273
Rubber products	188	357	1,506	2,482	3.211	2.516	443	1,164
Plastics & products	73	98	600	565	1.420	1.023	380	641
Non-metallic mineral products	175	175	1,614	1,449	1.796	1.104	526	1,215
Metal products	111	251	838	1,316	2.325	1.396	330	1,047
General machinery	125	196	1,063	1,265	1.854	1.159	447	771
Electric & precision machinery	151	187	812	1,407	2.643	1.452	299	7,113
Motor vehicles	125	509	898	3,472	3.605	1.242	414	1,646
Furniture	110	79	937	673	3.500	1.592	245	215
Jewellery	341	139	1,555	1,851	4.998	5.723	250	200

Source: Ramstetter (2002a: Appendix Table B2).

145 baht per hour or 73 per cent) than for non-production workers (1422 baht versus 1010 baht per hour, 41 per cent). By industry, positive differentials were more common for non-production workers (eleven of fourteen industries) than for production workers (nine of fourteen industries). Similar calculations from the 1998 survey again indicate that positive labour productivity differentials were somewhat larger in manufacturing on average and more common at the industry level in that year.[14]

Average capital productivity differentials in all manufacturing were relatively small in absolute value but negative (e.g. 1.98 versus 2.45 or −19 per cent), indicating lower average capital productivity in MNCs than in local plants. Similarly negative differentials were also observed in ten of the fourteen individual industries examined. The tendency for capital productivity to be relatively low in MNCs is also reflected in extremely high levels of capital intensity in MNCs. Overall, MNCs used an average of 1919 baht of fixed capital per worker hour but local plants used only 436 baht, a 340 per cent differential. These differentials were also 100 per cent or larger in half of the fourteen individual industries and positive in twelve industries. Calculations from the industrial survey for 1998 also suggest a strong tendency for MNCs to be more capital-intensive, but indicate smaller capital-intensive differentials, as well as little overall difference in average capital productivity.[15]

To sum up, these descriptive statistics suggest that MNCs did not have higher labour productivity in several industries in 1996 and tended to have relatively low capital productivity in most. However, these data also suggest that MNCs tended to be more capital-intensive than local plants. It is also true that MNCs tended to be much larger than local plants, which could make it easier for them to benefit from scale economies. Thus, it is clearly important to control for the influences of factor intensity, scale and other related factors when making comparisons of productivity in MNCs and local plants. It is also important to emphasize that productivity levels and differentials apparently vary greatly across industries. This makes it crucial to account for industry-level differences when making such comparisons.

5.4   Are productivity differentials significant?

This section examines productivity differentials more rigorously, after removing the influences of plant-level variation in factor intensities, scale and other factors related to technology. In addition, some of the results also account for differences between old plants (more than twelve years old) and newer plants as well as between plants promoted by the Thai BOI and those that are not. The logic for these controls is explained in other papers (Ramstetter 2002a, 2004) and this section will not dwell on the technical details. Rather, this section focuses on two sets of results for 1996, evaluating how alternative assumptions about technology affect the observation of productivity differentials and comparing the implications of the results presented to those of other studies as relevant.

5.4.1 Comparisons assuming Cobb-Douglas technology

In the Thai case, the most common approach towards examining productivity differentials has been to estimate Cobb-Douglas production functions and then to test for differences between MNCs and local firms or plants in various ways. These studies began by examining relatively small samples of BOI-promoted firms in the early 1980s (Khanthachai et al. 1987) as well as 1974 and 1986 (Tambunlertchai and Ramstetter 1991). Ramstetter (1993, 1994) then used similar methodologies to examine a larger sample for 1990, but this sample also consisted mainly of BOI-promoted firms. The results of these studies suggested that differences in productivity levels, as well as more general differences in production functions were often statistically insignificant in Thai manufacturing, especially at the industry level. When the results were interpreted, it was speculated that the BOI-promoted firms, which dominated these samples, might be among the more efficient of local firms, thereby making it difficult to find statistically significant differences in these samples.

After the industrial census for 1996 and subsequent surveys for 1998 and 2000 became available, it became possible to avoid this potential sampling bias, especially for the census year. Ramstetter (2001a, 2001b, 2004) thus re-examined productivity differentials among MNCs and local plants using alternative Cobb-Douglas specifications. The Cobb-Douglas approach is restrictive because the elasticity of substitution between factors for production (i.e. the percentage change in the capital-labour ratio that results from a one percentage point change in the ratio of the price of capital to the price of labour) is assumed to be one. However, the approach can be useful because its simplicity minimizes the potential for econometric problems such as multicollinearity and allows for easy interpretation of the results. These advantages are especially pronounced if constant returns to scale are assumed. In this case, the addition of a dummy variable for MNCs allows easy comparison of average factor (usually labour) productivity between MNCs and local firms or plants. Alternatively, one can define a number of dummies identifying ownership or nationality groups of MNCs, thereby facilitating comparisons between the MNC groups identified and local firms or plants. Some studies (e.g. Ramstetter 1994, 2001a, 2001b, 2004) have adopted this approach primarily because it is the only practical way to simultaneously compare a number of MNC groups and local plants.

Table 5.4 summarizes some results using this methodology, first showing statistically significant average labour productivity differentials between all MNCs and local plants in fourteen major manufacturing industries, after accounting for plant-level variation in capital intensity (the ratio of fixed assets to employment), non-production labour intensity (the share of non-production workers in employment), BOI promotional status, vintage (plants twelve years and older and newer plants), and size (differences between large plants and other plants in each industry).[16] Separate estimates were also performed for samples of all plants and samples of large plants with output of 25 million baht (about US$1 million) or more in order to examine the sensitivity of the results.[17] The results suggested that, after accounting for the other influences on labour productivity, MNCs had significantly higher average labour productivity in only two of the fourteen industries in both samples, chemicals and metal products, and in one more, jewellery, in the sample of all plants. In most industries, these differentials were statistically insignificant, suggesting that average labour productivity was generally not different in MNCs than in local plants. Similar results from the more limited industrial survey samples indicated that statistically significant differentials were somewhat more common in 1998 but even rarer in 2000.[18]

One reason why comparisons of MNCs and local plants might fail to reveal significant productivity differentials would be if differences among groups of MNCs were important. As explained in section 5.2, the distinction among ownership groups of MNCs, especially between those with large ownership shares and those with smaller ones, are often thought to be important. Thus, another set of regressions examines the differences between wholly-foreign, majority-foreign and minority-foreign MNCs on the one hand, and local plants, on the other.[19] Results of these estimates (Table 5.4) are similar to the results described above in that the vast majority of the productivity differentials are not statistically significant. However, these results do suggest there may have been positive differentials in textiles involving majority-foreign plants (both samples) and wholly-foreign plants (all plants) that the previous analysis did not reveal. The results also indicate that the productivity differentials observed in chemicals and metal products were concentrated in wholly-foreign MNCs as theory would suggest.

Table 5.4 Percentage differences in mean value added per hour worked between foreign MNCs and local plants assuming Cobb-Douglas technology, large 1996 sample

Industry	All plants				Large plants			
	All MNCs	Minority-foreign	Majority-foreign	Wholly-foreign	All MNCs	Minority-foreign	Majority-foreign	Wholly-foreign
Food	ns	ns	ns	ns	−28	−30	ns	ns
Textiles	ns	ns	68	88	ns	ns	79	ns
Apparel	ns	ns	ns	ns	ns	ns	ns	ns
Leather & footwear	ns	ns	ns	ns	ns	ns	ns	ns
Chemicals & products	44	34	ns	82	39	ns	ns	77
Rubber products	ns	ns	ns	ns	ns	ns	ns	ns
Plastics & products	ns	ns	ns	ns	ns	ns	ns	ns
Non-metallic mineral products	ns	ns	ns	ns	ns	ns	ns	ns
Metal products	32	ns	ns	63	28	ns	ns	ns
General machinery	ns	ns	ns	ns	ns	ns	ns	ns
Electric & precision machinery	ns	ns	ns	ns	−32	ns	−40	−54
Motor vehicles	ns	ns	ns	ns	ns	ns	ns	ns
Furniture	ns	ns	ns	ns	ns	−56	ns	ns
Jewellery	33	ns	ns	ns	ns	ns	ns	ns

Notes: Controls are capital intensity, non-production labour intensity, BOI promotional status, vintage and size; ns = difference not statistically significant at the 5 per cent level; all significance tests use heteroscedasticity-consistent standard errors; estimates for all MNCs assume that value added per hour was the same in all MNC ownership groups (minority-, majority- and wholly-foreign MNCs); large plants are plants with output of 25 million baht or more.

Source: Ramstetter (2004: Table 3).

Similar specifications have also been used to examine productivity differentials among nationality groups of MNCs and local plants in the census sample for 1996 and the survey samples for 1998 and 2000 (Ramstetter 2004). These comparisons also revealed a few productivity differentials that were not present in the aggregated comparison of all MNCs and local plants. They also suggested a weak tendency for labour productivity to be relatively high in MNCs from Europe, Japan and the United States compared to other MNCs, most of which come from other Asian economies. Significant productivity differentials were again relatively common in the 1998 sample, but rather rare in the 1996 and 2000 samples. In short, the most conspicuous result of analyses assuming Cobb-Douglas technology with constant returns is the fact that labour productivity differentials between MNCs and local plants are usually found to be statistically insignificant.

It should also be noted that relaxing the assumption of constant returns did not change this basic result in census samples for 1996 and survey samples for 1998 (Ramstetter 2001a). Several older studies mentioned above (Khanthachai et al. 1987; Ramstetter 1993; Ramstetter and Tambunlertchai 1991) also assumed Cobb-Douglas technology with variable returns, but failed to find many statistically significant productivity differentials.

5.4.2   Comparisons assuming translog technology

All the Cobb-Douglas-based approaches described above impose the unrealistic assumption that the elasticity of substitution among factors equals one. To get around this assumption a few studies (Brimble 1993; Ramstetter 2002a) have employed translog production functions which allow for a variable elasticity of substitution, in addition to variable returns to scale. Similarly, the productivity differentials reported in this section are calculated from simple translog production function estimates, where value added is specified as a function of labour and fixed assets.[20] Separate production functions are first estimated for MNCs and local plants, and a statistical test is then performed to see whether the functions are identical for both groups.[21] If the null hypothesis that the functions are identical is rejected, marginal products and production shift factors (the constant in the production function) are then calculated from the estimates and compared. If this null hypothesis cannot be rejected at the standard (5 per cent) level, differentials are reported as insignificant.

The first set of results assumes two types of labour, production and non-production workers, as in the preceding section (Table 5.5).[22] These results also suggest identical production functions in most of the industries

Table 5.5 Percentage differences in various productivity measures between all MNCs and local plants assuming translog technology and heterogeneous labour, small 1996 sample

Industry	Marginal product of production labour		Marginal product of non-production labour		Marginal product of fixed capital		Production shift factor	
	All plants	Large plants	All plants	Large plants	All plants	Large plants	All plants	Large plants
Food	ns	ns	ns	ns	ns	ns	ns	ns
Textiles	237	871	55	−70	−110	−94	4.0	4.8
Apparel	ns	ns	ns	ns	ns	ns	ns	ns
Leather & footwear	ns	smpl	ns	smpl	ns	smpl	ns	smpl
Chemicals & products	−378	−336	−214	−669	40	89	2.5	2.2
Rubber products	ns	ns	ns	ns	ns	ns	ns	ns
Plastics & products	ns	ns	ns	ns	ns	ns	ns	ns
Non-metallic mineral products	−124	ns	179	ns	−85	ns	0.7	ns
Metal products	−80	−18	−108	−1,014	38	27	1.9	1.5
General machinery	ns	ns	ns	ns	ns	ns	ns	ns
Electric & precision machinery	ns	ns	ns	ns	ns	ns	ns	ns
Motor vehicles	ns	ns	ns	ns	ns	ns	ns	ns
Furniture	ns	−154	ns	54	ns	35	ns	−0.1
Jewellery	39	ns	−108	ns	−80	ns	1.6	ns

Notes: ns = difference not statistically significant at the 5 per cent level; all signficance tests use heteroscedasticity-consistent standard errors; smpl = sample too small to faciliate reliable estimates (i.e. less than 30 local plants and/or less than 30 foreign plants); large plants are plants with output of 25 million baht or more.

Source: Ramstetter (2002a: Appendix Tables C1a, C2a, C3a, C4a, C5a, C6a, C7a, C8a, C9a, C10a, C11a, C12a, C13a, C14a).

examined, nine of fourteen samples for all plants and nine of thirteen samples for large plants. Moreover, significant differences were observed in both samples in only three industries: textiles, chemicals and metal products. Significant differences were also observed in non-metallic mineral products and jewellery in samples of all plants, and in furniture in samples of large plants. When significant, factor productivity differentials were usually negative, however. For example, the only cases of positive productivity differentials in favour of MNCs were observed for production labour in textiles (both samples) and jewellery (large plants), non-production labour in textiles (all plants), non-metallic mineral products (all plants) and furniture (large plants), as well as for capital in chemicals (both samples), metal products (both samples) and furniture (large plants). On the other hand, when there were statistically significant differences in production functions, the production shift factor was almost always higher in MNCs, a very small negative differential in the sample of large plants for furniture being the single exception. Thus, in this one respect, more general assumptions about technology seem to reveal a few more statistically significant differences than previously found.

There are two potential problems with the translog estimates presented above. First, the large number of parameters to be estimated means that small sample size could be a problem, especially for samples of large MNCs.[23] Second, high correlations among interaction terms in a translog specification create potential multicollinearity problems.[24] One way to reduce the potential severity of both of these problems is to reduce the number of factors in the production function. This can be done by assuming only one labour input, for example. Although it is theoretically preferable to identify two types of labour because their productivity levels are so different, the statistical benefits of simplifying the model may be more important in this context. Correspondingly, Table 5.6 reports the results of estimates assuming translog technology with homogeneous labour.[25] Results are very similar to those in Table 5.5 in that consistent differences between MNCs and local plants are only observed in three industries: textiles, chemicals and metal products. They are also consistent in suggesting significant differences in jewellery in the sample of all plants. However, the results differ in general machinery, where significant differences are found in the sample of large plants, and in non-metallic mineral products and furniture, where no significant differences are suggested. In this specification, results regarding factor productivity are mixed in the industries with significant differences. Labour is more productive in MNCs in textiles (all plants, but not large plants), chemicals (both samples) and

Table 5.6 Percentage differences in various productivity measures between all MNCs and local plants assuming translog technology and homogeneous labour, small 1996 sample

Industry	Marginal product of labour		Marginal product of fixed capital		Production shift factor	
	All plants	Large plants	All plants	Large plants	All plants	Large plants
Food	ns	ns	ns	ns	ns	ns
Textiles	155	−435	−106	−108	2.8	2.8
Apparel	ns	ns	ns	ns	ns	ns
Leather & footwear	ns	smpl	ns	smpl	ns	smpl
Chemicals & products	114	100	66	123	2.9	3.0
Rubber products	ns	ns	ns	ns	ns	ns
Plastics & products	ns	ns	ns	ns	ns	ns
Non-metallic mineral products	ns	ns	ns	ns	ns	ns
Metal products	−45	−39	47	30	1.3	1.3
General machinery	ns	262	ns	−71	ns	1.2
Electric & precision machinery	ns	ns	ns	ns	ns	ns
Motor vehicles	ns	ns	ns	ns	ns	ns
Furniture	ns	ns	ns	ns	ns	ns
Jewellery	−41	ns	−83	ns	1.6	ns

Notes: ns = difference not statistically significant at the 5 per cent level; smpl = sample too small to facilitate reliable estimates (i.e. less than 30 local plants and/or less than 30 foreign plants).
Source: Ramstetter (2002a: Appendix Tables C1c, C2c, C3c, C4c, C5c, C6c, C7c, C8c, C9c, C10c, C11c, C12c, C13c, C14c).

general machinery (large plants), while capital productivity differentials are positive in chemicals and metal products. However, negative differentials are as common as positive ones. On the other hand, the production shift factor is always higher in MNCs than in local plants, when differences are statistically significant.

5.5   Spillovers and explanations for the lack of productivity differentials

Both descriptive statistics and the statistical analysis accounting for other factors affecting productivity suggest that productivity differentials are not very common between MNCs and local plants in Thailand.

Moreover, similar results have been obtained from several studies spanning almost three decades and employing several alternative methodologies. One possible reason for this result would be if local plants were able to imitate MNCs quickly and thereby keep the technology gap between local plants and MNCs relatively small. As noted in section 5.2, MNCs are hypothesized to create productivity spillovers to local plants, which are realized through direct links with local plants, labour mobility between MNCs and local plants, and increased competition resulting from MNC presence. These spillovers are often examined by estimating a production function for local plants in a large cross-section of all manufacturing industries, and adding a measure of the MNC share of economic activity in each individual industry. If the coefficient on the MNC share is positive, it indicates that local plant productivity is higher in industries with large MNC presence and is interpreted as evidence of positive productivity spillovers.

As illustrated in Chapter 4's analysis of productivity spillovers in Indonesia, it is also common to examine how the extent of spillovers varies depending on foreign ownership shares or upon the nature of the industry involved. For example, Chapter 4 suggests that spillovers were positive and relatively large in industries where (1) MNCs with high foreign ownership shares were relatively small; (2) technological gaps between MNCs and local plants were relatively small; (3) capital intensity was relatively low; and (4) local plants had research and development activities. The only known study of spillovers in Thailand (Kohpaiboon 2003) examines another dimension of this issue, suggesting that spillovers were again positive and tended to be larger in industries with low levels of import protection.

In this chapter, the primary purpose is to ascertain whether positive spillovers might be able to explain the inability to find evidence of widespread productivity differentials in the previous section. The first step is thus to see if the evidence is consistent with spillovers in the three models used to examine productivity differentials. These models are distinguished by their alternative assumptions of (1) Cobb-Douglas technology with constant returns to scale; (2) translog technology with heterogeneous labour; and (3) translog technology with homogeneous labour.

Estimates assuming spillovers were identical for all MNCs all indicate that these spillovers were positive, statistically significant and of similar magnitude (Table 5.7). However, there was a 15 per cent variation in the estimates, with Cobb-Douglas estimates suggesting the smallest spillovers and translog estimates assuming homogeneous labour indicating the largest.

Estimates allowing the spillovers to vary depending on the type of MNC suggested a somewhat larger variation. The Cobb-Douglas estimates indicated that the largest spillovers involved majority-foreign MNCs, but both translog estimates suggested that the largest spillovers came from minority-foreign MNCs. Results from all specifications suggested spillovers from wholly-foreign MNCs were smaller than from the other two groups and 22–29 per cent smaller than from the top group. Thus, these results are similar to those for Indonesia in Chapter 4 in that they suggest spillovers were always positive but that spillovers involving wholly-foreign MNCs tended to be relatively small.

There are two fundamental problems with these spillover estimates that mandate caution in their interpretation. First, there is a potential simultaneity problem, which can be especially severe in simple cross-sections such as this one.[26] Namely, MNCs may be attracted to industries in which local plants have high productivity. Kohpaiboon's (2003) estimates are notable in this regard, because they suggest that positive spillovers still exist after accounting for this kind of simultaneity. Second, in contrast to the industry-level estimates of productivity differentials

Table 5.7   Estimates of spillover coefficients under alternative assumptions and equation explanatory power, small 1996 sample

Industry	Cobb-Douglas technology	Translog technology, heterogeneous labour	Translog technology, homogeneous labour
EQUATIONS ASSUMING IDENTICAL SPILLOVERS FROM ALL MNCs			
All MNCs	0.42	0.46	0.49
Adjusted R-squared	0.093	0.520	0.515
EQUATIONS ASSUMING SPILLOVERS VARY BY FOREIGN OWNERSHIP SHARE			
Minority-foreign MNCs	0.42	0.52	0.56
Majority-foreign MNCs	0.49	0.51	0.49
Wholly-foreign MNCs	0.39	0.40	0.46
Adjusted R-squared	0.093	0.519	0.515

Notes: All coefficients statistically significant at the 5 per cent level; all equations allow the production shift factor (the constant) to differ for BOI-promoted plants, old plants, and large plants; all tests of coefficient significance use White's standard errors that correct for heteroscedasticity; for detailed estimation results see Appendix Table 5.2.
Source: Appendix Table 5.2

in the previous section, estimates of spillovers must, by their nature, assume that production technology is identical across industries. In other words, it is impossible to account for the large industry-wise variation in productivity levels and productivity differentials that were observed in sections 5.3 and 5.4, and at the same time measure spillovers using the standard methodology. Because the spillover calculations are based on different assumptions about industry-wise variation in technology, it is thus a technical contradiction to argue that the observation of positive spillovers in Table 5.7 was a reason that calculations reported in Tables 5.4, 5.5 and 5.6 revealed relatively few significant productivity differentials.

Even if one accepts this evidence and concludes there were positive spillovers which contributed to the lack of significant productivity differentials in 1996, it also seems hard to argue that the existence of spillovers could explain evidence suggesting that significant productivity differentials were rare in numerous previous years (e.g. 1974, 1982–83, 1990). To the contrary, if there were positive spillovers in 1996, wouldn't that suggest positive productivity differentials in past years? Of course, as mentioned above, the evidence for past years comes from much more limited samples and it is possible that the results would be different if more comprehensive samples could be used for past years as well. On the other hand, the patterns observed in the older data sets and the 1996 data set are so similar in important respects that results for previous years might have been similar even if more comprehensive data sets were available.

If that is indeed the case, perhaps the only way to reconcile the existence of positive spillovers with the lack of productivity differentials would be if the spillovers were extremely rapid. Rapid spillovers are a possibility in Thailand for at least two reasons. First, labour, especially skilled labour, tends to be very mobile, which increases the diffusion of ideas from MNCs to local plants (and vice versa). Second, in most manufacturing industries, technologies are relatively standardized and easily imitated. This factor may be important in industries like food, apparel, leather and footwear, rubber, plastics, furniture and jewellery, for example.

Another possibility is that relatively large MNC presence intensifies competitive pressure in an industry and motivates local firms to increase productivity, even though productivity differentials are not statistically significant. In other words, it may be that there is such large variation in the productivity levels of MNCs and local plants in most industries that the differences between the groups have not been significant, even though positive spillovers exist. For example, some local firms are known to operate relatively efficient plants in industries such as food (e.g. Charoen Pokphand Foods) and non-metallic minerals (e.g. Siam Cement), while there are also many other local plants in these industries that have rather low productivity. On the other hand, there is a wide range of performance among both MNCs and local plants as illustrated in case studies of the automobile industry (Chapter 6; Ito 2004a; Umemoto and Ramstetter 2004). Very clearly, the data examined in this chapter and previous studies of productivity differentials suggest that large variation is the norm and the proximate cause of the prevalence of insignificant productivity differentials between MNCs and local plants. Unfortunately, it is impossible to evaluate the extent to which positive spillovers may be responsible for this observation with any precision.

5.6   In conclusion: the puzzle remains

This chapter has reviewed evidence suggesting that productivity differentials between MNCs and local plants, as well as more general differences in production functions, have not been very common in Thai manufacturing. In order to minimize possible sample selection biases, the focus has been on a large sample of manufacturing plants from the industrial census of 1996. Simple comparisons of average factor productivity levels suggested that MNCs tended to have higher average labour productivity, but that productivity differentials were not usually that large and sometimes negative. MNCs also had higher capital intensity in most industries and these differences were often very large. Correspondingly, MNCs had lower average capital productivity than local plants in most industries.

Because simple comparisons have the disadvantage of ignoring other influences on productivity levels, production functions were then estimated to examine productivity differentials after accounting for other controls such as factor intensities, scale, vintage and BOI-promotional status. Three alternative sets of assumptions regarding technology were examined but the results were remarkably consistent, suggesting that productivity differentials were generally insignificant in most industries in 1996.[27] Textiles, chemicals and metal products were the major exceptions, but productivity differentials were not consistently positive even in these industries.

Finally, the chapter examined evidence suggesting positive productivity spillovers from MNCs to local plants and considered the possibility that extremely rapid spillovers could be one reason for the prevalence of insignificant productivity differentials. However, the extent of positive spillovers is still unclear at the industry level and the causes of large variation in productivity levels among MNCs and local plants remain unclear. In short, the puzzle remains.

Notes

1. The term MNCs refers to foreign-owned MNCs in this chapter.
2. These studies include analyses of limited data sets primarily covering firms promoted by the BOI for 1973–74 and 1985–86 (Tambunlertchai and Ramstetter 1991), 1982–83 (Khanthachai et al. 1987) and 1990 (Ramstetter 1993, 1994), as well as from analyses of the comprehensive 1996 census data set used here and smaller samples of similar survey data for 1998 and 2000 (Ito 2004a; Ramstetter 2001a, 2001b, 2002b, 2004).
3. Results from Hill (1988: 107–20), Ito (2004b), Okamoto and Sjöholm (2000), Sjöholm (1998), Takii (2004) and Takii and Ramstetter (2005) indicate that productivity differentials were rather common in Indonesia.
4. Oguchi et al. (2002) suggest productivity differentials were generally small while both Oguchi et al. (2002) and Menon (1998) find that productivity growth was generally no faster in MNCs than in local plants.
5. See Chapter 8 and evidence for Indonesia, Singapore, Thailand and Vietnam in Phan and Ramstetter (2004), Ramstetter (1994, 1999, 2002a), and Ramstetter and Takii (2005).
6. Evidence for Indonesia also comes from Blomström and Sjöholm (1999); Sjöholm (1998, 1999); Takii (2004); Takii and Ramstetter (2005); while Blomström (1990) provides evidence for Mexico.
7. In the Thai case, the census data cover a much larger portion of manufacturing than available data for other years (e.g. 1990, 1998, 2000; see Ramstetter 1994, 2004). Differences between survey coverage in subsequent years and the census year make it very difficult to ascertain which trends result from changes in coverage between the census and subsequent surveys and which trends result from actual changes in economic activity (Ramstetter 2003, 2004).
8. See Ramstetter (2001a, 2003, 2004) for more details on the methodology for eliminating duplicates.
9. Please see Appendix Table A5.1 for details on sample size.
10. For example, census estimates are much larger than national accounts estimates in rubber, plastics, motor vehicles and chemicals, and much smaller in jewellery, apparel and leather and footwear.
11. The 1998 sample contained 4773 plants, while the 2000 sample contained 2520 plants. See Ramstetter (2003: Appendix Tables 9b–9c, 11b–11c) for compilations of the data cited.
12. Similar comparisons show MNCs had lower average labour productivity in only two industries (leather and footwear and jewellery) in 1998 and one (plastics) in 2000 (Ramstetter 2003: Appendix Tables 9b–9c).
13. In addition, both MNCs and local plants had markedly higher average labour productivity for both types of labour in the small sample than observed in the large sample, suggesting that the 1542 plants excluded from

the small sample had extremely small value added and low average labour productivity.

14. In the 1998 sample, average productivity was 107 per cent higher in MNCs for production workers and 87 per cent higher for non-production workers. MNCs also had higher average productivity in twelve of fourteen industries for production workers and eleven of fourteen for non-production workers (Ramstetter 2002a: Appendix Table B2).

15. In the 1998 sample, capital intensity was 136 per cent higher in MNCs and MNCs also had higher capital intensity in twelve of fourteen industries. However, in the 1998 sample, average capital productivity was 25 per cent higher in MNCs on average in manufacturing and higher in six of fourteen industries (Ramstetter 2002a: Appendix Table B2).

16. The exact specification is given in equation (1) of Ramstetter (2004).

17. Comparisons of MNCs and local plants are also likely to be more appropriate in samples of large plants because most MNCs are large.

18. In 1998, MNCs had significantly higher labour productivity in nine of fourteen industries in samples of all plants and in five of thirteen industries in samples of large plants. For 2000, these frequencies were two of fourteen and zero of thirteen, respectively (Ramstetter 2004: Tables 5, 7).

19. The exact specification is given in equation (4) of Ramstetter (2004).

20. Although the differentials reported here come from estimates that include no other controls in an attempt to minimize potential multicollinearity problems, Ramstetter (2002a: Tables 4, 5) shows that results do not differ much when additional dummy variables are added to control for BOI-promoted plants, large plants, old plants and plants that export half of their output or more, or import half or more of their inputs.

21. This test comes from Greene (1997) and is described in detail in Ramstetter (2002a: 4).

22. The exact specification is given in equation (1) of Ramstetter (2002a).

23. For example, no estimates are made for large plants in leather and footwear because the number of MNCs was less than thirty. Most samples are much larger, however (Appendix Table A5.1 Ramstetter 2002a: Appendix Table A1).

24. Note that all independent variables are defined relative to their means to reduce potential for multicollinearity, but correlations among independent variables are still high in many cases.

25. The exact specification is given in equation (3) of Ramstetter (2002a).

26. Note that this problem is not generally thought to be as severe in panels such as those used in Chapter 4. Unfortunately, it is impossible to obtain panel data for Thailand.

27. Significant differentials were also noted to be somewhat more common in a more limited set of data for 1998, but quite rare in an even smaller data set for 2000.

References

Blomström, Magnus (1990) *Foreign Investment and Spillovers*, London: Routledge.

Blomström, Magnus and Fredrik Sjöholm (1999) 'Technology Transfer and Spillovers: Does Local Participation with Multinationals Matter?' *European Economic Review*, 43: 915–23.

Brimble, Peter John (1993) 'Industrial Development and Productivity Change', PhD Dissertation, Johns Hopkins University.

Buckley, Peter J. and Mark Casson (1991) *The Future of the Multinational Enterprise*, second edition, London: Macmillan.

Casson, Mark (1987) *The Firm and the Market: Studies on the Multinational and the Scope of the Firm*, Cambridge, MA: MIT Press.

Caves, Richard E. (1996) *Multinational Enterprise and Economic Analysis*, second edition, Cambridge: Cambridge University Press.

Chao, C.-C. and Eden Yu (1996) 'Are Wholly Foreign-Owned Enterprises Better Than Joint Ventures?' *Journal of International Economics*, 40: 225–37.

Dunning, John H. (1988) *Explaining International Production*, London: Unwin Hyman.

Dunning, John H. (1993) *Multinational Enterprises and the Global Economy*, Workingham, UK: Addison-Wesley Publishing Co.

Greene, William H. (1997) *Econometric Analysis*, third edition, Upper Saddle River, NJ: Prentice-Hall.

Hill, Hal (1988) *Foreign Investment and Industrialization in Indonesia*, Singapore: Oxford University Press.

Hymer, Stephen H. (1960) 'The International Operations of National Firms: a Study of Direct Foreign Investment', PhD dissertation, MIT (published by MIT Press, 1976).

International Monetary Fund (2005) *International Financial Statistics*, January, CD-ROM, Washington, DC: International Monetary Fund.

Ito, Keiko (2004a) 'Foreign Ownership and Plant Productivity in the Thai Automobile Industry in 1996 and 1998: a Conditional Quantile Analysis', *Journal of Asian Economics*, 15: 321–53.

Ito, Keiko (2004b) 'Foreign Ownership and Productivity in the Indonesian Automobile Industry: Evidence from Establishment Data for 1990–1999', in Takatoshi Ito and Andrew K. Rose, eds, *Growth and Productivity in East Asia*, Chicago: University of Chicago Press, pp. 229–70.

Khanthachai, Nathabhol, Kanchana Tanmavad, Tawatchai Boonsiri, Chantana Nisaisook and Anucha Arttanuchit (1987) *Technology and Skills in Thailand*, Singapore: Institute of Southeast Asian Studies.

Kohpaiboon, Archanun (2003) 'Foreign Direct Investment and Technology Spillover: a Cross-industry Analysis of Thai Manufacturing', University of Western Australia 2003 PhD conference papers (downloaded from http://www.econs.ecel.uwa.edu.au/erc/erc/PhD%20Conference%20Web/2003%20Conference%20Papers.htm).

Markusen, James R. (1991) 'The Theory of the Multinational Enterprise: a Common Analytical Framework', in Eric D. Ramstetter, ed., *Direct Foreign Investment in Asia's Developing Economies and Structural Change in the Asia-Pacific Region*, Boulder, Co: Westview Press, pp. 11–32.

Menon, J. (1998) 'Total Factor Productivity Growth in Foreign and Domestic Firms in Malaysian Manufacturing', *Journal of Asian Economics*, 9: 251–80.

Moran, Theodore H. (2001) *Parental Supervision: the New Paradigm for Foreign Direct Investment and Development*, Washington, DC: Institute for International Economics.

National Statistical Office (1999) *Report on the 1997 Industrial Census of the Whole Kingdom*, Bangkok: National Statistical Office.

Oguchi, Noriyoshi, Nor Aini Mohd Amdzah, Zainon Bakar, Rauzah Zainal Abidin and Mazlina Shafii (2002) 'Productivity of Foreign and Domestic Firms in Malaysian Manufacturing Industry', *Asian Economic Journal*, 16: 215–28.

Okamoto Yumiko and Fredrik Sjöholm (2000) 'Productivity in the Indonesian Automotive Industry', *ASEAN Economic Bulletin*, 17: 60–73.

Phan, Minh Ngoc and Eric D. Ramstetter (2004) 'Foreign Ownership Shares and Exports of Multinational Firms in Vietnamese Manufacturing', Working Paper 2004–32, Kitakyushu: International Centre for the Study of East Asian Development.

Ramstetter, Eric D. (1993) 'Production Technology in Foreign and Local Firms in Thai Manufacturing', Discussion Paper No. 8, Nagoya: Graduate School of International Development, Nagoya University.

Ramstetter, Eric D. (1994) 'Comparisons of Japanese Multinationals and Other Firms in Thailand's Non-oil Manufacturing Industries', *ASEAN Economic Bulletin*, 11: 36–58.

Ramstetter, Eric D. (1999) 'Comparisons of Foreign Multinationals and Local Firms in Asian Manufacturing Over Time', *Asian Economic Journal*, 13: 163–203.

Ramstetter, Eric D. (2001a) 'Labor Productivity in Foreign Multinationals and Local Plants in Thai Manufacturing, 1996 and 1998', Working Paper 2001–13, Kitakyushu: International Centre for the Study of East Asian Development.

Ramstetter, Eric D. (2001b) 'Labor Productivity in Local Plants and Foreign Multinationals by Nationality in Thai Manufacturing, 1996 and 1998', Working Paper 2001–31, Kitakyushu: International Centre for the Study of East Asian Development.

Ramstetter, Eric D. (2002a) 'Does Technology Differ in Local Plants and Foreign Multinationals in Thai Manufacturing? Evidence from Translog Production Functions for 1996 and 1998', Working Paper 2002–04, Kitakyushu: International Centre for the Study of East Asian Development.

Ramstetter, Eric D. (2002b) 'Trade Propensities and Foreign Ownership Shares in Thai Manufacturing, 1996', Working Paper 2002–03, Kitakyushu: International Centre for the Study of East Asian Development.

Ramstetter, Eric D. (2003) 'Labor Productivity, Wages, Nationality, and Foreign Ownership Shares in Thai Manufacturing, 1996–2000', Working Paper 2003–15, Kitakyushu: International Centre for the Study of East Asian Development.

Ramstetter, Eric D. (2004) 'Labor Productivity, Wages, Nationality, and Foreign Ownership Shares in Thai manufacturing, 1996–2000', *Journal of Asian Economics*, 14: 861–84.

Ramstetter, Eric D. and Sadayuki Takii (2005) 'Exporting and Foreign Ownership in Indonesian Manufacturing, 1990–2000', Working Paper 2005–15, Kitakyushu: International Centre for the Study of East Asian Development.

Rugman, Alan M. (1980) 'Internalization as a General Theory of Foreign Direct Investment: a Re-appraisal of the Literature', *Weltwirtschaftliches Archiv*, 116: 365–79.

Rugman, Alan M. (1985) 'Internalization is Still a General Theory of Foreign Direct Investment', *Weltwirtschaftliches Archiv*, 121: 570–5.

Sjöholm, Fredrik (1998) 'Joint Ventures, Technology Transfer and Spillovers: Evidence from Indonesian Establishment Data', in Economic Planning Agency, ed., *Foreign Direct Investment in Asia*, papers and proceedings of an international symposium, 22–23 October, Tokyo: Economic Planning Agency, pp. 587–616.

Sjöholm, Fredrik (1999) 'Technology Gap, Competition and Spillovers from Direct Foreign Investment: Evidence from Establishment Data', *Journal of Development Studies*, 36: 53–73.

Takii, Sadayuki (2004) 'Productivity Differentials between Local and Foreign Plants in Indonesian Manufacturing, 1995', *World Development*, 32: 1957–69.

Takii, Sadayuki and Eric D. Ramstetter (2005) 'Multinational Presence and Labor Productivity Differentials in Indonesian Manufacturing, 1975–2001', *Bulletin of Indonesian Economic Studies*, 41: 181–202.

Tambunlertchai, Somsak and Eric D. Ramstetter (1991) 'Foreign Firms in Promoted Industries and Structural Change in Thailand', in Eric D. Ramstetter, ed., *Direct Foreign Investment in Asia's Developing Economies and Structural Change in the Asia-Pacific Region*, Boulder, CO: Westview Press, pp. 65–104.

Umemoto, Masaru and Eric D. Ramstetter (2004) 'The Boom in Vehicle Exports from Thailand: Protection, Markets, and Multinationals', Working Paper 2004–01, Kitakyushu: International Centre for the Study of East Asian Development.

Appendix: production functions used to measure spillovers

This appendix details the specifications and results of previously unpublished production functions estimates used to evaluate spillovers in Thai manufacturing for 1996. As in the comparison of productivity levels, three types of production functions are used. These are (1) the Cobb-Douglas function, (2) a translog function with two types of labour, and (3) a translog with one type of labour. All equations include controls for BOI promotional status, plant size, and vintage, while the Cobb-Douglas function also includes a control for the share of white-collar workers in the workforce. This control was omitted from the translog with one type of labour because the primary concern was to reduce the number of independent variables and thus the chances of multicollinearity. Each function is then estimated two times, once to evaluate the average effect of all MNCs on productivity in local plants and once to see if spillovers were different for minority-foreign, majority-foreign or wholly-foreign MNCs. The resulting equations are given below and the estimation results are reported in Table A5.2, after Table A5.1 provides details about the samples used in the chapter.

$$(1)\ \ln(V_{ij}/E_{ij}) = a1 + a2[\ln(EN_{ij}/E_{ij})] + a3[\ln(K_{ij}/E_{ij})] + a4(Dboi_{ij}) + a5(Dold_{ij}) + a6(Dlg_{ij})$$
$$+ a7(FS_j)$$

$$(2)\ \ln(V/E_{ij}) = b1 + b2[\ln(EN_{ij}/E_{ij})] + b3[\ln(K_{ij}/E_{ij})] + b4(Dboi_{ij}) + b5(Dold_{ij}) + b6(Dlg_{ij})$$
$$+ b7(FSmn_j) + b8(FSmj_j) + b9(FSwh_j)$$

$$(3)\ \ln(V_{ij}) = c1 + c2[\ln(EN_{ij})] + c3[\ln(EP_{ij})] + c4[\ln(K_{ij})] + c5[(\ln(EN_{ij}))^2] + c6[(\ln(EP_{ij}))^2]$$
$$+ c7[(\ln(K_{ij}))^2] + c8[\ln(EN_{ij})\cdot\ln(EP_{ij})] + c9[\ln(EN_{ij})\cdot\ln(K_{ij})] + c10[\ln(EP_{ij})\cdot\ln(K_{ij})]$$
$$+ c11(Dboi_{ij}) + c12(Dold_{ij}) + c13(Dlg_{ij}) + c14(FS_j)$$

$$(4)\ \ln(V_{ij}) = d1 + d2[\ln(EN_{ij})] + d3[\ln(EP_{ij})] + d4[\ln(K_{ij})] + d5[(\ln(EN_{ij}))^2] + d6[(\ln(EP_{ij}))^2]$$
$$+ d7[(\ln(K_{ij}))^2] + d8[\ln(EN_{ij})\cdot\ln(EP_{ij})] + d9[\ln(EN_{ij})\cdot\ln(K_{ij})] + d10[\ln(EP_{ij})\cdot\ln(K_{ij})]$$
$$+ d11(Dboi_{ij}) + d12(Dold_{ij}) + d13(Dlg_{ij}) + d14(FSmn_j) + d15(FSmj_j) + d16(FSwh_j)$$

$$(5)\ \ln(V_i) = e1 + e2[\ln(E_i)] + e3[\ln(K_i)] + e4[(\ln(E_i))^2] + e5[(\ln(K_i))^2] + e6[\ln(E_i)\cdot\ln(K_i)]$$
$$+ e7(Dboi_{ij}) + e8(Dold_{ij}) + e9(Dlg_{ij}) + e10(FS_j)$$

$$(6)\ \ln(V_i) = f1 + f2[\ln(E_i)] + f3[\ln(K_i)] + f4[(\ln(E_i))^2] + f5[(\ln(K_i))^2] + f6[\ln(E_i)\cdot\ln(K_i)]$$
$$+ f7(Dboi_{ij}) + f8(Dold_{ij}) + f9(Dlg_{ij}) + f10(FSmn_j) + f11(FSmj_j) + f12(FSwh_j)$$

where

$Dboi_{ij} = 1$ if plant i in industry j is BOI-promoted, = 0 otherwise,

$Df_{ij} = 1$ if the foreign ownership share of plant i in industry j is 1% or greater, = 0 otherwise,

$Dfmj_{ij} = 1$ if the foreign ownership share of plant i in industry j is 50%–99%, = 0 otherwise,

$Dfmn_{ij} = 1$ if the foreign ownership share of plant i in industry j is 1%–49%, = 0 otherwise,

$Dfwh_{ij} = 1$ if the foreign ownership share of plant i in industry j is 100%, = 0 otherwise,

$Dlg_{ij} = 1$ if the output of plant i in industry j is larger than mean output for the industry plus one standard deviation or more, = 0 otherwise,

$Dold_{ij} = 1$ if plant i in industry j has been in operation for 11 or more years, = 0 otherwise,

E_{ij} = hours worked by all workers in plant i in industry j,

EN_{ij} = hours worked by non-production workers in plant i in industry j,

FS_j = MNC share of employment in industry j,

$FSmn_j$ = minority-foreign MNC share of employment in industry j,

$FSmj_j$ = majority-foreign MNC share of employment in industry j,

$FSwh_j$ = wholly-foreign MNC share of employment in industry j,

K_{ij} = average book value of fixed assets in plant i in industry j, multiplied by the percentage of hours used each year,

V_{ij} = value added in plant i in industry j.

Appendix Table A5.1   Number of sample plants in Thai manufacturing, 1996

Industry	Large samples					Small samples	
	Local plants	*MNC total*	*Minority-foreign*	*Majority-foreign*	*Wholly-foreign*	*Local plants*	*MNC total*
Manufacturing	8,672	1,822	1,142	379	301	7,214	1,738
Food	1,293	190	139	32	19	1,069	186
Textiles	580	136	105	21	10	474	127
Apparel	642	101	77	17	7	508	99
Leather & footwear	250	39	18	14	7	206	36
Chemicals & products	366	146	94	31	21	343	146
Rubber products	209	75	49	15	11	197	71
Plastics & products	490	114	67	24	23	431	108
Non-metallic mineral products	905	59	43	13	3	689	57
Metal products	706	125	80	21	24	581	117
General machinery	373	107	68	19	20	333	103

Electric & precision machinery	264	276	104	75	97	237	258
Office & computing machinery	3	32	3	9	20	2	30
Miscellaneous electric machinery	162	102	51	30	21	142	94
Radio, TV, communication	56	109	37	29	43	54	102
Precision machinery	43	33	13	7	13	39	32
Motor vehicles	376	79	56	20	3	330	76
Furniture	416	45	31	8	6	326	43
Jewellery	104	73	38	18	17	81	72

Sources: Large samples from Ramstetter (2003: Appendix Table 11a); small samples from Ramstetter (2002a: Appendix Table A1).

Appendix Table A5.2   Alternative spillover estimates

Independent variables, indicator	Spillovers assumed to be identical for all MNCs		Spillovers assumed to differ by foreign ownership share	
	Coefficient	*Significance*	*Coefficient*	*Significance*
COBB-DOUGLAS TECHNOLOGY				
(Equations (1) & (2); dependent variable $= \ln(V_{ij}/E_{ij})$)				
Constant	3.448	0.00	3.446	0.00
$\ln(EN_{ij}/E_{ij})$	0.170	0.00	0.170	0.00
$\ln(K_{ij}/E_{ij})$	0.201	0.00	0.201	0.00
$Dboi_{ij}$	−0.149	0.01	−0.150	0.01
$Dold_{ij}$	0.058	0.04	0.058	0.04
Dlg_{ij}	0.751	0.00	0.750	0.00
FS_j	0.424	0.00	–	–
$FSmn_j$	–	–	0.423	0.02
$FSmj_j$	–	–	0.492	0.03
$FSwh_j$	–	–	0.389	0.00
F-statistic	124.99	0.00	93.73	0.00
White test	88.90	0.00	120.59	0.00
Adjusted R-squared	0.093	–	0.093	–
No. observations	7,214	–	7,214	–
TRANSLOG TECHNOLOGY WITH HETEROGENEOUS LABOUR				
(Equations (3) & (4); dependent variable $= \ln(V_{ij})$)				
Constant	15.829	0.00	15.814	0.00
$\ln(EN_{ij})$	0.229	0.00	0.230	0.00
$\ln(EP_{ij})$	0.387	0.00	0.387	0.00
$\ln(K_{ij})$	0.217	0.00	0.217	0.00

Appendix Table A5.2   (Continued)

Independent variables, indicator	Spillovers assumed to be identical for all MNCs		Spillovers assumed to differ by foreign ownership share	
	Coefficient	Significance	Coefficient	Significance
$\ln(EN_{ij})^2$	0.038	0.01	0.038	0.01
$\ln(EP_{ij})^2$	0.061	0.00	0.061	0.00
$\ln(K_{ij})^2$	0.029	0.00	0.029	0.00
$\ln(EN_{ij})*\ln(EP_{ij})$	−0.104	0.00	−0.104	0.00
$\ln(EN_{ij})*\ln(K_{ij})$	−0.031	0.01	−0.031	0.01
$\ln(EP_{ij})*\ln(K_{ij})$	−0.034	0.03	−0.034	0.03
$Dboi_{ij}$	0.026	0.65	0.027	0.63
$Dold_{ij}$	0.113	0.00	0.113	0.00
Dlg_{ij}	1.347	0.00	1.347	0.00
FS_j	0.455	0.00	–	–
$FSmn_j$	–	–	0.519	0.00
$FSmj_j$	–	–	0.507	0.02
$FSwh_j$	–	–	0.401	0.00
F-statistic	600.89	0.00	520.67	0.00
White test	196.03	0.00	249.78	0.00
Adjusted R-squared	0.520	–	0.519	–
No. observations	7,214	–	7,214	–

TRANSLOG TECHNOLOGY WITH HOMOGENEOUS LABOUR
(Equations (5) & (6); dependent variable $= \ln(V_{ij})$)

	Coefficient	Significance	Coefficient	Significance
Constant	15.822	0.00	15.808	0.00
$\ln(E_{ij})$	0.590	0.00	0.590	0.00
$\ln(K_{ij})$	0.233	0.00	0.233	0.00
$\ln(E_{ij})^2$	−0.010	0.48	−0.010	0.48
$\ln(K_{ij})^2$	0.028	0.00	0.028	0.00
$\ln(E_{ij})*\ln(K_{ij})$	−0.059	0.00	−0.059	0.00
$Dboi_{ij}$	0.018	0.75	0.020	0.73
$Dold_{ij}$	0.126	0.00	0.126	0.00
Dlg_{ij}	1.369	0.00	1.370	0.00
FS_j	0.486	0.00	–	–
$FSmn_j$	–	–	0.556	0.00
$FSmj_j$	–	–	0.486	0.03
$FSwh_j$	–	–	0.455	0.00
F-statistic	851.80	0.00	696.78	0.00
White test	148.75	0.00	194.91	0.00
Adjusted R-squared	0.515	–	0.515	–
No. observations	7,214	–	7,214	–

Source: Author's calculations.

6
Foreign Ownership and Productivity in the Indonesian and Thai Automobile Industries

Keiko Ito

6.1 Introduction

Many developing countries have sought to develop the automobile industry as a major element of their industrialization efforts. This industry has been targeted because it has a number of characteristics thought to be conducive to overall industrial development. First, the automobile industry is a large industry, which accounts for a large portion of employment and gross domestic product (GDP) in many countries. Second, it is a synthetic industry with strong linkages to other industries. Thus, technological progress in the automobile industry can affect both the automobile industry itself and many other industries.

Like many other developing economies, Indonesia and Thailand have attempted to develop their automobile industries by utilizing foreign direct investment (FDI) from foreign multinational corporations (MNCs). In response to these efforts, major foreign automakers started operating in these countries in the 1960s and 1970s. Although there were some differences in industrial policies and policies towards foreign automakers, the automobile industry grew rapidly in both countries during the first half of the 1990s until the 1997 financial crisis. This rapid growth resulted mainly from rapid economic expansion in these and neighbouring countries, as well as from policy changes.

In traditional MNC theory, FDI is often regarded as the movement of managerial resources. In other words, FDI facilitates the movement of firm-specific assets related to production technology and marketing, as well as managerial know-how. Correspondingly, a large body of literature emphasizes that the transfer of superior managerial resources and other firm-specific assets makes MNC affiliates more productive than local companies (e.g. Dunning 1988; Caves 1996; Markusen 1991). Moreover, the entry of MNCs may also affect overall productivity levels by introducing new ideas or increasing the level of competition in the market and generating spillovers to local firms. This suggests that MNCs may play an important role in increasing productivity levels of a host country, both by replacing low-productivity, domestic production with high-productivity, foreign-owned production and by stimulating productivity increases in domestic production as previously discussed in Chapters 4 and 5. Recognition of these productivity increases and expectations of technology transfer from foreign MNCs were two major reasons why Indonesian and Thai policy-makers encouraged foreign automakers to set up joint ventures with local partners. As a result, foreign (particularly Japanese) firms have been dominant players in the assembly and component sectors in the two countries. However, the two governments also adopted a number of policies promoting domestic producers, including the establishment of local content requirements for automakers that were designed to promote the localization of parts and components.

In line with theoretical expectations, previous academic studies have generally found foreign-owned establishments to be more efficient than local ones. However, as emphasized in Chapters 4 and 5, there are many exceptions to this general result in Thailand and a few in Indonesia, especially if productivity differentials are examined at the industry level.[1] Results of studies focused more narrowly on the automobile sector have also been mixed, indicating that labour productivity was higher in foreign-owned plants than in locally-owned plants, but that total factor productivity (TFP) was not significantly different between the two groups.[2] According to these studies, the low level of capacity utilization and the small scale of production are the main obstacles to higher TFP levels and growth rates.

The purpose of this chapter is to analyse representative evidence on productivity determinants and sources of productivity growth in the Indonesian and Thai automobile industries and to compare productivity levels and growth in locally-owned plants and foreign-owned plants. To this end, section 6.2 provides a brief overview of the automobile industries in the two countries and describes their major characteristics. Section 6.3 then uses plant-level data to calculate various partial measures of productivity and compares them between the two countries and between local and foreign plants in each country. Section 6.4 continues by investigating the determinants of the partial productivity measures and TFP with regression analyses. Finally, the concluding section summarizes the major results and discusses their implications for the automobile industries in the two countries.

6.2　The automobile industries in Indonesia and Thailand

This section first summarizes major aspects of the automobile industry's development in Indonesia and Thailand and then provides a closer analysis of ownership patterns and market structures in the industry in both countries.

6.2.1　Industrial development

The Indonesian government has promoted the development of the automobile industry since the late 1960s.[3] As in other Asian or Latin American countries, foreign automakers have played an important role in the development of the local automobile industry. On the other hand, since the 'New Order' government assumed power in 1968, local automakers have been promoted with local content rules, entry barriers and foreign ownership restrictions (Hill 1996; Aswicahyono, Anas and Rizal 2000). An import ban on completely built-up (CBU) cars was introduced in 1971 and remained in force until 1993, when it was replaced by tariffs ranging from 175 to 275 per cent.

In 1977 the government introduced a deletion programme, which specified components that had to be produced in Indonesia and penalized automobile manufacturers if they used imported products for the designated components. This programme was intended to foster the development of supporting industries, but was unsuccessful. Poor technological capabilities in local producers, high profit requirements among distributors, small production scale resulting from market fragmentation, and joint venture agreements that limited local partners to distribution rather than full manufacture, all contributed to the failure of this policy (Aswicahyono, Anas and Rizal 2000).

Moreover, in order to ensure a minimum production scale, the government used a licensing system that limited production of certain functional components such as transmissions and brake systems, to one or two companies each. In addition to hindering competition within the parts industry, this system also led to cost increases resulting from small-scale production of a wide variety of products, because the one or two licensed companies were compelled to produce multiple parts under multiple brand names (Takayasu et al. 1996). As a result, although final automobile sales were about two-thirds of Thai levels in 1995, the number of auto parts manufacturers was only about one-quarter of

Thai levels in the same year or less (Table 6.1). On the other hand, quite a few foreign auto parts suppliers (most of them Japanese) have established Indonesian affiliates in order to supply major parts to automobile assemblers, partly in response to the local content requirements.

The government implemented a number of deregulation packages in the 1990s. For example, the deletion programme was replaced by an incentive programme in 1993 in a move to promote local parts makers. The new programme provided incentives to parts suppliers in the form of lower import duties on imported components, sub-components, semi-finished parts and raw materials, and these duties were lower for

Table 6.1 Automobile industries in ASEAN countries

Indicator, year	Indonesia		Thailand		ASEAN-4	
AUTOMOBILE MARKETS						
ASEAN market sales: units (import shares in per cent)						
1995	384,449	28%	571,580	37%	1,369,983	na
1996	337,399	27%	589,126	31%	1,453,409	na
1997	392,185	31%	363,156	23%	1,304,612	na
1998	167,234	na	201,055	na	653,837	na
1999	93,814	na	218,330	na	675,106	na
Sales by Japanese manufacturers: units (market shares in per cent)						
1995	365,520	95%	514,704	90%	1,075,425	78%
Sales by US and European manufacturers: units (market shares in per cent)						
1995	17,137	5%	46,322	8%	86,292	6%
STRUCTURE OF AUTOMOBILE PARTS INDUSTRY (AS OF JANUARY)						
Total number of parts manufacturers						
1998	150–200		750–800		1300–1500	
Japanese affiliates or subsidiaries (shares in per cent)						
1998	82	47%	209	27%	406	30%
U.S. and European affiliates or subsidiaries (shares in per cent)						
1998	7	4%	21	3%	52	4%
AUTOMOTIVE TARIFFS AND NON-TARIFF BARRIERS						
Average applied tariff rates						
	Parts	Vehicles	Parts	Vehicles	Parts	Vehicles
1998	22%	86%	43%	43%	27%	47%
Share of imports subject to non-tariff barriers						
	Parts	Vehicles	Parts	Vehicles	Parts	Vehicles
1998	0%	70%	2%	45%	3%	65%

Sources: Takayasu et al. (1996: Tables 3, 8, 13, 17); Nikkan Jidosha Shinbun-sha (various years); Poapongsakorn and Wangdee (2000: Table 2); Farrel and Findlay (2001: Table 2.8).

production lines in which high local content was achieved. In 1995, duties on remaining components (40 per cent for commercial vehicles and 60 per cent for passenger cars) were exempted for vehicles exceeding local content requirements and restrictions on investments in the production of new cars were removed. These policy changes, combined with the expansion of automobile production in the early-to-mid-1990s, led to establishment of many new parts plants, both local and foreign.[4] As in all four large members of the Association of Southeast Asian Nations (ASEAN-4), most of the automobiles sold in Indonesia are made by Japanese automakers (Table 6.1).

In Thailand, major foreign automakers started operating in the 1960s and 1970s. Moreover, since the late 1980s, many Japanese auto parts suppliers have set up production and marketing networks in Thailand. The Thai government first began to provide investment incentives by enacting the 1960 Industrial Promotion Act as part of its strategy to promote import substitution. In response to the investment promotion policy, the first automobile assembly plant in Thailand, the Anglo-Thai Motor Company, started operating in 1961. After that, at least nine assembly plants were set up in 1961–69. In the 1970s and early 1980s, many Japanese automobile parts suppliers established production companies or concluded licensing agreements with local manufacturers, mainly in response to the strengthening of local content requirements. On the other hand, some European and US automakers discontinued assembly operations because of the intensified competition.[5]

Throughout the process of promoting the automobile industry, the Thai government protected local producers by imposing high tariffs on completely built-up automobiles (CBU) and attracted foreign automakers by offering them various incentives to invest in the country. The intention was to achieve import substitution by promoting joint-ventures between foreign automakers and local firms. In addition, the government set local content requirements for automakers in an attempt to promote the localization of parts and components. This policy led Japanese automakers to encourage related parts suppliers to invest in Thailand.

In the early 1990s, the government reversed this policy, reduced tariff rates, and removed restrictions limiting foreign ownership to 49 per cent. This liberalization and high overall economic growth led to rapid expansion of the Thai automobile market, as well as large FDI inflows into Thailand's automobile industry during the first half of the 1990s. Annual automobile sales peaked at 589,129 in 1996 (Table 6.1), which is less than one-tenth of the corresponding figure in Japan, for example. Thus, even though it was the biggest market in the ASEAN-4 and grew rapidly through the mid-1990s, the Thai automobile market remained rather small by global standards. As in other developing countries, small market size prevents the establishment of larger, more efficient plants and has been a major obstacle to the development of Thailand's auto parts industry.[6]

6.2.2   Ownership and market structure

In the Indonesian automobile industry, foreign (particularly Japanese) firms have always been dominant players in the assembly and component sectors, except for the small-scale replacement parts segment. The dominance of foreign firms in automobile production is commonly observed in developing countries. In Indonesia, most major automobile manufacturing companies are joint ventures between local conglomerates and Japanese, European or US automakers, because local conglomerates sought to gain access to world-class technology through joint ventures with foreign automakers (Table 6.2).[7] In 1995, there were fourteen major automobile assemblers, all of which rely on foreign partners, though the modalities of MNC entry have varied depending on the regulatory environment and foreign partners' preferences.[8] Before the 1997 crisis, foreign partners were not usually able to acquire majority ownership.

Another key feature is the small number of local joint-venture participants. In 1995 and 1998, there were only three local groups with market shares over 2 per cent: the Astra group with three manufacturers, the Indomobil (Salim) group with four, and the Krama Yudha group with two. The small number of local participants derives in part from the government's *de facto* selection of the major domestic business groups that were to participate in the industry (Aswicahyono, Basri and Hill 2000). As a result, the Astra group holds a market share of over 50 per cent, and the sum of the market shares of these three major groups reaches about 90 per cent. Moreover, some assemblers produce more than one foreign brand name. As Aswicahyono, Basri and Hill (2000) point out, this feature reduces the incentives for foreign partners to develop close relationships with local partners or make commitments to upgrade their technological capabilities.

The Astra group, which has its core business activities in the manufacturing of automobiles and machinery, also owns a number of firms producing automobile components. According to FOURIN (2000), there were 158 automobile companies in Indonesia in the late 1990s, of which 23 were under the control of the Astra group. There were 76 firms affiliated with Japanese MNCs, 18 of which were joint ventures with Astra group firms. Sato (1996) documents a high degree of vertical integration from bodies and general components to

Table 6.2 Major auto manufacturers in Indonesia (as of 1995 and 1998)

No.	Group	Market share	Ethnic group	Local firm	Start up	Foreign partners joint venture (ownership)	Contract
<1995>							
(1)	Astra	55%	Govt. + Chinese	(a) Toyota Astra Motor	1972	Toyota (49%)	
				(b) Gaya Motor	(1955)		Daihatsu, Isuzu, Nissan, etc.
				(c) Pantja Motor	1974		Isuzu, Nissan
(2)	Indomobil (Salim)	21%	Chinese	(a) Indomobil Suzuki	1991	Suzuki (49%)	
				(b) Ismac	1973		Nissan, Chrysler
				(c) National Assemblers	1974		Mazda, Volvo, Hino
				(d) GM Buana Indonesia		General Motors (60%)	
(3)	Krama Yudha	20%	Pribumi	(a) Krama Yudha Kesuma	1981		Mitsubishi
				(b) Krama Yudha Ratu Motor	1973		Mitsubishi
(4)	Imora	1%	Chinese	Prospect Motor	1975		Honda
(5)	Bimantara	2%	Pribumi	(a) German Motor	(1970)	Mecedes Benz (35%)	
				(b) Tricitra Karya	1995		Hyundai
(6)	Starsauto	na		Starsauto Dinamika	1995		Daewoo
(7)	Humpus	0%	Pribumi	Kia-Timor Motors		Kia (35%)	
<1998>							
(1)	Astra	51%	Govt. + Chinese	(a) Toyota Astra Motor	1972	Toyota (49%)	
				(b) Gaya Motor	(1955)		Isuzu, BMW, Ford, Peugeot
				(c) Pantja Motor	1974	Isuzu (12.5%)	
				(d) Astra Daihatsu Motor	(1992)	Daihatsu (40%)	
				(e) Astra Nissan Diesel	1996	Nissan Diesel (12.5%)	

Table 6.2   (Continued)

No.	Group	Market share	Ethnic group	Local firm	Start up	Foreign partners joint venture (ownership)	Contract
(2)	Indomobil (Salim)	21%	Chinese	(a) Indomobil Suzuki	1991	Suzuki (49%)	
				(b) Ismac Nissan Manufacturing	1996	Nissan (35%)	Audi, Volvo, Ssangyong
				(c) Ismac	1973		Mazda, Volvo, VW, Audi, etc.
(3)	Krama Yudha	18%	Pribumi	(a) Krama Yudha Kesuma Motor	1981	MKM (Mitsubishi Krama Yudha Motors & Mfg. (99%)	
				(b) Krama Yudha Ratu Motor	1975		Mitsubishi
(4)	Imora	2%	Chinese	Honda Prospect Motor	(1992)	Honda Group (49%)	
(5)	Bimantara	1%	Pribumi	Tricitra Karya	1995		Hyundai, Ford
(6)	Starsauto	0%		Starsauto Dinamika	1995		Daewoo
(7)	Mercedes-Benz	1%	Europe	Mercedes-Benz Group	(1970)	DaimlerChrysler (95%)	
(8)	General Motors	1%	U.S.A.	GM Buana Indonesia	1994	General Motors (100%)	

Notes: Pribumi is an Indonesian language term referring to indigenous groups; start-up generally indicates the year the firm started operation but figures in parentheses indicate the year of establishment.
Sources: Aswicahyono, Basri and Hill (2000: Table 3, pp. 220–1); Nomura (1996: Table I-5, pp. 96–9); FOURIN (2000).

core components within the Astra group. She also shows that the Astra group was the only Indonesian automaker that procured the six major functional components from within the group.[9] After the 1997 Asian economic crisis, several local partners ran into financial difficulties creating a need for injections of new capital in many joint ventures. There was also another sweeping policy liberalization that allowed foreign investors to increase their ownership shares in old joint ventures or acquire new shares in Indonesian automobile firms. As a result, foreign ownership shares were markedly higher many foreign firms after the crisis (Table 6.2). However, the Astra group was still able to maintain its leading position in the Indonesian automobile industry.

Before the 1997 economic crisis, all foreign-owned auto manufacturers in Thailand were also joint ventures with local partners. However, the ownership structure contrasted markedly with Indonesia, partially because each foreign automaker cooperated with only one Thai business group (Table 6.3). This conspicuous difference made it possible for foreign automakers to make deeper commitments to technological upgrading in their Thai partners. Foreign ownership restrictions were then dismantled after the 1997 crisis and many local partners in joint ventures ran into financial difficulties in Thailand as well. Thus, most foreign automakers now hold majority shares in their Thai affiliates, enhancing the management power of the MNCs involved. The automobile market is also more competitive in Thailand than in Indonesia, with six firms having market shares of 8 per cent or more and no firm having a market share over 30 per cent as of 2001.

Despite the protection afforded by both governments, automobile production did not take off until the late 1980s in either country (Figure 6.1). As indicated above, the industry subsequently grew rapidly through the mid-1990s until the financial crisis hit in 1997. The crisis hit the industry hard in both countries. In 1998, automobile production declined to only 58,079 units in Indonesia and to 158,130 units in Thailand, representing large declines of 85 per cent and 72 per cent, respectively, compared to previous peaks (1997 for Indonesia, 1996 for Thailand). Although automobile production recovered rapidly after 1999, annual production did not reach pre-crisis peaks until 2002 (Thailand) or 2003 (Indonesia).

To sum up, rigorous protection and state intervention did help Indonesian automobile production to grow more rapidly than other manufacturing production. The automobile industry's share of manufacturing GDP increased from 1.6 per cent in 1975 to 5.3 per cent in 1990 before falling some to 4.6 per cent in 1996 (Aswicahyono, Anas and Rizal 2000). On the other hand, the industry's share of manufacturing

Table 6.3 Major auto manufacturers in Thailand (as of 2001)

No.	Assemblers	Market share	Local business group or family	Start up	Foreign partners	Brand
(1)	Toyota Motor	28%	Siam Cement (10%–>10%)	1964	Toyota (59.6%–>86.4%)	Toyota
(2)	Hino Motors	1%		1964	Hino (35%–>34.1%)	Hino
(3)	MMC Sittipol	8%	Lee group (52%–>0%)	1966	Mitsubishi (48%–>97.2%)	Mitsubishi
(4)	Isuzu Motors	24%		1966	Isuzu (47.9%–>48%)	Isuzu
(5)	Honda Automobile	14%		1984	Honda (49%–>91.3%)	Honda
(6)	Thai Honda Manufacturing			1967	Honda (60%–>83%)	Honda
(7)	Thai-Swedish Assembly	1%		1975	Volvo (52%–>100%)	Volvo
					Renault (20%–>0%)	Land Rover
(8)	AutoAlliance	8%		1998	Ford (50%), Mazda (45%)	Ford
						Mazda
(9)	General Motors Thailand Assembly Center	1%		2000	GM (77%), Holden (23%)	Chevrolet
(10)	BMW Manufacturing	1%		2000	BMW (100%)	BMW
(11)	Siam Motors & Nissan	11%	Siam Group (75%–>75%)	1962	Nissan (25%–>25%)	Nissan
(12)	Siam Nissan Automobile		Siam Motors (75%–>75%)	1977	Nissan (25%–>25%)	Nissan
(13)	Nissan Diesel Thailand		Siam Motors (40%–>15%)	1987	Nissan Diesel (30%–>49%)	Nissan
(14)	Thonburi Automotive Assembly Plant		Thonburi Automotive Group (100%–>100%)	1962		Mercedes Benz
(15)	Bangchan General Assembly		Phra Nakorn Automobile Group (66%)	1968		Honda, Daihatsu, GM, Hyundai, etc.
(16)	YMC Assembly		(Local 100%)	1974		BMW, Peugeot, VW

Notes: Figures in parentheses indicate ownership share of local groups or of foreign partners. The ownership share at the starting point of each arrow corresponds to the share for the year 1996 and the share at the end of the arrow corresponds to the share for 2001. Honda Automobile was formerly called Honda Cars Manufacturing.

Sources: Brooker Group Public Co. Ltd. (2003); Sakura Institute of Research (1996).

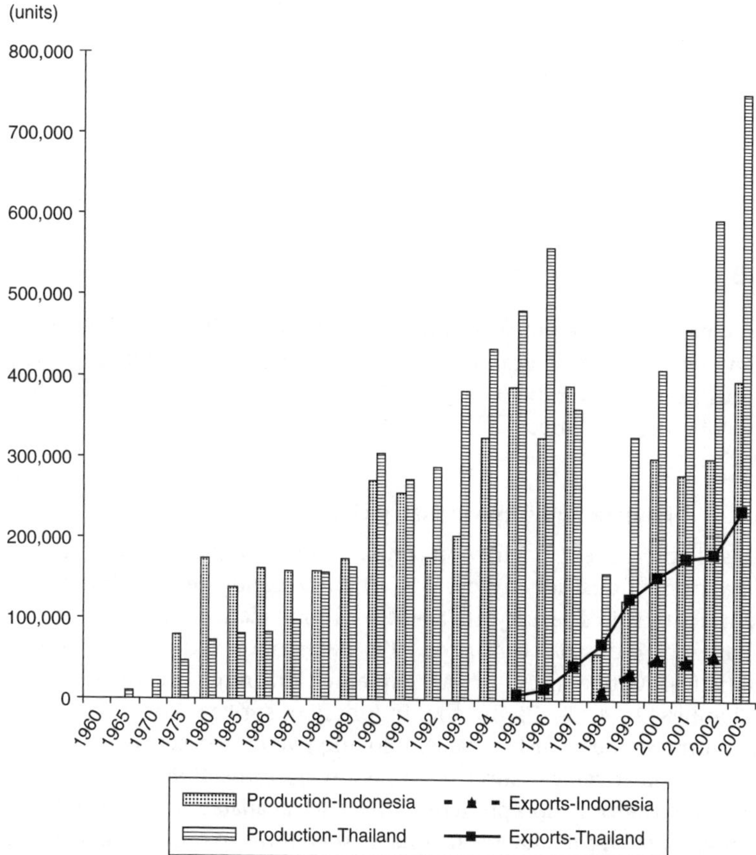

Figure 6.1   Motor vehicle production and exports in Indonesia and Thailand
Sources: Nikkan Jidosha Shinbun-sha (various years); FOURIN (various years); Thailand Automotive Institute (2005).

employment remained only 1.4–1.5 per cent throughout this period. In Thailand, the automobile industry has always been larger, though the lack of good statistics creates some question over the actual size of the industry. For example, official compilations from industrial statistics similar to those cited for Indonesia above suggest that the automobile industry was quite large in 1996, accounting for about 14 per cent of manufacturing value added and 4.5 per cent of manufacturing employment in 1996 (National Statistical Office 1999a). On the other hand, national accounts estimates suggest that the industry accounted for only 7.1 per cent of manufacturing value added in 1996, and that this share then plunged to 1.8 per cent in 1998 before recovering strongly to 9.3 per cent in 2003 (National Economic and Social Development Board 2004). In Thailand, the strong recovery of production in recent years was partly the result of rapidly growing exports (see Figure 6.1 and Chapter 8). This is another aspect in which the Thai industry contrasts markedly with its Indonesian counterpart, which is still domestic-market-oriented.

6.3 Productivity differentials

The major purpose of this section is to analyse productivity differentials between foreign and local plants in the Indonesian and Thai automobile industries. However, before proceeding to this analysis, it is necessary to describe the data used and relevant patterns observed from descriptive statistics.

6.3.1 The data and some industry characteristics

This chapter relies primarily on compilations of unpublished plant-level data from industrial surveys for 1990–99 conducted by Indonesia's central statistical agency (BPS-Statistics or Badan Pusat Statistik) and Thailand's industrial census of 1996 data conducted by the National Statistical Office (NSO).[10] As explained in more detail elsewhere (Chapters 1, 4, 5, 7, 8), the Indonesian surveys cover large and medium-sized establishments employing twenty workers or more with rather good coverage rates (75–85 per cent) for the 1990s, but the 1996 census is the only comprehensive data set available for Thailand. The samples used in this chapter are smaller than those in official compilations for both countries because plants with incomplete data or entries that were believed to be unreliable are excluded from these samples.[11]

Compilations from these samples again indicate that the Thai automobile industry in 1996 was much larger than the Indonesian industry in 1995, with 3.7 times the number of establishments, 2.3 times the number of employees, and 4.9 times the value added (Table 6.4). Foreign shares of motor vehicles were relatively small in terms of the number of establishments and employees, but relatively large in terms of production (measured as value added or gross output). Foreign shares were also much larger in Thailand by most measures, although differences in shares of value added, both of which exceeded four-fifths, were rather small. In both countries, motor vehicles assembly accounted for the largest shares of production (value added or gross output), but assembly shares of industry totals were markedly larger in Thailand. Assembly operations also accounted for the largest share of automobile industry employment in Thailand but the

Table 6.4   Basic indicators for sample plants in the mid-1990s

Country, year, industry, indicator	Number of plants/firms		Number of workers		Gross output (US$ millions)		Value added (US$ millions)	
	Number	*Share*	*Number*	*Share*	*Value*	*Share*	*Value*	*Share*
INDONESIA 1995 (local currency = rupiah; US$1 = 2,249 rupiah)								
Motor Vehicles Sector Total (shares of motor vehicles' total in parentheses)								
Total	111	(100%)	33,667	(100%)	2,506	(100%)	1,046	(100%)
Local	100	(90%)	23,586	(70%)	871	(35%)	186	(18%)
Foreign	11	(10%)	10,081	(30%)	1,635	(65%)	860	(82%)
Motor Vehicle Assembly (shares of motor vehicles' total in parentheses)								
Total	7	(6%)	7,626	(23%)	1,295	(52%)	679	(65%)
Local	4	(4%)	1,853	(6%)	237	(9%)	53	(5%)
Foreign	3	(3%)	5,773	(17%)	1,058	(42%)	626	(60%)
Motor Vehicle Bodies (shares of motor vehicles' total in parentheses)								
Total	60	(54%)	9,723	(29%)	80	(3%)	26	(2%)
Local	60	(54%)	9,723	(29%)	80	(3%)	26	(2%)
Foreign	0	(0%)	0	(0%)	0	(0%)	0	(0%)
Motor Vehicle Parts and Accessories (shares of motor vehicles' total in parentheses)								
Total	44	(40%)	16,318	(48%)	1,131	(45%)	340	(33%)
Local	36	(32%)	12,010	(36%)	554	(22%)	107	(10%)
Foreign	8	(7%)	4,308	(13%)	577	(23%)	234	(22%)

Table 6.4   (Continued)

Country, year, industry, indicator	Number of plants/firms		Number of workers		Gross output (US$ millions)		Value added (US$ millions)	
	Number	*Share*	*Number*	*Share*	*Value*	*Share*	*Value*	*Share*
THAILAND 1996 (local currency = baht; US$1 = 25.343 baht)								
Motor Vehicles Sector Total (shares of motor vehicles sector total in parentheses)								
Total	406	(100%)	78,253	(100%)	16,590	(100%)	5,106	(100%)
Local	330	(81%)	32,808	(42%)	1,711	(10%)	542	(11%)
Foreign	76	(19%)	45,445	(58%)	14,879	(90%)	4,564	(89%)
Motor Vehicle Assembly (shares of motor vehicles sector total in parentheses)								
Total	46	(11%)	33,062	(42%)	12,811	(77%)	4,076	(80%)
Local	28	(7%)	3,433	(4%)	308	(2%)	60	(1%)
Foreign	15	(4%)	29,629	(38%)	12,504	(75%)	4,016	(79%)
Motor Vehicle Bodies and Trailers (shares of motor vehicles' total in parentheses)								
Total	186	(46%)	15,425	(20%)	1,999	(12%)	473	(9%)
Local	178	(44%)	10,918	(14%)	592	(4%)	174	(3%)
Foreign	8	(2%)	4,507	(6%)	1,407	(8%)	299	(6%)
Motor Vehicle Parts and Accessories (shares of motor vehicles' total in parentheses)								
Total	177	(44%)	29,766	(38%)	1,780	(11%)	557	(11%)
Local	124	(31%)	18,457	(24%)	811	(5%)	309	(6%)
Foreign	53	(13%)	11,309	(14%)	969	(6%)	248	(5%)

Sources: Ito (2004a: Table 7.5; 2004b: Table 1); International Monetary Fund (2005).

share of parts and accessories was of similar size. In Indonesia, parts and accessories plants had the largest number of employees. The largest number of plants were involved in bodies (and trailers), but parts and accessories also had a large number of affiliates in both countries.

If direct comparisons are made for 1996 (Table 6.5), Thai establishments were more numerous in the motor vehicles industry overall and

Table 6.5 Performance indicators for sample plants in 1996

Indicator	Indonesia		Thailand	
	Int'l $	*US$*	*Int'l $*	*US$*
Number of establishments	139		406	
Assembly	8		43	
Herfindahl index	0.596		0.116	
Bodies	63		186	
Herfindahl index	0.089		0.128	
Parts	68		177	
Herfindahl index	0.141		0.051	
Simple Averages for All Motor Vehicles' Establishments				
Number of employees per establishment	277		193	
Output per establishment ($1,000)	58,670	19,455	90,838	40,931
Value added per establishment ($1,000)	31,089	10,309	27,958	12,598
Capital stock per establishment ($1,000)	17,054	5,655	20,439	9,210
Years in operation	12.5		10.1	
Productivity measures				
Output per employee ($1,000)	84.6	28.1	126.7	57.1
Value added per employee ($1,000)	36.1	12.0	37.4	16.9
Capital-labour ratio (($1,000)	71.0	23.5	41.9	18.9
Share of non-production workers (%)	20.3		17.1	
Inventory ratios (% of output)				
Total inventory	32.0		16.2	
Final goods inventory	4.9		3.0	
Work-in-process inventory	4.1		2.3	
Raw materials inventory	25.0		10.8	
Other indicators				
Production worker wages ($, annual)	5,007	1,660	7,347	3,310
Non-production worker wages ($, annual)	9,396	3,116	12,699	5,722
Price-cost margin (%)	35.3		20.9	

Notes: $ = US or international dollars; all values first calculated in local currencies and translated to US dollars at official exchange rates (Thailand = 25.3 baht/$, Indonesia = 2342.3 rupiah/$) or to international dollars using PPP exchange rates (Thailand = 11.4 baht/$, Indonesia = 776.7 rupiah/$) capital stock for Indonesia valued at 1993 prices; average variable cost is the sum of labour and intermediate input costs divided by output; the price-cost margin is (value added – wages paid)/output.
Sources: BPS-Statistics (various years b); National Statistical Office (1999b); World Bank (1998).

in all three sub-categories (assembly, bodies, parts). The Indonesian industry was much more concentrated (i.e. Herfindahl indices were higher) in assembly and parts, but somewhat less concentrated in bodies. The price–cost margin was also higher in the Indonesian industry, indicating a lower degree of competition. Indonesian plants were larger in terms of employment, but smaller in terms of capital and most production measures, though differences were relatively small in terms of value added.[12] Labour productivity measures (average output per employee or average value added per employee) and wage rates were higher in Thailand than those in Indonesia, suggesting that labour was more efficient in Thai plants than in their Indonesian counterparts. The facts that Indonesian plants used relatively large amounts of high cost factors of production (capital and non-production workers) and carried more inventory than Thai plants also suggest they were relatively inefficient.

6.3.2 Productivity differences between foreign and local establishments

Productivity levels and related indicators are first compared in foreign and local establishments using descriptive statistics similar to those analysed in the previous section. Ratios of foreign to local plants are calculated for a number of indicators and t-tests are performed to see if the differences are statistically significant. If the differences between foreign and local plants are relatively large and the plant-wise variation among each group is relatively small, the differences being considered tend to be statistically significant. However, these measures of differences do not account for other influences on the variable being measured.

In Indonesia foreign establishments tended to be larger than local plants in terms of employment, output, value added and capital stock (Table 6.6). These differences are statistically significant in assembly as well as in parts and accessories in 1990–96, but only in the latter industry in 1999. Labour productivity (both output per employee and value added per employee) and TFP were significantly higher for foreign establishments in the parts and components industry in 1990–96 and a few other years.[13] However, these differences are not statistically significant in the motor vehicle assembly industry, partly as a result of heterogeneity among the establishments and the small sample size. The capital–labour ratio was larger for foreign establishments in most years in both industries (1990 was the exception in both industries) but differences in capital intensity were usually statistically insignificant (1999 in parts and accessories being the sole exception).[14]

Table 6.6 Economic performance in foreign plants relative to local plants in Indonesian motor vehicle industries

Indicator	Motor vehicle assembly								Motor vehicle parts and accessories							
	1990–96		1990		1995		1999		1990–96		1990		1995		1999	
	MNC/ local	T-test	MNC/ local	T-test	MNC/ local	T-test	MNC/ local	T-test	MNC/ local	T-test	MNC/ local	T-test	MNC/ local	T-test	MNC/ local	T-test
No. of employees per establishment	4.32	***	4.48		4.15		3.77		1.77	***	1.76		1.62		2.11	*
Output per establishment	6.27	**	29.05		5.90		33.58		5.41	***	8.08		4.70		6.48	**
Value added per establishment	12.56	**	33.59		16.27		27.03		7.17	***	7.03		9.42		6.14	**
Capital stock per establishment	6.97	***	2.88		5.89		9.06		2.59	***	2.09		1.92		2.66	**
Years in operation	0.84		0.86		0.77		1.27		0.97		0.97		0.97		0.72	
Capital-labour ratio	1.70		0.61		1.80		3.23		1.50		0.97		1.11		2.77	*
Productivity measures																
Output/employee	0.84		4.13		0.65		6.15		2.49	***	2.49		2.53		5.04	*
Value added/employee	1.52		4.85		1.82		5.02		2.92	***	2.80		4.01		5.32	*
TFP (in logarithm)	1.01		1.14		1.15		1.06		1.28	***	1.27	**	1.34	*	1.14	
Production worker wages	1.32		1.34		1.20		1.20		1.87	***	2.17	**	2.16	**	4.10	**
Non-production worker wages	1.15		1.70		1.41		2.28		1.55	***	2.33	*	1.01		6.15	

Notes: Pecuniary values are calculated in 1993 rupiah; see Ito (2004a: 263) for details on price deflators; some observations are excluded because of missing values or recording mistakes; t-tests assume unequal variances and test the hypothesis that values are equal for foreign and local plants (i.e. that the foreign/local ratio equals 1); * = significant at 10%, ** = significant at 5%, *** = significant at 1% level (two-tailed tests).
Sources: BPS-Statistics (various years b); Ito (2004a: Table 7.7).

In the Thai case, four labour productivity measures (output or value added per production worker hour or output or value added per employee) were all higher in foreign plants and all these differences were statistically significant at the 5 per cent level (Table 6.7). The two capital productivity measures (ratios of output or value added to fixed assets) were significantly higher in foreign plants only in the assembly industry. Capital productivity was lower in foreign plants in the other two industries and most of these differences were statistically significant (the ratio of value added to fixed assets in parts and accessories being the single exception). Foreign plants also had significantly higher capital–labour ratios and were significantly larger in terms of registered capital or employment per plant in all but one case (employment per plant in parts and accessories being the exception). Results for TFP differed among industries, however. TFP was significantly higher in foreign plants in assembly and in the sample of all motor vehicle establishments. TFP was also markedly higher on average in bodies and trailers, but this difference was not significant. In parts and accessories, TFP levels were roughly equal in foreign and local plants.[15]

In sum, the results in Tables 6.6 and 6.7 show that labour productivity tends to be relatively high in foreign plants both in Indonesia and Thailand. In addition, limiting samples to relatively large establishments generates similar results (Ito 2004a, 2004b). However, foreign plants also tended to be larger and more capital intensive. These differences should be taken into account when comparing productivity, because differences in size and capital intensity, not differences in ownership, might explain the observation of relatively high labour productivity in foreign plants.

6.4   Determinants of total factor productivity and its growth

This section presents the results of regression analyses conducted to see if foreign plants still have higher productivity than local plants after controlling for the influences of size and capital intensity and other factors thought to affect productivity. Utilizing the panel data for Indonesia, it is also possible to examine the determinants of TFP growth using a cost function framework.

6.4.1   Productivity and the managerial resources of MNCs

For Indonesia, it is assumed that productivity levels are determined by industry-wide time effects and observable plant-specific characteristics. Plant size and plant age are the two plant-specific characteristics

Table 6.7 Economic performance in foreign plants relative to local plants in Thai motor vehicle industries, 1996

	Assembly		Bodies and trailers		Parts and accessories		Total	
	Foreign/local	*T-test*	*Foreign/local*	*T-test*	*Foreign/local*	*T-test*	*Foreign/local*	*T-test*
Employment per establishment	16.11	***	9.18	***	1.43		6.01	***
Registered capital per establishment	28.70	**	17.79	**	5.19	***	19.79	***
Years in operation	1.79	*	0.88		0.66	***	0.94	
Capital-labour ratio	2.86	*	8.00	*	3.41	***	3.98	***
Productivity measures								
Output per production worker hour	10.19	***	8.03	**	2.52	***	5.12	***
Value added per production worker hour	10.16	***	6.18	**	2.55	***	4.08	***
Output per employee	14.48	***	9.45	**	2.59	***	5.90	***
Value added per employee	15.43	***	6.57	**	2.41	***	4.79	***
Output per 1 baht of fixed assets	3.95	**	0.25	***	0.31	**	0.46	***
Value added per 1 baht of fixed assets	1.88	**	0.16	***	0.26		0.29	***
Relative TFP	−3.16	***	−2.59		0.99		−0.39	**
Production worker wages	2.55	***	1.84	**	1.38	***	1.58	***
Non-production worker wages	1.65	**	2.20	**	2.13	***	2.28	***

Notes: Pecuniary values are in current market prices; negative ratios for TFP reflect negative TFP for local plants and positive TFP for foreign plants in three categories (assembly, body and trailers, total); in the other category (part and accessories) TFP was negative for both foreign and local plants; t-tests assume unequal variances and test the hypothesis that values are equal for foreign and local plants (i.e. that the foreign/local ratio equals 1); * = significant at 10%, ** = significant at 5%, *** = significant at 1% level (two-tailed tests).
Source: Calculated from Ito (2004b: Tables 2, B.1).

included because larger plants and older plants may be more productive if they realize economies of scale or benefit from learning by doing. If foreign-owned plants are still more productive than local plants after controlling for size and age, the remaining differences in productivity are attributed to the MNCs' possession of superior managerial resources and other firm-specific assets. This methodology is implemented by using the 1990–99 panel of all motor vehicles plants and regressing plant-level productivity on year- and industry-specific dummies, plant size, plant age, and a dummy variable for foreign establishments. Four productivity measures are examined for 1990–99 in this framework: average variable cost, output per employee (in real terms), value added per employee (in real terms), and TFP.[16]

For Thailand, two productivity measures – labour productivity and relative TFP – are estimated as a function of various plant-specific characteristics. The labour productivity equation can be derived from a production function and assumes that labour productivity is determined by factor intensities (capital intensity, the non-production worker share) and other plant-specific characteristics factors such as age (a dummy for plants starting up in 1986 or earlier), size, Board of Investment (BOI) status (a dummy for BOI-promoted plants), exporting status (a dummy for exporting plants) and importing status (a dummy for importing plants). Similar to the Indonesian case, the TFP equation excludes factor intensities as an explanatory variable because this total measure of productivity already accounts for the influences of factor intensities. Both the labour productivity and TFP equations also include a dummy for foreign plants in order to examine the effects of ownership after controlling for the other influences described above.[17]

More specifically, the coefficients on the foreign ownership dummy reveal the marginal difference in productivity levels between foreign and local plants after controlling for influence of the other factors included in the equation examined. Coefficients on the foreign ownership dummy are expected to be positive, because the traditional theory suggests that MNCs will be more productive than local plants (see section 6.1), which are predominantly non-MNCs in Indonesia and Thailand. Table 6.8 presents estimated coefficients on the dummy variable for foreign ownership for representative specifications of the equations described above.[18]

In the Indonesian case, coefficients on the foreign ownership dummy were positive and significant for the two labour productivity measures, but not in the average variable cost or TFP equations. The Indonesian results also indicated that labour productivity measures

Table 6.8 Estimated differences in productivity measures between MNCs and local plants in motor vehicles, OLS results

Productivity measure	Estimated coefficients and T-values		No. of observations
	Coefficient	T-value	
INDONESIAN REGRESSIONS, UNBALANCED PANEL, 1990–99			
(controls = size, age, time & industry dummies)			
Average variable cost	0.470	(0.88)	1,134
Output per employee	1.593	(2.24)**	1,134
Value added per employee	1.427	(2.06)**	1,124
TFP	–0.363	(–0.76)	1,125
THAI LABOUR PRODUCTIVITY REGRESSIONS, 1996 CROSS-SECTION			
(controls = fixed assets per production worker, non-production workers per production worker, age, BOI promotional status, exporting status, importing status)			
Value added per production worker hour	0.244	(1.25)	406
THAI LABOUR PRODUCTIVITY REGRESSIONS, 1996 CROSS-SECTION			
(controls = fixed assets per production worker, non-production workers per production worker, age, BOI promotional status, exporting status, importing status, industry)			
Value added per production worker hour	0.168	(0.87)	406
THAI TFP REGRESSIONS, 1996 CROSS-SECTION			
(controls = size, size & foreign ownership, age, BOI promotional status, exporting status, importing status, industry)			
TFP	–1.391	(–1.08)	406
THAI TFP REGRESSIONS, 1996 CROSS-SECTION			
(controls = size, size & foreign ownership, size & industry dummies, size & foreign ownership & industry dummies, age, BOI promotional status, exporting status, importing status, industry)			
TFP	–1.421	(–0.70)	406

Notes: t-statistics based on White's robust standard errors (White 1980); ** = significant at 5% level (two-tailed tests).
Sources: Ito (2004a: Table 7.8; 2004b: Tables 4 and 6).

(output per employee and value added per employee) and TFP were positively correlated with plant age and plant size (Ito 2004a: Table 7.8). For Thailand, coefficients on the foreign ownership dummy were never significant. As in the Indonesian case, negative coefficients on the foreign ownership dummy in the TFP equations are also conspicuous, though one cannot attach much meaning to these results as they are statistically insignificant. In other words, these results suggest that there was not a strong tendency for foreign plants to have higher productivity than local plants in the Thai motor vehicle industry.[19] On the other hand, results from alternative quantile regressions (Ito 2004b) can be interpreted as evidence that foreign ownership does matter, but only among the relatively productive plants. As expected, in most specifications, these results also suggested positive correlations between labour productivity, on the one hand, and capital intensity or the ratio of non-production workers to production workers, on the other. Both labour productivity and TFP were also positively correlated with plant size, but there was no evidence that the importance of scale economies differs between foreign and local plants.

The regression results thus provide only weak evidence that foreign plants have higher productivity after controlling for factor intensities and other related plant-specific characteristics in the Indonesian and Thai automobile industries. Although there is some indication that labour productivity was higher in foreign plants in Indonesia, this was not the case in Thailand and differences in TFP levels were insignificant in both countries. In marked contrast, the results suggested that large plants had consistently higher productivity by any measure, and that scale economies were a key determinant of both labour productivity and TFP.

6.4.2 Determinants of TFP growth

Utilizing the plant-level panel data on the Indonesian automotive industry, it is also possible to examine the determinants of TFP growth, employing a cost function framework. This framework is advantageous because it endogenizes the impact of capacity utilization.[20] The cost function analysis focuses on 1990–96 because it would be very difficult to distinguish the effects of scale economies from the crisis-related effects of low demand after 1996.

Following Fuss and Waverman (1992), Nadiri and Nandi (1999), Kawai (2000) and others, a variable cost function is used as the basis to decompose TFP growth into three components.[21] The first is a scale effect which refers to changes in TFP resulting from changes in output levels. The second, capacity-utilization effect, results from expansion of production capacity and the differences between long- and short-run equilibrium conditions as firms adjust to short-run fluctuations in demand. The third effect describes the effects of technological change on TFP. These effects are in turn influenced by both supply- and demand-side factors. On the

Table 6.9 Decomposition of average annual TFP growth rate in Indonesian motor vehicles, 1990–96 (per cent)

Sample	Scale effect	Capacity utilization effect	Technological change effect	TFP
All establishments	0.117	–1.511	–0.011	–1.405
Foreign establishments	–0.441	–3.257	–0.018	–3.717
Local establishments	–0.468	–1.506	–0.010	–1.984

Source: Reproduced from Ito (2004a: 259).

supply-side, economies of scale arise if average cost falls as output rises, and result from the technological characteristics of a plant. However, at the same time, sufficient market size is necessary before a firm will decide to increase output. Therefore, the scale effect reflects both supply-side and demand-side factors. On the other hand, the capacity-utilization effect captures the effects resulting from short-run changes in demand.

The average annual TFP growth rate was negative for both local and foreign establishments and much lower in foreign plants (–3.7 per cent) than in local plants (–2.0 per cent, Table 6.9). The capacity-utilization effect was much larger in absolute value than the other two effects and again negative for both local and foreign plants. The negative capacity-utilization effect accounted for the vast majority of the negative TFP growth observed for both local (over three-quarters) and foreign (over six-sevenths) establishments. This might reflect the fact that expectations of continued rapid growth in the Indonesian automobile market led many establishments to invest in large amounts of machinery, equipment and other fixed capital in the early 1990s. In addition, quite a few foreign and local establishments were first established in the mid-1990s, which also may have contributed to a negative capacity-utilization effect on TFP growth. Although it was much smaller than the capacity-utilization effect, the scale effect was also negative and of similar magnitude for foreign and local establishments. In contrast, the technological change effect was negligible for all plants in the Indonesian motor vehicle industry.

6.5   Concluding remarks

According to economic theory, manufacturing plants owned by multi-national corporations are likely to be more productive than local plants because they possess superior managerial resources and other firm-specific assets. This chapter has examined productivity differences between foreign-owned and local establishments in the Indonesian and Thai automobile industries in the 1990s. Several alternative productivity measures and specifications were examined in order to generate robust and comprehensive results.

Descriptive statistics indicated that foreign establishments tend to be larger, enjoy higher labour productivity, and pay higher wages than local plants. The results of the regression analyses also showed that foreign establishments had significantly higher labour productivity than local plants in Indonesia but not in Thailand. Moreover, there was no indication that MNCs' ownership-specific advantages led to higher TFP in MNCs as economic theory would suggest. Rather the results indicated that the scale effect was an important determinant of productivity levels in both countries. This in turn suggests that plants must operate at a more efficient scale and improve capacity utilization in order to improve productivity in these countries.

Decomposition analysis suggested that inefficient capacity utilization accounted for the vast majority of the negative TFP growth in Indonesia, and that this effect was particularly large in foreign plants. The scale effect was much smaller and the technological change was negligible for both foreign and local establishments. This suggests that demand-side factors were rather important determinants of productivity growth in Indonesia.[22]

Notes

1. See Lipsey (2004) for a survey of the literature. The evidence for Indonesia suggests that MNCs had relatively high productivity in Indonesian industries, including transportation machinery (which is primarily automobiles), as well as the existence of positive productivity spillovers (see Chapter 4 for details). More limited evidence for Thailand also suggests the existence of positive spillovers, but that productivity differentials were generally small and insignificant in a wide range of industries, including motor vehicles (see Chapter 5 for details).
2. These results come from Ito (2004a, 2004b) and Okamoto and Sjöholm (2000). Note that results for Thai labour productivity from Ito (2004a) contrast to some of the results in Chapters 5, probably because of differences in aggregation and methodology. TFP is a preferred measure of productivity because it takes account of the differences in factor intensities.
3. The automobile industry is considered strategic in Indonesia because (1) it supplies equipment used to fulfil public transportation requirements; (2) it creates employment opportunities and facilitates the introduction of high technology into its own and other markets; and (3) it generates income for the government from import duties and other taxes (Aswicahyono, Anas and Rizal 2000).

4. Although deregulation packages suggested a shift from protectionism towards a more market-oriented approach, the Soeharto administration later launched the National Car Project, which contradicted the earlier, market-oriented reforms in many respects. However, after the 1997–98 crisis, the government discontinued special tax, customs and credit privileges for the National Car Project (Aswicahyono, Anas and Rizal 2000).

5. As a result, most of the automobiles sold in the country have been made by Japanese automakers, which accounted for 90 per cent of the units sold in 1995 (Table 6.1) and 80 per cent in 2001 (Nikkan Jidosha Shinbun-sha, various years).

6. For example, the Thai case is discussed in Yahata and Mizuno (1988), Maruhashi (1995), Buranathanung (1996) and Terdudomtham (1997). Under the AICO (ASEAN Industrial Cooperation) scheme, preferential tariff rates were set in November 1996 with the aim of broadening the ASEAN market, allowing ASEAN producers to benefit from the resulting economies of scale, and encouraging cooperative production among ASEAN producers. However, ASEAN member governments have often required trade flows under this scheme to be balanced, which severely limits the scope and effectiveness of the programme (Farrell and Findlay 2001).

7. The government required foreign automakers to establish joint ventures in order to facilitate access to technology and to create opportunities for local conglomerates to profit by participating in the automobile manufacturing business.

8. See Aswicahyono, Basri and Hill (2000) for details.

9. These groups include engines, chassis frames, brakes, transmissions, clutch systems and propeller shafts. As described above, the government used a licensing system for these components and the Astra group was in a favourable position to secure the limited number of licences offered (Sato 1996).

10. Data sources are BPS-Statistics (various years b) and the National Statistical Office (1999b) while official compilations are BPS-Statistics (various years a) and National Statistical Office (1999a).

11. For example, official compilations (BPS-Statistics various years a) put the number of motor vehicle assemblers at fourteen in 1995 but after eliminating plants with incomplete or unreliable data, this number is reduced to seven in this sample (Table 6.4). The original Thai data also include some establishments with ten to nineteen employees, but they are not included in these data sets primarily because comparisons of these small plants, which are primarily local, and MNCs, which are primarily large, are not thought to be meaningful. The Thai data also have relatively severe coverage and duplication problems as described in Chapters 1, 3, 5 and 8. For more details on these samples, see Ito (2004a, 2004b).

12. Note that value added per establishment was larger in Indonesia if measured at purchasing power parity (in international dollars) but smaller if measured at market exchange rates (in US dollars).

13. TFP is calculated slightly differently for Indonesia and for Thailand. For Indonesia, the methodology is explained in Ito (2004a: 247). For Thailand, see Ito (2004b: 346–7).

14. In a pattern similar to that observed in labour productivity measures, wages were often significantly higher for foreign establishments in the parts and

accessories industry, but not in assembly (see additional indicators in Ito 2004a: Table 7.7). Results for inventory ratios varied greatly across industry and time, and were usually insignificant, except for parts and accessories in 1999 where they were significantly lower in foreign plants. On the other hand, the import ratio was much higher for foreign establishments in both industries and differences were statistically significant in 1990–96 and also in 1999 for parts and accessories

15. The TFP results in Table 6.7 are slightly confusing because the negative signs result from negative denominators, which measure TFP in local plants relative to average TFP. In addition, according to results for samples of all motor vehicle plants in Ito (2004b: Appendix Table B.1), wages are significantly higher for foreign plants in the Thai motor vehicle industry. Foreign assembly plants also managed their inventory relatively efficiently, while foreign plants in the other two industries still held large inventories in 1996.

16. Squares of plant size and plant age are also included in the regression equation in order to take the non-linear effects into account. Average variable cost is defined as the sum of labour and intermediate input costs divided by output in real terms. See Ito (2004a: 251–4, 262–3) for details on the equations and variable definitions.

17. See Ito (2004b: 332–47) for details on the equations and variable definitions used in the Thai case.

18. For results of estimating alternative specifications, which are broadly similar, see Ito (2004a: Table 7.8; 2004b: Tables 4 and 6).

19. This is a result similar to corresponding results obtained using alternative methodologies to estimate productivity differentials in Thai motor vehicles and described in Chapter 5.

20. An alternative is to calculate utilization impacts from the data, but there is no information on the number of hours worked in the Indonesian data and although the survey asks the percentage of actual production to production capacity during the year, the quality of the capacity utilization data was judged to be too poor for use in this analysis.

21. See Ito (2004a: 255–8) for a formal derivation and further details.

22. According to Rhys (1998), the minimum efficient scale is about 250,000 units per year for automobile assembly and about 1 million units per year for the casting of engine blocks and pressing of panel parts. In Indonesia, however, even the largest assembly plant only assembles at most about 75,000 automobiles per year, which is much lower than the production scale of a major Japanese assembly plant (approximately 600,000 units per year) or a major Thai assembly plant (approximately 150,000 units per year). Information on units of cars assembled in a year was taken from various yearbooks of the automobile market and interviews by the author.

References

Aswicahyono, Haryo, Titik Anas and Jose Rizal (2000) 'The Indonesian Automotive Industry', *ASEAN Automotive Report* (retrieved from www.asean-auto.org, 3 May 2002).

Aswicahyono, Haryo, M. Chatib Basri and Hal Hill (2000) 'How Not to Industrialise? Indonesia's Automotive Industry', *Bulletin of Indonesian Economic Studies*, 36: 209–41.

BPS-Statistics (various years a) *Statistik Industri: Besar Dan Sedang [Industrial Statistics: Large and Medium Manufacturing Statistics]*, 1990–9 issues, Jakarta: BPS-Statistics.

BPS-Statistics (various years b). Unpublished plant-level data underlying *Statistik Industri: Besar Dan Sedang [Industrial Statistics: Large and Medium Manufacturing Statistics]*, 1990–9 issues, Jakarta: BPS-Statistics.

Brooker Group Public Co. Ltd. (2003) *Thailand's Automotive Industry*, Bangkok: Brooker Group Public Co. Ltd.

Buranathanung, Noppadol (1996) 'The Organization of Parts Procurement in the Thai Automobile Industry', *Chulalongkorn Journal of Economics*, 8: 67–99.

Caves, Richard E. (1996) *Multinational Enterprise and Economic Analysis*, second edition, Cambridge: Cambridge University Press.

Dunning, John H. (1988) *Explaining International Production*, London: Unwin Hyman.

Farrell, Roger and Christopher Findlay (2001) 'Japan and the ASEAN4 Automotive Industry: Developments and Inter-relationships in the Regional Automotive Industry', Working Paper 2001–24. Kitakyushu: International Centre for the Study of East Asian Development.

FOURIN (2000) *2000 Asean Taiwan Jidosha Buhin Sangyo [Directory of the Automobile Parts Industry in ASEAN and Taiwan 2000]*, Nagoya: FOURIN.

FOURIN (various years) *Sekai Jidousha Tokei Hakusho [FOURIN's Global Automotive Statistics]*, Nagoya: FOURIN.

Fuss, Mevyn A. and Leonard Waverman (1992) *Costs and Productivity in Automobile Production: the Challenge of Japanese Efficiency*, Cambridge: Cambridge University Press.

Hill, Hal (1996) 'Indonesia's Industrial Policy and Performance: "Orthodoxy" Vindicated', *Economic Development and Cultural Change*, 45: 147–74.

International Monetary Fund (2005) *International Financial Statistics CD-ROM*, January 2005 issue, Washington, DC: International Monetary Fund.

Ito, Keiko (2004a) 'Foreign Ownership and Productivity in the Indonesian Automobile Industry: Evidence from Establishment Data for 1990–1999', in Takatoshi Ito and Andrew K. Rose, eds, *Growth and Productivity in East Asia*, Chicago and London: University of Chicago Press, pp. 229–70.

Ito, Keiko (2004b) 'Foreign Ownership and Plant Productivity in the Thai Automobile Industry in 1996 and 1998: a Conditional Quantile Analysis', *Journal of Asian Economics*, 15: 321–53.

Kawai, Hiroki (2000) 'Japan', in Pacific Economic Cooperation Council (PECC), ed., *Pacific Economic Outlook Structure Project: Productivity Growth and Industrial Structure in the Pacific Region: Background Papers*, Osaka: Japan Committee for Pacific Economic Outlook, pp. 197–229.

Lipsey, Robert E (2004) 'Home- and Host-Country Effects of Foreign Direct Investment', in Robert E. Baldwin and L. Alan Winters, eds, *Challenges to Globalization: Analyzing the Economics*, Chicago and London: University of Chicago Press, pp. 333–79.

Markusen, James R. (1991) 'The Theory of the Multinational Enterprise: a Common Analytical Framework', in Eric D. Ramstetter, ed., *Direct Foreign Investment in Asia's Developing Economies and Structural Change in the Asia-Pacific Region*, Boulder, Co.: Westview Press, pp. 11–32.

Maruhashi, Hiroko (1995) *Japanese Subcontracting System in Thailand: a Case Study of the Thai Automobile Industry*, Master's thesis, Bangkok: Faculty of Economics, Thammasat University.

Nadiri, M. Ishaq and Banani Nandi (1999) 'Technical Change, Markup, Divestiture, and Productivity Growth in the US Telecommunications Industry', *Review of Economics and Statistics*, 81: 488–98.

National Economic and Social Development Board (2004) *National Income of Thailand*, 2003 edition, Bangkok: NESDB.

National Statistical Office (1999a) *Report of the 1997 Industrial Census: Whole Kingdom*, Bangkok: National Statistical Office.

National Statistical Office (1999b) Unpublished plant-level data underlying *Report of the 1997 Industrial Census: Whole Kingdom*, Bangkok: National Statistical Office.

Nikkan Jidosha Shinbun-sha (various years) *Jidosha Sangyo Handbook [Handbook of the Automobile Industry]*, Tokyo: Nikkan Jidosha Shinbun-sha.

Nomura, Toshiro (1996) 'Indonesia no Kokuminsha Keikaku to Humpus Kia no Jidosha Shijo Sannyu [The National Car Project and the Entry of Humpus and Kia into Indonesia's Automobile Market]', *Shokei Ronso*, 46: 81–154.

Okamoto, Yumiko and Fredrik Sjöholm (2000) 'Productivity in the Indonesian Automotive Industry', *ASEAN Economic Bulletin*, 17: 60–73.

Poapongsakorn, Nipon and Chayanit Wangdee (2000) 'The Impact of Technological Change and Corporate Reorganization in the ASEAN Automobile Industry', *ASEAN Automotive Report* (retrieved from www.asean-auto.org, 3 May 2002).

Rhys, Garel (1998) 'The Motor Industry', in B. J. Atkinson, F. Liversey and B. Hilward, eds, *Applied Economics*, Basingstoke: Macmillan, pp. 250–72.

Sakura Institute of Research (1996) 'Tounan Ajia no Jidosha Sangyo no Hatten to Ikinai Kyoryoku Suishin ni kansuru Sogo Chosa [Comprehensive Survey on the Development of Automotive Industry in Southeast Asia and the Promotion of Regional Cooperation]', Tokyo: Center for Pacific Business Studies, Sakura Institute of Research.

Sato, Yuri (1996) 'The Astra Group: a Pioneer of Management Modernization in Indonesia', *Developing Economies*, 34: 247–80.

Takayasu, Kenichi, Yukiko Ishizaki and Minako Mori (1996) 'The Imminent Advent of the Age of Global Competition for the Automobile Industry in Southeast Asia', *RIM Pacific Business and Industries*, 3, 33, Tokyo: Center for Pacific Business Studies, Sakura Institute of Research.

Terdudomtham, Tammavit (1997) *The Automobile Industry in Thailand*, Bangkok: Thailand Development Research Institute.

Thailand Automotive Institute (2005) *Car Statistic Report* (retrieved from www.thaiauto.or.th/Records/eng/vehicleproduction_eng.asp, 3 May 2005).

White, Halbert (1980) 'A Heteroskedasticity-Consistent Covariance Matrix Estimator and a Direct Test for Heteroskedasticity', *Econometrica*, 48: 813–38.

World Bank (1998) *World Development Indicators 1998*, Washington, DC: World Bank.

Yahata, Shigemi and Junko Mizuno (1988) *Nikkei Shinshutsu Kigyo to Genchi Kigyo to no Kigyo-kan Bungyo Kozo to Gijutsu Iten: Tai no Jidosha Sangyo wo Jirei to shite [The Division of Labour and Technology Transfer among Japanese Affiliates and Local Firms: a Case Study of the Thai Automobile Industry]*, Tokyo: Institute of Developing Economies.

Part IV

Exports and Foreign Ownership

7
Multinational Companies and Exports in Indonesian Manufacturing

Fredrik Sjöholm and Sadayuki Takii

7.1 Introduction

Indonesia liberalized its trade regime in the mid-1980s, which resulted in a large increase in manufacturing exports. Indonesian firms seem, hence, to react to changing incentives and base their export choices on costs and benefits of production for domestic and foreign markets. Our knowledge about which Indonesian firms are in a position to enter foreign markets through exports is more limited. Typically, most firms produce only for the domestic market even in industries where Indonesia has large export levels.

Empirical studies on countries other than Indonesia find persistence in exports: a plant that has started to export tends to continue.[1] Moreover, firm-wise characteristics that affect the costs of production and the quality of the products seem to be important to explain firm-level exports. For instance, exporters tend to be large; to have high productivity levels; and to have high shares of white-collar workers.[2] However, low costs and good quality are necessary but presumably not sufficient to facilitate exports. Success in foreign markets requires that the exporters take foreign market conditions into consideration. Information on foreign preferences, regulations, distribution channels and other market characteristics has to be gathered and analysed. This type of information can be costly, and the higher the costs are the less likely it is that the firm will find it profitable to initiate exports. More importantly, the cost can be expected to decrease with the amount of foreign networks since knowledge on foreign conditions may increase with such networks.

Foreign-owned multinational corporations (MNCs) possess extensive foreign networks, which can allow them easier access to foreign markets compared to local non-MNCs. This is one reason why governments in developing countries offer preferential treatment to export-oriented projects by MNCs. During the decade before the drastic deregulation of foreign direct investment (FDI) in June 1994, Indonesia also granted export-oriented projects by MNCs exemptions from foreign ownership restrictions as well as requirements for divestment and minimum capital investment (see Pangestu 1996: 164). The exemptions were one response to the slow growth of exports after the sharp decline in oil prices and the Plaza Accord in the mid-1980s. There were also other important reforms designed to stimulate non-oil and gas exports and investment. The result was a sharp recovery which was mainly driven by growth in non-oil and gas exports, particularly manufactures (Hill 1997: 302–3).

This chapter examines Indonesia's manufacturing exports with a special focus on the role of foreign-owned companies. Our analysis is based on plant-level industrial surveys, which have been conducted annually by BPS-Statistics (Indonesia's central agency of statistics) since 1975. The data include all manufacturing plants with twenty employees or more for thirty-seven years, 1975–2001. We will use data for 1990–2000, when export figures are included.

7.2   Determinants of export participation: theory and empirical results

The heterogeneity of firms has been a core aspect of both theoretical and empirical literature on international trade in recent years. As previously mentioned, the decision to export to a foreign market requires information on different consumer preferences, distribution channels and marketing. Moreover, it is necessary to identify the main competitors and to learn about the foreign institutional framework. Consequently, there are considerable costs incurred when collecting information before exporting can take place. These costs are normally referred to as sunk entry costs, which are expenses incurred from entering a foreign market that must be written off whether the firm decides to export or not.[3] On the other hand, once the firm has invested in collecting the information, it can be utilized without incurring many additional costs. Hence, there will be large degrees of persistence in trade flows as firms that have entered the foreign market tend to continue to export.

Export entry costs can be expected to vary between firms. For instance, recent theoretical studies predict that more productive firms engage in exporting and less productive firms stay in domestic markets

(Bernard et al. 2003; Melitz 2003; Helpman et al. 2004; Head and Ries 2003). Moreover, Roberts and Tybout (1997: 561) suggest that foreign networks will reduce the cost of collecting information on new markets for a firm. In particular, face-to-face communication facilitates the understanding of foreign markets, as firms have the opportunity to secure clarifications or additional information.

Foreign ownership may have a positive effect on export propensities since multinational corporations by definition have an international network. Frequently, the multinational is not only familiar with its home country conditions, but also has information on other markets. One would therefore expect firms with foreign ownership to be relatively likely to export.

Most of the previous studies, thus, have asserted that a firm's decision to engage in exporting is dependent on related sunk costs and the level of productivity, as well as the size and skills of the labour force. As discussed in Chapter 4, MNCs' affiliates tend to have higher productivity than locally-owned plants. Moreover, Chapter 2 showed MNCs to have a more educated labour force than locally-owned plants. More importantly, MNCs' affiliates are thought to have more information about foreign consumer preferences, distribution systems, legal frameworks and numerous other aspects of foreign markets. These advantages are especially pronounced when the export market is the MNC's home country.

There are a few important previous studies that empirically examine the relationship between foreign ownership and a firm's decision to export. For instance, Aitken et al. (1997) examine the issue for Mexican manufacturing data and find plants with foreign ownership to be more likely to export than domestically-owned plants. Athukorala et al. (1995) used cross-sectional data for Sri Lankan manufacturing firms in 1981 to examine whether MNCs' affiliates are more export-oriented than local firms in a given developing-country environment. The results suggest that Third World MNCs are more likely to export than local firms, while there is no statistical difference between developed-country MNCs and local firms once other characteristics are controlled for.

7.3   MNCs and export in the Indonesian manufacturing sector

Trade policy in Indonesia has changed considerably over the years.[4] Through the mid-1980s, import substitution was pursued as a way to promote industrialization. However, trade reforms were initiated in the beginning of the 1980s when declining prices of oil and other raw materials resulted in a balance of payments crisis. The reforms continued throughout the 1980s and 1990s. More specifically, the exchange rate was depreciated, tariffs and non-tariff barriers were substantially reduced, various import bans were abolished, local content regulations relaxed, the FDI regime liberalized, and customs procedures improved.[5] Equally important were other economic and political factors that also helped to attract FDI and spur export growth, including a stable macroeconomic policy, low wages, political stability and abundant supplies of natural resources (Hill 1988: 140).

The far-reaching liberalization resulted in a large increase in manufacturing output and exports. For example, the economy grew at annual rates of 6.3 and 7.2 per cent during 1985–90 and 1990–96, respectively (Takii 2005). Over the whole period, merchandise exports increased from US$19 billion in 1985 to US$50 billion in 1997. The share of manufacturing in total exports increased from around 14 per cent in 1985 to around 65 per cent in 1996. The financial and political crisis starting in 1997 had a negative effect on manufacturing exports but they recovered to pre-crisis levels by the turn of the century (Ramstetter and Takii 2005: 2). In addition, the annual inflow of FDI as measured in the balance of payments statistics also increased from only US$310 million in 1985 to US$6.2 billion in 1997 (Takii 2005).

For the first years after the liberalization in 1986, the expansion of output and exports appears to have been concentrated in domestically-owned firms. For instance, Hill (1988: 128) notes that domestically-owned firms were almost exclusively responsible for the strong expansion of the garment and plywood exports. Hill (1996: 78) also shows that annual FDI inflows as a share of GDP rarely exceeded 1 per cent during the period 1969–92, and that the share of FDI in gross capital formation was typically lower than 4 per cent. Moreover, Okamoto and Sjöholm (2003: 383) show that, although the number of foreign plants in the manufacturing sector increased around 80 per cent between 1980 and 1990, the foreign share of employment and value added decreased over the same period. One likely explanation is that domestically-owned firms were in a better position to quickly understand and react to the broad economic reforms and liberalization in the mid-1980s. Foreign actors presumably needed more time to gather information and react to the new economic environment in Indonesia.

Once foreign firms understood the changes in Indonesia, they invested and expanded in Indonesia in an unprecedented way. Luckily for Indonesia, the liberalization coincided with a search for low cost export platforms by large multinational companies, which were mainly from Japan and other Asian countries. Hence, the liberalization triggered inflows of export-oriented FDI, often from other Asian countries. As a result, the real gross output in foreign-owned plants increased by around 214 per cent between 1990 and 1995 compared to around 87 per cent for domestically-owned plants (Okamoto and Sjöholm 2005: 164). Accordingly, employment increased 250 per cent in foreign-owned plants over the same period compared to 50 per cent in domestically-owned ones.

Ramstetter (1999) confirms that foreign-owned firms in Indonesia exported a larger portion of their output than domestically-owned firms, and that they therefore were an important factor behind the growth of exports. In particular, some important Indonesian export industries, such as electronics, are heavily dominated by foreign-owned firms.

This is not to say that MNCs are the only source of increased exports in Indonesia. Foreign trading houses, customers, and suppliers of technology and capital have also helped Indonesian firms with marketing know-how and information on export markets. The extent of this type of assistance is difficult to estimate but case studies suggest that they are important in industries such as textiles, wood products and machine parts.[6]

7.3.1　Export propensities

The structure of the Indonesian manufacturing sector is shown in Table 7.1. The number of plants increased about 34 per cent from 16,536 in 1990 to 22,174 in 2000. The relative size of different sectors changed over time. For example, the share of food (including beverages and tobacco) has declined and the shares of textiles (including apparel, leather and footwear) and metal products and machinery have increased. Textiles was the largest employer in the year 2000, accounting for almost one-third of manufacturing employment in sample plants. Metal products and machinery was the largest sector in terms of value added with a share of about 27 per cent.

Moreover, these two sectors combined account for almost 47 per cent of total manufacturing exports.[7] Other sectors with large exports include food, wood and furniture, and chemicals (including rubber and plastics). The share of manufacturing output that is exported has increased from about 17 per cent in 1990 to about 26 per cent in 2000.

Every industry within manufacturing has become more export-oriented. Despite this increase in exports, the vast majority of output was supplied to the domestic market. Wood and furniture was the only sector

Table 7.1 Descriptive statistics on the Indonesian manufacturing sector in 1990 and 2000

ISIC	Sector	Number of plants		Share of total manufacturing (%)						Share of total output that is exported (%)		Share of total plants that export (%)	
				Value added		Employment		Exports					
		1990	2000	1990	2000	1990	2000	1990	2000	1990	2000	1990	2000
	Total	16,536	22,174	100	100	100	100	100	100	16.9	26.4	11.7	16.5
31	Food, beverages, tobacco	4,616	5,482	27.5	21.2	23.1	19.3	11.9	12.6	8.5	16.4	6.4	9.6
32	Textiles, apparel, leather, footwear	3,958	4,876	14.6	16.1	27.5	32.7	22.6	24.0	24.0	37.1	13.5	17.1
33	Wood products, furniture	1,946	3,147	11.0	6.6	15.3	13.1	31.5	15.1	47.4	59.8	29.3	37.7
34	Paper products, printing & publishing	702	967	4.6	6.3	3.3	3.8	2.2	4.6	7.7	15.7	2.8	5.2
35	Chemicals, rubber, plastics	2,059	2,622	14.3	14.8	14.4	11.5	17.2	14.5	17.2	24.7	14.2	16.0
36	Non-metallic mineral products	1,323	1,907	3.8	3.5	4.3	3.9	1.9	2.6	9.1	23.0	4.4	6.2
37	Basic metals	95	239	9.0	3.4	1.2	1.2	6.8	3.1	14.4	18.4	18.9	16.3
38	Metal products, machinery	1,595	2,434	14.8	27.3	9.8	12.4	5.4	22.6	5.9	24.1	7.0	13.7
39	Miscellaneous manufacturing	242	500	0.4	0.8	1.1	2.0	0.4	1.0	15.9	34.3	14.9	30.8

Source: Sjöholm and Takii (2003: Table 1).

in which more than 50 per cent of output was exported. The importance of production for the domestic market compared to exports is even more striking if the share of plants with positive exports is considered; the share has increased over time, but was still only about 17 per cent in 2000. Even in the industry with the highest export propensity – wood and furniture – less than 38 per cent of the plants were engaged in exporting.

The figures raise the obvious question: which firms export? Some indications that MNCs are important exporters are seen in Table 7.2. The foreign share of exports increased from around 23 per cent in 1990 to around 45 per cent in 2000. The foreign share of exports varies among industries. Shares in metal products and machinery were more than 70 per cent in 1990 and over 94 per cent in 2000, while the corresponding shares for wood and furniture were around 13 per cent in both years. There was a remarkable decrease in the foreign share of exports in the paper industry (including printing and publishing) from

Table 7.2 Foreign shares of exports, employment and value added in 1990 and 2000

ISIC	Sector	Foreign share of export		Foreign share of employment		Foreign share of value added	
		1990	*2000*	*1990*	*2000*	*1990*	*2000*
	Total	23.1	45.3	10.3	21.6	22.2	38.9
31	Food, beverages, tobacco	4.8	30.3	4.4	7.7	8.1	16.6
32	Textiles, apparel, leather, footwear	21.7	39.0	11.6	24.4	18.4	35.0
33	Wood products, furniture	12.8	13.5	7.1	10.6	10.1	8.9
34	Paper products, printing & publishing	52.2	5.0	9.1	16.9	30.4	22.4
35	Chemicals, rubber, plastics	26.7	41.1	15.6	20.5	34.3	45.6
36	Non-metallic mineral products	15.6	44.9	7.0	14.7	20.6	39.8
37	Basic metals	52.1	27.2	24.4	19.5	24.0	39.1
38	Metal products, machinery	70.9	94.5	17.5	48.0	46.5	65.6
39	Miscellaneous manufacturing	32.2	54.1	15.4	45.5	18.5	45.3

Source: Authors' calculation from BPS-Statistics (various years).

over 50 per cent in 1990 to only 5 per cent in 2000. The foreign share of exports also decreased in basic metals. In all other industries the foreign share of exports has increased, with very large increases taking place in, for instance, food, non-metallic minerals, metal products and machinery, and miscellaneous manufacturing. Finally, the foreign share of exports tended to be higher than the foreign share of value added and employment with some exceptions, suggesting that MNCs are export-oriented compared to local firms.

Alternative calculations confirm that foreign plants were more common among exporters than among non-exporters (Table 7.3). Foreign plants accounted for 13 per cent of all exporting plants in 1990 and 27 per cent in 2000. Conversely, foreign plants accounted for only 3 and 7 per cent, respectively, of non-exporting plants. Foreign plants were also a larger percentage of the total among exporters than among non-exporters in all sectors. The share of foreign plants among exporters is especially high in metal products and machinery (60 per cent) and basic metals (45 per cent). On the other hand, the share of

Table 7.3 Ownership shares for exporters and non-exporters in 1990 and 2000

ISIC	Sector	Share of foreign plants (%)			
		Exporters		Non-exporters	
		1990	*2000*	*1990*	*2000*
	Total	13	27	3	7
31	Food, beverages, tobacco	5	16	1	2
32	Textiles, apparel, leather, footwear	11	24	1	4
33	Wood products, furniture	6	9	2	2
34	Paper products, printing & publishing	19	23	2	4
35	Chemicals, rubber, plastics	18	37	8	19
36	Non-metallic mineral products	7	26	2	5
37	Basic metals	33	45	17	18
38	Metal products, machinery	38	60	7	21
39	Miscellaneous manufacturing	22	23	3	8

Source: Sjöholm and Takii (2003: Table 3).

foreign plants among exporters in wood and furniture was low, even though there were substantial exports in this industry (Table 7.1).

The previous analysis clearly shows that MNCs were an important source of Indonesian exports in 2000. Foreign plants accounted for 45 per cent of total manufacturing exports and 27 per cent of exporting plants were MNCs. A slightly different question is: how important is exporting for foreign-owned plants located in Indonesia? To examine this issue we look at the share of MNCs' output that is exported and sold on the Indonesian market. It should be noted that the figures are in some sense likely to underestimate the importance of export for some types of plants. More precisely, some of the plants sell inputs to assembly plants that export most of their production, and it might be that this behaviour is more important for, for instance, domestically-owned plants than for foreign-owned plants.

Table 7.4 shows simple averages of export propensities (shares of exports in output) by ownership group. Export propensities increased in most industries and groups during the decade. From the table, it is clear that MNCs' affiliates tend to have higher export propensities than locally-owned plants. Foreign plants exported 36 per cent of output in 1990 and around 52 per cent in 2000. Corresponding figures for domestically-owned firms are 7.7 and 21 per cent, respectively. Foreign-owned plants tended to have particularly high export propensities in wood and furniture as well as in textiles. Moreover, foreign- and domestically-owned plants were similar in that both ownership groups had high export propensities in roughly the same industries. Finally, majority-foreign plants tend to have higher export propensities than minority-foreign plants.

These results suggest that foreign MNCs are considerably more export-oriented than local firms are. This could lead us to conclude that the presence of MNCs' foreign networks is a crucial determinant of export propensities. It is not obvious, however, that the higher export orientation is solely due to foreign ownership itself. It could also be the case that part of the higher foreign export orientation in MNCs is the result of other plant characteristics that enable MNCs to export more easily. Such characteristics could include, for instance, size and produc-tivity. Table 7.5 compares some of these characteristics for exporters and non-exporters. Labour productivity was about two times higher in exporters than in non-exporters and the difference seems to have increased over time. Relatively high labour productivity in exporters is observed in every sector for 1990 and 2000. Moreover, exporters were considerably larger than non-exporters. The number of employees per

Table 7.4 Mean export propensities by industry and foreign ownership share in 1990 and 2000

ISIC	Sector	1990				2000			
		Local	Foreign	Minority-foreign	Majority-foreign	Local	Foreign	Minority-foreign	Majority-foreign
	Total	7.7	36.0	0.0	45.8	21.1	52.3	37.5	54.5
31	Food, beverages, tobacco	4.2	12.5	10.2	14.6	6.1	34.9	30.6	36.5
32	Textiles, apparel, leather, footwear	8.5	42.9	42.7	43.0	10.5	48.9	44.4	49.6
33	Wood products, furniture	21.5	52.7	51.3	54.3	31.4	69.9	65.6	70.9
34	Paper products, printing & publishing	0.7	13.5	18.4	7.0	2.3	19.5	4.5	25.0
35	Chemicals, rubber, plastics	7.9	18.0	10.7	20.9	7.7	25.5	22.8	26.2
36	Non-metallic mineral products	2.1	9.1	3.5	14.0	2.8	22.2	14.6	27.2
37	Basic metals	4.3	10.4	0.0	17.9	7.1	23.4	4.3	26.3
38	Metal products, machinery	1.9	13.5	12.5	14.3	3.7	28.2	18.8	30.1
39	Miscellaneous manufacturing	7.7	36.0	0.0	45.8	21.1	52.3	37.5	54.5

Source: Authors' calculation from BPS-Statistics (various years).

Table 7.5 Plant characteristics for exporters and non-exporters in 1990 and 2000

ISIC	Sector	Labour productivity (value added per worker, 1000 rupiahs)				Size (number of workers)				Share of white-collar workers (%)			
		Exporters		Non-exporters		Exporters		Non-exporters		Exporters		Non-exporters	
		1990	2000	1990	2000	1990	2000	1990	2000	1990	2000	1990	2000
	Total	4,037	18,779	2,154	8,273	197	297	45	47	16	16	14	14
31	Food, beverages, tobacco	2,672	13,561	1,000	4,643	117	170	33	35	18	18	13	12
32	Textiles, apparel, leather, footwear	2,511	12,575	1,386	5,990	258	475	42	47	11	12	9	10
33	Wood products, furniture	3,771	9,814	2,278	6,841	174	146	42	32	14	12	15	12
34	Paper products, printing & publishing	9,245	12,860	2,316	10,871	279	258	46	54	26	18	19	19
35	Chemicals, rubber, plastics	5,347	34,268	4,628	15,813	196	237	54	54	21	24	20	23
36	Non-metallic mineral products	2,938	22,640	1,438	6,473	225	263	56	64	15	17	13	12
37	Basic metals	27,996	66,959	9,601	22,646	270	312	132	78	27	20	28	23
38	Metal products, machinery	5,988	36,403	2,635	13,284	202	294	58	68	18	19	18	19
39	Miscellaneous manufacturing	2,142	6,897	1,236	6,084	195	121	32	35	12	12	9	10

Source: Sjöholm and Takii (2003: Table 2).

plant was about four times larger in 1990 and six times larger in 2000. Again, exporters were relatively large in all sectors in both years. Finally, exporters seem to use a larger share of white-collar workers, but the difference is relatively small and not consistent over sectors.

The figures in Table 7.5 suggest that exporters and non-exporters differ substantially in various respects. Again, it is possible that this difference, rather than access to foreign networks, explains some of the higher export orientation among foreign MNCs. To examine the role of ownership in exporting we would like to compare 'identical' plants with different owners. The most obvious way to approach this issue is through econometric estimation where one tries to control for differences among plants such as those depicted in Table 7.5. This is done by Ramstetter (1999) where a tobit model is used to estimate export propensities in Indonesian manufacturing plant data for 1992 and 1994. The estimates control for a number of plant characteristics that might affect export propensities, such as capital- and skill-intensities, age and size of the plant. Ramstetter finds that foreign-owned plants were significantly more export-oriented even after controlling for differences in plant characteristics. He also finds that the share of foreign ownership mattered: export propensities were highest in plants with large majority shares, followed by plants with medium foreign ownership, plants with low foreign ownership, and locally-owned plants.

Ramstetter and Takii (2005) conduct a similar analysis but using pooled samples covering the years 1990–2000 and estimated at the industry level. The results show again that foreign-owned plants had higher export propensities than domestically-owned plants even after controlling for various plant characteristics. However, there is less evidence of a difference in export propensities between plants with different shares of foreign ownership (heavily-foreign, majority-foreign and minority-foreign). Such effects seem to be confined to a few industries: metal products, plastics, electric and precision machinery, and textiles (narrowly defined to exclude apparel, leather and footwear).

7.3.2   Entry into exporting

So far we have showed that foreign-owned plants are more export-oriented than local firms, and that they are more export-oriented even after we control for various characteristics that also affect export propensities. There is one additional problem that we have not examined which could affect our conclusion that access to foreign networks controlled by MNCs facilitates exporting. More precisely, it is possible that plants with foreign ownership have large exports simply because foreign owners have acquired plants that already export. If this is the case, the causality would go from exporting to foreign ownership and not the other way around. One possible way to examine this issue is to look at plants that initiate exports. In a sample of plants that only produce for the local Indonesian market, which plants will start to export in a future year?

Table 7.6 tries to shed some further light on the issue and shows the pattern of entry and exit. The share of non-exporters that start to export in the following year has been rather stable at around 5 per cent over the years. However, there are differences among sectors. For instance, plants in wood and furniture and miscellaneous manufacturing were relatively likely to become exporters, while plants in food and paper were relatively unlikely to become exporters. The exit rate from

Table 7.6   Entry and exit rates for exporting in 1990 and 1999

ISIC	Sector	Entry rate to export (share of non-exporters who start export the following year)		Exit rate from export (share of exporters who stop export the following year)	
		1990	*1999*	*1990*	*1999*
	Total	4.5	5.2	33	20
31	Food, beverages, tobacco	2.5	2.8	47	24
32	Textiles, apparel, leather, footwear	5.2	6.2	34	21
33	Wood products, furniture	9.4	11.6	25	15
34	Paper products, printing & publishing	2.8	2.1	50	29
35	Chemicals, rubber, plastics	6.1	5.7	33	19
36	Non-metallic mineral products	2.9	2.0	47	21
37	Basic metals	16.9	6.6	33	31
38	Metal products, machinery	3.0	5.0	30	23
39	Miscellaneous manufacturing	12.1	11.2	19	21

Source: Sjöholm and Takii (2003: Table 4).

exporting was very large; about one-third of exporters in 1990 ceased exporting the following year. However, the exit rate declined over time to about 20 per cent in 1999. A portion of the high export rate is accounted for by several plants that ceased exporting and then resumed at a later date. For instance, the exit rate was only about 20 per cent among plants that did not export in the following three years (not shown in the table). Hence, about one-third of the plants that ceased exporting in 1991 reinitiated exports in the following two years.

Table 7.7 shows indicators of foreign networks in 1995 for non-exporting plants that started to export in 1996 relative to the same indicators for plants that continued to produce only for the domestic market. Plants that exported in 1995 are excluded because the causality between exporting and the other variables would otherwise be unclear. Ratios between the two groups are calculated for foreign ownership, as well as for two additional variables that capture other aspects of foreign networks, imports and spillovers from foreign MNCs. Foreign ownership is the share of foreign plants. Secondly, spillovers are defined as the share of a district's gross output produced in plants with foreign ownership. Finally, imports are defined as the share of plants with imports from abroad.[8] Table 7.7 reports the ratio of the mean value of each indicator for plants that initiated exports in 1996 to the corresponding mean value for plants that continue producing only for the domestic market. If the ratio is one, the mean value is the same in both groups; if it is greater than one the mean value is greater in plants that initiated exports and suggests relatively extensive foreign networks in 1995 among plants that initiated exports. Likewise a value below one suggests that the indicator of foreign networks was relatively low among plants that initiated exports.

Table 7.7 first shows that foreign ownership shares were much larger among plants that initiated exports in 1996 and this difference was observed consistently across industries. This suggests that plants with foreign ownership were more likely to start exporting than plants with domestic owners in all industries. Plants also tended to be located in districts with a relatively large foreign presence, though there were exceptions in a few industries. Finally, plants with imports in 1995 were relatively likely to start exporting in 1996, and this result is also obtained in all industries examined.

The preceding figures indicate that foreign networks are an important determinant of the decision to export in the Indonesian manufacturing sector, but other factors may also affect the decision. To further examine the issue an econometric approach is required. Sjöholm (2003)

Table 7.7 Foreign networks and exports: ratios between establishments that became exporters in 1996 and establishments that did not become exporters

Sector	ISIC	Foreign ownership	Spillovers	Import
Total		6.1	1.3	2.4
Food products	311/12	9.1	1.1	2.4
Beverages	313	–	2.4	4.1
Tobacco products	314	19.3	1.3	6.7
Textiles	321	6.2	1.5	2.6
Clothing	322	14.8	1.1	4.1
Leather products	323	9.7	1.4	2.0
Footwear	324	11.0	1.3	4.1
Wood products	331	5.1	1.3	8.4
Furniture	332	12.3	1.1	1.7
Paper products	341	1.2	1.3	3.5
Printing	342	6.4	0.4	1.9
Industrial chemicals	351	1.8	1.2	1.7
Other chemicals	352	4.2	1.1	1.4
Petrol refineries	353	–	–	–
Coal products	354	–	0.6	–
Rubber products	355	18.7	1.0	1.1
Plastic products	356	7.5	1.4	1.6
Pottery	361	–	1.0	1.4
Glass products	362	–	1.2	3.2
Cement	363	20.6	3.4	10.5
Clay products	364	–	2.8	–
Non-metal products	369	–	0.9	2.8
Iron and steel	371	1.5	1.2	2.6
Non-ferrous metals	372	4.1	0.8	2.7
Metal products	381	5.2	1.2	2.9
General machinery	382	7.9	1.3	2.2
Electric machinery	383	3.1	1.2	1.5
Transportation machinery	384	4.7	1.8	3.9
Precision machinery	385	–	1.4	2.5
Other manufacturing	390	8.3	1.2	1.8

Source: Sjöholm (2003: Table 2).

estimated a probit model with a sample of non-exporters in 1995 and examined the export status in 1996. The results of this cross-sectional analysis suggest that both foreign ownership and importing increased the probability that a plant would initiate exports, but there is no statistically significant evidence of a spillover effect. It should be noted that spillovers are notoriously difficult to estimate and estimation requires various strong assumptions regarding the nature and mechanisms of such spillovers.

One weakness with cross-section analysis, such as in Sjöholm (2003), is that it does not take into account unobserved firm characteristics. In other words, some firms might start to export not because they are foreign-owned but because they have some superior quality that is not observed in the data. Examples of such qualities might include superior management or employees with various types of qualifications and experience. Sjöholm and Takii (2003) elaborate on the issue by analysing entry into export in a panel of plants, which together with various econometric techniques, allow them to control for unobserved plant characteristics.

Table 7.8 shows alternative estimates of a coefficient measuring the effect of foreign ownership on the probability that a plant would export in Indonesian manufacturing during 1990–2000, as well as associated significance levels.[9] Three different types of estimators were used: ordinary least squares (OLS), a fixed effect estimator, and a general method of moment estimator (GMM). The latter two models control for plant-specific effects and use variations within plants to estimate the issue at hand. All estimates included a number of other variables that might affect export propensities: size, productivity, public owner-ship, capital intensity, the share of white-collar workers and importing status.

The results of all models and specifications suggest that foreign ownership was an important determinant of the exporting decision. The estimated effect ranges from foreign-owned plants being around 6 per cent more likely to export, after controlling for firm characteristics, to 10 per cent in the fixed effect estimation, and almost 25 per cent in the GMM esti-mation. Other results from the same estimates (not shown) suggest that

Table 7.8   Foreign ownership and exports: estimates from panel data 1990–2000

Independent variables	*Coefficients and t-statistics*		
	OLS	*Fixed effect*	*GMM*
Foreign ownership	0.0631* (12.7)	0.0973* (5.0)	0.2457* (3.0)

Notes: t-statistics within brackets are based on robust standard errors.
* Significant at the 1 per cent level.
Full estimation details are reported in the source.
Source: Sjöholm and Takii (2003: Table 5).

there is a persistent sunk cost involved in exporting. In other words, plants that initiate exports tend to continue exporting. Other explanatory variables, such as size, capital intensity and labour productivity, were also positively associated with exporting. Results for imports, and for a few other variables, were mixed and differed among models.

The findings are broadly consistent with the results from other countries (Bernard and Jensen 1999, 2001; Bernard and Wagner 2001) in suggesting that sunk costs are important in explaining exports as is size. Previous studies have also found that high productivity levels positively affect the decision to export but that the effect of growth in productivity (fixed effect model) is more uncertain. The size of the sunk cost effect seems to be higher in other studies, suggesting that its effect on entry into and exit from exporting is more pronounced in Indonesia.

Sjöholm and Takii (2003) also examine whether different types of foreign ownership have different effects on exporting. The results suggested that this does not seem to be the case. Firstly, foreign ownership is an important determinant to export but it does not seem to be important if the plant is majority-foreign owned or not. This result differs from results obtained by Ramstetter and Takii (2005), but it should be noted that the questions asked in the papers differ. Ramstetter and Takii examine whether export propensities differ depending on the foreign ownership share, whereas Sjöholm and Takii (2003) examine whether the foreign ownership share affects the likelihood that plants will initiate exports. As noted by Ramstetter and Takii, wholly-owned foreign plants were for a long time only allowed in Indonesia if at least 80 per cent of the output was exported. Hence, these plants were usually engaged in exporting from the beginning of their operations in Indonesia.

Finally, Sjöholm and Takii (2003) examine whether the effect of foreign ownership differed between greenfield investments and foreign takeovers of domestic plants. The hypothesis of equal coefficients for the two types of foreign plants could not be rejected, suggesting that the form of foreign entrance makes little difference to the likelihood that a plant will become an exporter.

7.4   Concluding remarks

Indonesia's manufacturing exports increased dramatically after the mid-1980s. The initial increase was largely the result of exports by domestically-owned firms, but MNCs have become increasingly important exporters over time. This chapter has shown that increases in manufacturing exports during the 1990s were largely the result of increased exports from MNCs. By 2000, foreign-owned plants accounted for about 45 per cent of Indonesia's manufacturing exports. Exports in metal products and machinery were heavily dominated by foreign-owned plants. Moreover, foreign-owned plants were substantially more export-oriented, exporting close to half of their output, while domestically-owned plants exported only about one-fifth of their output. Part of the higher export orientation results from differences in firm characteristics such as size and productivity. However, a survey of econometric studies shows that MNCs were more export-oriented even after controlling for such differences. We conclude that MNCs' international networks enable them to export more of their output than local Indonesian firms.

Moreover, the results in this chapter suggest that the high export propensities observed among foreign plants are not only a result of high export orientation when the plants are established. Rather, even foreign plants which began by producing only for the domestic market were more likely than purely domestic plants to initiate exports. Hence, foreign-owned plants show a higher degree of flexibility and a better ability to seek new markets when conditions make it necessary or favourable. Again, foreign and domestic plants differ in many other respects that are likely to affect export behaviour. However, the effect of foreign ownership on the initiation of exports remains robust after controlling for such characteristics at the plant level.

Hence, our study clearly confirms the relatively high export orientation of foreign-owned plants and the importance of foreign-owned plants as a source of Indonesian exports. That foreign MNCs are important sources of Indonesian exports should not come as a surprise. Exporting requires access to an international distribution system and information on foreign markets. We have shown that foreign MNCs are one important channel through which developing countries can get access to foreign markets and increase exports.

Notes

1. See Roberts and Tybout (1997) and Bernard and Wagner (1997).
2. See, for instance, Roberts and Tybout (1997), Bernard and Wagner (1997, 2001), Aw et al. (2000), Clerides et al. (1998) and Bernard and Jensen (1999).
3. See e.g. Baldwin (1988, 1989), Baldwin and Krugman (1989), Dixit (1989a, 1989b) and Krugman (1989).
4. See e.g. Guillouet (1990), Thee and Pangestu (1998) and Pangestu (1997).
5. See e.g. Fane and Cordon (1996), Hill (1996) and Pangestu (1997, 1998).
6. See Berry and Levy (1994), Cole (1998) and Okamoto and Sjöholm (2003).

7. It should be noted that the coverage of the export data differs among years. Ramstetter and Takii (2005) find the coverage to be relatively poor in 1990–91 and 1998–2000. Figures on total exports or on exports as a share of output might therefore be biased, but there is no *a priori* reason to expect comparisons of exports between plants with different ownership to be biased.

8. As an example, foreign ownership is calculated as (foreign firms that started to export/total firms that started to export)/(foreign firms that did not start to export/total firms that did not start to export).

9. See Sjöholm and Takii (2003) for more information on the estimations and results.

References

Aitken, Brian, Gordon H. Hanson and Ann E. Harrison (1997) 'Spillovers, Foreign Investment, and Export Behavior', *Journal of International Economics*, 43: 103–32.

Athukorala, Premachandra, Sisira Jayasuriya and Edward Oczkowski (1995) 'Multinational Firms and Export Performance in Developing Countries: Some Analytical Issues and New Empirical Evidence', *Journal of Development Economics*, 46: 109–22.

Aw, Bee Yan, Sukkyun Chung and Mark J. Roberts (2000) 'Productivity and Turnover in the Export Market: Micro-level Evidence from the Republic of Korea and Taiwan (China)', *The World Bank Economic Review*, 14: 65–90.

Baldwin, R. Edward (1988) 'Hysteresis in Import Prices: the Beachhead Effect', *American Economic Review*, 78: 773–85.

Baldwin, R. Edward (1989) 'Sunk-Cost Hysteresis', NBER Working Paper Series No. 2911.

Baldwin, R. Edward and Paul R. Krugman (1989) 'Persistent Trade Effects of Large Exchange Rate Shocks', *Quarterly Journal of Economics*, 104: 635–54.

Bernard, Andrew B. and J. Bradford Jensen (1999) 'Exceptional Exporter Performance: Cause, Effect, or Both?' *Journal of International Economics*, 47: 1–25.

Bernard, Andrew B. and J. Bradford Jensen (2001) 'Why Some Firms Export', NBER Working Paper Series No. 8349.

Bernard Andrew B. and Joachim Wagner (1997) 'Exports and Success in German Manufacturing', *Weltwirtschaftliches Archiv*, 133: 134–57.

Bernard, Andrew B. and Joachim Wagner (2001) 'Export Entry and Exit by German Firms', *Weltwirtschaftliches Archiv*, 137: 105–23.

Bernard, Andrew B., Jonathan Eaton, Bradford Jensen and Samuel Kortum (2003) 'Plants and Productivity in International Trade', *American Economic Review*, 93: 1268–90.

Berry, Albert and Brian Levy (1994) 'Indonesia's Small and Medium-size Exporters and Their Support Systems', World Bank Policy Research Working Paper No. 1402.

BPS-Statistics (various years). Unpublished plant-level data underlying *Statistik Industri: Besar Dan Sedang* [Industrial statistics: Large and Medium Manufacturing Statistics], 1990–2000 issues, Jakarta: BPS-Statistics.

Clerides, Sofrans K., Saul Lach and James R. Tybout (1998) 'Is Learning by Exporting Important? Micro-Dynamic Evidence from Colombia, Mexico, and Morocco', *Quarterly Journal of Economics*, 113: 903–47.

Cole, William (1998) 'Bali's Garment Export Industry', in Hal Hill and Kian Wie Thee, eds, *Indonesia's Technological Challenge*, Canberra: Australian National University.

Dixit, Avinash (1989a) 'Entry and Exit Decisions under Uncertainty', *Journal of Political Economy*, 97: 620–38.

Dixit, Avinash (1989b) 'Hysteresis, Import Penetration, and Exchange Rate Pass-Through', *Quarterly Journal of Economics*, 104: 205–28.

Fane, George and Timothy Condon (1996) 'Trade Reform in Indonesia, 1987–95', *Bulletin of Indonesian Economic Studies*, 32: 33–54.

Guillouet, Alain (1990) *Booming Economies of South East Asia*, Singapore: Longman.

Head, Keith and John Ries (2003) 'Heterogeneity and the FDI Versus Export Decision of Japanese Manufacturers', *Journal of Japanese and International Economics*, 17: 448–67.

Helpman, Elhanan, Marc J. Melitz and Stephen R. Yeaple (2004) 'Export Versus FDI with Heterogeneous Firms', *American Economic Review*, 94: 300–16.

Hill, Hal (1988) *Foreign Investment and Industrialization in Indonesia*, Oxford: Oxford University Press.

Hill, Hal (1996) *The Indonesian Economy Since 1966: Southeast Asia's Emerging Giant*, Cambridge: Cambridge University Press.

Hill, Hal (1997) *Indonesia's Industrial Transformation*, Singapore: Institute of Southeast Asian Studies.

Krugman, Paul R. (1989) *Exchange Rate Instability*, Cambridge, MA: MIT Press.

Melitz, Marc J. (2003) 'The Impact of Trade on Intra-Industry Reallocations and Aggregate Industry Productivity', *Econometrica*, 71: 1695–1725.

Okamoto, Yumiko and Fredrik Sjöholm (2003) 'Technology Development in Indonesia', in Sanjaya Lall and Shujiro Urata, eds, *Competitiveness, FDI and Technological Activity in East Asia*, London: Edward Elgar, pp. 375–96.

Okamoto, Yumiko and Fredrik Sjöholm (2005) 'FDI and the Dynamics of Productivity in Indonesian Manufacturing', *Journal of Development Studies*, 41: 160–82.

Pangestu, Mari (1996) *Economic Reform, Deregulation and Privatization: the Indonesian Experience*, Jakarta: Centre for Strategic and International Studies.

Pangestu, Mari (1997) 'The Indonesian Textile and Garment Industry: Structural Change and Competitive Challenges', in Mari Pangestu and Yuri Sato, eds, *Waves of Change in Indonesia's Manufacturing Industry*, Tokyo, Institute of Developing Economies, pp. 29–62.

Pangestu, Mari (1998) 'The Indonesian Textile and Garment Industry: Structural Change and Corporate Responses', in Yuri Sato, ed., *Changing Industrial Structures and Business Strategies in Indonesia*, Tokyo: Institute of Developing Countries, pp. 1–33.

Ramstetter, Eric D. (1999) 'Trade Propensities and Foreign Ownership Shares in Indonesian Manufacturing', *Bulletin of Indonesian Economic Studies*, 35: 43–66.

Ramstetter, Eric D. and Sadayuki Takii (2005) 'Exporting and Foreign Ownership in Indonesian Manufacturing, 1990–2000', Working Paper 2005–15, Kitakyushu: International Centre for the Study of East Asian Development.

Roberts, Mark J. and James R. Tybout (1997) 'The Decision to Export in Colombia: an Empirical Model of Entry with Sunk Costs', *American Economic Review*, 87: 545–64.

Sjöholm, Fredrik (2003) 'Which Indonesian Firms Export? The Importance of Foreign Networks', *Papers in Regional Science*, 82: 333–50.

Sjöholm, Fredrik and Sadayuki Takii (2003) 'Foreign Networks and Exports: Results from Indonesian Panel Data', Working Paper 2003–33, Kitakyushu: International Centre for the Study of East Asian Development.

Takii, Sadayuki (2005) 'Indonesia', *East Asian Economic Perspectives [Recent Trends and Prospects for Major Asian Economies]*, 16, 1: 101–18.

Thee, Kian Wie and Mari Pangestu (1998) 'Technological Capabilities and Indonesia's Manufactured Exports', in Dieter Ernst, Tom Ganiatsos and Lynn Mytelka, eds, *Technological Capabilities and Export Success in Asia*, United Nations Committee on Trade and Development, pp. 211–65.

8
Exports and Foreign Ownership in Thai Manufacturing

Eric D. Ramstetter and Masaru Umemoto

8.1   Introduction

Previous research suggests that foreign-owned multinational corporations (MNCs) often export a much larger portion of their output than local plants in Asian economies and that these exports represent one of the largest direct contributions of MNCs to the host economies involved.[1] This has been observed in economy-wide data or industry-level data for the manufacturing sectors of Hong Kong, Indonesia, Malaysia, Singapore, Taiwan, Thailand and Vietnam, for example (Ramstetter 1994, 1998, 1999a; Phan and Ramstetter 2004a). Additional evidence from the manufacturing sectors of Indonesia, Singapore, Thailand and Vietnam also suggests that export propensities are higher in MNCs with relatively large foreign ownership shares (Ramstetter 1994, 1998, 1999b, 2002b; Phan and Ramstetter 2004b).

Previous evidence on these points for Thailand comes from a rather limited sample of firms for 1990, most of which were promoted by the Thai Board of Investment (BOI).[2] The first contribution of this chapter is thus to add evidence regarding the relationship between exports and foreign ownership in Thai manufacturing using a much more comprehensive sample of plants from the industrial census for 1996 (section 8.3). The second contribution is to examine the relationship more closely in the context of the recent boom in the exports of automobiles and automobile parts that began in the late 1990s (section 8.4). This case is of particular interest because there were also large changes in foreign ownership shares during this period, partially as a result of the 1997–98 economic crisis. These empirical analyses are preceded by a review of analytical principles and previous literature (section 8.2) and followed by a concluding section that summarizes the major findings of the chapter.

8.2 Analytical principles and the previous literature

As discussed in Chapter 1, most theorists recognize that MNCs tend to possess relatively sophisticated firm-specific assets, such as production technology, marketing networks and management know-how, and that this feature distinguishes MNCs sharply from non-MNCs.[3] If MNCs possess firm-specific assets in relatively large amounts, they can be expected to differ systematically from non-MNCs. Moreover, the vast majority of local Thai firms do not have overseas operations yet. Thus, comparisons of foreign-owned MNCs and local firms in Thailand are essentially comparisons of MNCs and non-MNCs. Two differences are particularly important when analysing differences in export propensities between MNCs and non-MNCs.

First, by virtue of their superior production technology and management know-how, MNCs may be more productive than non-MNCs, making it relatively easy for them to produce internationally marketable products. If this is the case, it then follows that export propensities will be higher in MNCs than in non-MNCs. However, the existing evidence for Thailand suggests that, although MNCs tend to be more productive than local firms or plants in several respects, there is large variation in productivity among MNCs and local firms or plants. Correspondingly, productivity differentials between MNCs and local firms or plants have generally been found to be insignificant statistically (Chapter 5). This is in marked contrast to evidence from Indonesia, for example (Chapter 4).

Second, MNCs tend to possess relatively sophisticated marketing networks in general, and international marketing networks in particular. Thus, transactions costs associated with international trade may be relatively low for MNCs and MNCs may have relatively high export propensities compared to non-MNCs, even if there are no differences in production technology. Previous evidence from relatively small firm-level samples suggests that this may have been the case in Thai manufacturing in 1990 (Ramstetter 1993, 1994, 1998). Export propensities were generally higher in foreign firms than local firms, and those differences were statistically significant despite the rarity of statistically significant productivity differentials. One major purpose of this chapter is to analyse similar evidence from much more comprehensive samples of manufacturing plants in 1996, which when combined with evidence from Chapter 5, suggests a similar pattern. This pattern contrasts with patterns observed in Indonesia and Singapore, for example, where MNCs had both higher export propensities and higher productivity than local plants (Chapters 4, 7; Ramstetter 1998, 1999a, 1999b; Ramstetter and Takii 2005).

In addition to comparing MNCs and local plants, it may also be important to compare export propensities among MNCs with different foreign ownership shares. For example, it is often asserted that MNCs restrict technology transfer to affiliates they do not control (e.g. minority-owned affiliates) in order to protect intellectual property, which is an important source of competitiveness for the MNCs (Blomström and Kokko 1998; Moran 2001). If this is the case, there may be a positive correlation between productivity and foreign ownership shares. A positive correlation between export propensities and foreign ownership shares may result if higher productivity increases the ability of MNCs to produce internationally marketable products. Time-series evidence from manufacturing in Hong Kong and Singapore (Ramstetter 1999a) is consistent with this possibility, suggesting positive correlations between foreign ownership shares, on the one hand, and productivity or export propensities, on the other. Evidence from plant-level analysis of manufacturing in Indonesia (Chapter 4) suggests that minority-foreign plants tend to have lower productivity, but the correlation between foreign ownership and productivity varies greatly across industry. Similar evidence for Thailand (Chapter 5; Ramstetter 2001) suggests that positive correlations between productivity and foreign ownership are not common.

MNCs may also have a strong motive to restrict the access to international marketing networks by uncontrolled affiliates, even if they do not or cannot restrict access to technology and related firm-specific assets. This motive exists because lack of marketing coordination between uncontrolled affiliates on the one hand, and the parent and/or other affiliates on the other, could result in excess supply of a firm's products in specific markets. Accordingly, firms with larger foreign ownership shares may have higher export propensities than firms with lower foreign ownership shares, even if productivity differentials do not affect export performance or do not exist. Evidence for small samples of Thai manufacturing firms in 1990 (Ramstetter 1993, 1994, 1998) is consistent with this possibility. If combined with evidence from Chapter 5, the results of this chapter suggest a similar pattern in more comprehensive samples of manufacturing plants in 1996. Evidence from Indonesian manufacturing plants in the 1990s also indicates a stronger correlation between foreign ownership shares and export propensities (Ramstetter 1999b; Ramstetter and Takii 2005) than between foreign ownership shares and productivity (see above paragraph).[4]

On the other hand, multinational parents also have a strong motive to provide firm-specific assets, including marketing networks, to all affiliates in order to increase the profitability of the affiliates in question. Thus, the extent to which there is a relationship between foreign ownership shares and export propensities is clearly an empirical question and must be examined on a case-by-case basis.

8.3   Plant-level analysis of manufacturing industries

This section presents analysis of the relationship between export propensities and foreign ownership shares in several manufacturing industries using the plant-level data underlying the 1997 Thai industrial census (National Statistical Office 1999), which has data on economic activity in 1996. First, major characteristics of the data and major patterns observed in descriptive statistics are analysed. Second, the results of more rigorous analysis that controls for other factors thought to affect the relationship between exports and foreign ownership shares are presented.

8.3.1   The data and some descriptive statistics

As described in Chapter 5, official compilations of plant-level data from the Thai industrial census for 1996 show that this census covered only a little over one-half of manufacturing employment and slightly less than three-quarters of manufacturing value added (see Table 5.1). Perhaps more importantly, in order to be used for meaningful analysis of the relationship between foreign ownership and export propensities, the census samples must be further reduced to (1) remove duplicates, (2) remove incomplete records, and (3) remove records for very small plants.[5] As a result, the sample used in this analysis was reduced from the original 23,677 to 8952 plants, which is called the small sample in Chapter 5.[6] These plants accounted for 69 per cent of employment and 81 per cent of the value added reported by the census publication but only 36 per cent of total manufacturing employment and 58 per cent of total manufacturing value added for 1996. In addition, the value added estimates suggest large variation in coverage rates across industries. Given the low coverage rates and the data problems, caution is clearly mandated when interpreting patterns observed in these data. On the other hand, this is by far the most comprehensive data set on Thai manufacturing plants or firms that has been assembled to date, making analysis of these data important in the Thai context.

Distributions of export propensities from this census sample (Table 8.1) are largely consistent with previously observed patterns in firm-level data for 1990 (Ramstetter 1994, 1998). Specifically, they indicate that larger proportions of foreign plants tended to have relatively high export propensities than did local plants.[7] For example, in samples of all plants in all manufacturing industries, high export propensities equal to half or more of output were observed in more than half of all foreign plants (52 per cent), but only in less than one-sixth (15 per cent) of local plants. If the samples are limited to large plants with output equal to 25 million baht or more (about US$1 million), the gap between foreign and local plants is smaller but still large: 54 per cent versus 22 per cent. Conversely, only 24 per cent of all foreign plants or 21 per cent of large foreign plants had zero export propensities compared to 72 per cent and 61 per cent, respectively, for local plants.

Among the fourteen individual industry categories listed in Table 8.1, high export propensities were observed in a relatively large proportion (60 per cent or more) of all foreign plants in half of the industries (food, apparel, leather and footwear, rubber, electric and precision machinery, furniture and jewellery). High export propensities were also observed in a moderate proportion (30–59 per cent) of foreign plants in another five industries (textiles, plastics, non-metallic mineral products, metal products, general machinery) and in a low proportion of foreign plants (29 per cent or less) in only two industries (chemicals and motor vehicles). In contrast, high export propensities were never observed in a high proportion of local plants. They were observed in a moderate proportion of local plants in four industries (apparel, leather and footwear, rubber and jewellery), but in all other ten industries high export propensities were observed in a low proportion of local plants. Not surprisingly, industries in which relatively high export propensities were common also tended to have relatively large revealed comparative advantage indices as early as 1992 (Ramstetter 1997: Table 1).

If similar comparisons are made among minority-foreign plants, majority-foreign plants and wholly-foreign plants, the most conspicuous pattern is the strong tendency for a large proportion of minority-foreign plants to have relatively low export propensities. The proportion of wholly-foreign plants with high export propensities is also larger than that of majority-foreign plants, but differences between wholly-foreign plants and majority-foreign plants were much smaller than differences between minority-foreign plants and the other two

Table 8.1 Distribution of local and foreign plants by export propensity (XP) and industry, 1996 (% of industry-ownership group totals)

Industry	Percentage of plants with $XP=0\%$					Percentage of plants $50\% \leq XP \leq 100\%$				
	Local plants	All foreign	Minority-foreign	Majority-foreign	Wholly-foreign	Local plants	All foreign	Minority-foreign	Majority-foreign	Wholly-foreign
All manufacturing	72	24	31	13	8	15	53	41	70	81
Food	70	19	23	10	11	20	62	59	74	61
Textiles	72	31	38	5	0	14	39	27	79	100
Apparel	47	5	7	0	0	42	85	80	100	100
Leather & footwear	50	19	31	15	0	33	69	50	77	100
Chemicals & products	71	29	34	16	29	4	29	22	52	29
Rubber products	42	8	9	15	0	41	77	79	62	91
Plastics & products	73	29	39	23	5	10	44	30	50	77
Non-metallic mineral products	87	37	42	18	33	7	37	26	73	67
Metal products	84	39	49	19	24	5	34	16	62	71
General machinery	77	21	28	17	0	6	48	30	67	94
Electric & precision machinery	72	12	23	4	7	9	69	44	82	86
Motor vehicles	86	32	41	11	0	5	21	11	42	67
Furniture	70	14	14	13	17	21	72	69	75	83
Jewellery	35	6	11	0	0	53	94	89	100	100
All manufacturing, large plants	61	21	28	12	7	22	54	42	71	81

Note: Large plants are defined as plants with output of 25 million baht or more.
Source: Ramstetter (2002a: Tables 1, 3a, 3b).

groups. These comparisons also reveal similar patterns in most individual industries. Plants with high export propensities constituted a high proportion (60 per cent or more) of wholly-foreign plants in thirteen of fourteen industries (chemicals was the exception). This was also true in eleven of fourteen industries for majority-foreign plants (chemicals, plastics and motor vehicles were the exceptions), but in only four of fourteen industries for minority-foreign plants (apparel, rubber, furniture, jewellery). Conversely, plants with zero export propensities accounted for a small proportion (29 per cent or less) in all but one industry (non-metallic mineral products) for wholly-foreign plants and in all fourteen industries for majority-foreign plants (other manufacturing was the exception), but only in half of the industries for minority-foreign plants (food, apparel, rubber, general machinery, electric and precision machinery, furniture, jewellery).

8.3.2   Analysing the relationship between exports and foreign ownership

The preceding section shows rather clearly that MNCs tend to have relatively high export propensities with greater frequency than local plants and that high export propensities occur in wholly- and majority-foreign plants with much greater frequency than in minority-foreign plants. However, in a relatively low-wage economy like Thailand, export propensities are also likely to be negatively correlated with the amount of capital and the number of relatively high-wage, non-production workers used in the production process, because these factors are relatively scarce and thus expensive in Thailand. Similarly, transactions costs associated with exporting are likely to be relatively low for larger firms. In Thailand, BOI promotion status is another potentially important factor which may be positively correlated with trade propensities because the BOI offered substantial incentives to firms with high export propensities. Thus, if MNCs have relatively low capital- or non-production-worker intensities, are relatively large, or had a larger tendency to be promoted by the BOI, the observation of relatively high export propensities among MNCs may result from differences in factor intensities, size or promotion status, not from any differences in foreign ownership.[8]

Another plant-level characteristic that may affect export propensities is plant vintage, though the nature of this relationship is ambiguous *a priori*. If one believes the learning by doing hypothesis, vintage is likely to be positively correlated with export propensities because older firms are likely to have accumulated more experience exporting. On the other hand, Thailand gradually liberalized trade policies in the 1980s and the pace of liberalized trade accelerated markedly in the 1990s. Thus, newer firms may be better equipped to export as a result of being forced to compete with imports and encouraged to export more than older firms. If this is the case, the correlation could be negative and previous studies also suggest that the relationship was negative in 1990 (Ramstetter 1994, 1998).

To estimate the correlation between export propensities and foreign ownership shares, and at the same time account for the effects of the other factors described above, one must run a regression where the export propensity is first viewed as a function of the plant's capital intensity (fixed assets per worker), non-production-worker intensity (non-production-worker share of total employment), size (a dummy for large plants), vintage (plant age), and BOI promotional status (a dummy for BOI-promoted plants), and then add a dummy variable for all foreign plants or set of dummy variables for minority-, majority- and wholly-foreign plants. However, as highlighted in the previous section, trade propensities and foreign ownership shares are not reported as continuous variables (e.g. the percentage of production exported or the percentage of inputs imported) in the census data. Rather they are reported as ordered, discrete variables identifying four groups of firms by export propensity or foreign ownership group (0 per cent, 1–49 per cent, 50–99 per cent, 100 per cent). Correspondingly four equations are estimated with each of the alternative export propensity and foreign ownership definitions.

The first and simplest equation examines the relationship between the probability of exporting and the existence of foreign ownership. In other words, it defines both export propensities and foreign ownership shares in binomial terms, taking the value 1 for plants with a positive export propensity or a positive foreign ownership share and 0 for plants with no exports or no foreign ownership.[9] Because the resulting dependent variable is binary, a probit technique is used to estimate this equation. If the coefficient on the foreign ownership dummy is positive and statistically significant in this specification, foreign plants have a higher probability of exporting than local plants after controlling for the effects of factor intensities, age, size and BOI-promotional status.

The second equation examines the relationship between the probability a plant has a relatively high export propensity and the existence of foreign ownership. It differs from the first equation in that the export propensity is defined as multinomial or ordered variable taking the value 4 for plants that export all their output, 3 for plants that export

50–99 per cent of their output, 2 for plants exporting 1–49 per cent of their output, and 1 for plants with no exports.[10] Correspondingly, this equation is estimated with an ordered probit technique. If the coefficient on the foreign ownership dummy is positive and statistically significant, it indicates that the foreign plants have a higher probability of falling into a group with a relatively high export propensity than do local plants, again after accounting for the effects of the controls identified above.

The third and fourth equations correspond to the first and second equations, respectively, except that these equations relax the assumption that all MNCs have the same probability of exporting (third equation) or falling into a group with a relatively high export propensity (fourth equation). Rather, the equations allow for the possibility that these probabilities may depend on the extent of foreign ownership by including three separate dummy variables to distinguish minority-, majority- and wholly-foreign plants.[11] Thus, in the third equation, if the coefficient on one of the foreign ownership dummies is positive and statistically significant, the foreign plants in the ownership group represented by that dummy have a higher probability of exporting than local plants, after controlling for the effects of factor intensities, age, size and BOI-promotional status. Likewise, in the fourth equation, a positive and statistically significant coefficient on one of the foreign ownership dummies indicates that the foreign plants in the ownership group represented by the dummy have a higher probability of falling into a group with a relatively high export propensity than do local plants, again after accounting for the effects of the controls identified above.

The large inter-industry differences observed in the previous section suggest that it is also very important to account for industry affiliation when estimating the above equations. To do this, equations are first estimated in samples of all manufacturing plants, using industry dummies to allow the intercepts to differ across industries. This allows estimates of the average relationship between foreign ownership and export propensities to vary across industries. However, it has the disadvantage of forcing slope coefficients, including coefficients measuring the probability that all MNCs or a particular ownership group of MNCs will export or fall into a group with relatively high export propensities, to be equal across all industries. In order to relax this assumption and allow for possible inter-industry differences, separate estimates are then performed for each of fourteen individual industries with relatively large samples, when such estimates are possible.[12] In addition, estimates were performed both for samples of all plants, including a large number of small plants, and samples of larger plants in which output was 25 million baht or more to see if the exclusion of small, predominantly local plants would affect the results.

To conserve space, full results of estimating the four equations described above are omitted here and this chapter focuses on results for the coefficients on the foreign ownership dummies, which are the primary concern here.[13] Tables 8.2 and 8.3 also show goodness of fit measures for the estimated equations, which were generally in the expected range for cross-section estimates such as these. However, these estimates fail to correct for one potentially important statistical problem – heteroscedasticity – and if heteroscedasticity affects these estimates, the estimates reported in Tables 8.2 and 8.3 are inefficient, making the reported levels of statistical significance unreliable.[14] Another potentially important statistical problem is simultaneity, especially the possibility that export propensities may be a determinant of a plant's foreign ownership share. The potential for this problem is particularly relevant in Thailand and other Southeast Asian countries where foreign ownership restrictions have been relaxed for plants that export a lot of their output.[15] On the other hand, as explained above, there is a very strong theoretical expectation that MNCs will restrict access of non-controlled affiliates to their international marketing networks, and thus that causation would run from ownership shares to export propensities, not the other way around.

The results of estimating the first equation suggest that foreign plants had a higher probability of exporting than local plants and that this difference remained statistically significant after accounting for the effects of factor intensity, age, size and BOI status (Table 8.2). This was observed in all of the industry groups for which estimates could be made, both in the samples of all plants and in the samples of large plants. However, coefficients tended to be smaller in samples of large plants, suggesting that differences between local and foreign plants were relatively small, but still significant for large plants. Estimates of the second equation further suggest that foreign plants also had a higher probability of falling into a group with relatively high export propensities than did local plants, after accounting for the effects of the control variables. Here again these differences were significant in all industry groups in samples of all plants and in all but one industry (jewellery) in the samples of large plants. Coefficients also tended to be relatively small, but positive and significant for large plants.

Table 8.2 Significant coefficients on a dummy variable for all MNCs and goodness of fit from the first and second export propensity regressions

| Industry | Probit estimates (first equation) | | | | Ordered probit estimates (second equation) | | | |
| | All plants | | Large plants | | All plants | | Large plants | |
	Coefficient	Fit	Coefficient	Fit	Coefficient	Fit	Coefficient	Fit
All manufacturing	1.038	0.27	0.860	0.27	0.911	0.29	0.736	0.34
Food	1.181	0.22	1.013	0.18	0.959	0.22	0.792	0.21
Textiles	0.698	0.20	0.629	0.17	0.568	0.16	0.463	0.15
Apparel	1.441	0.15	1.321	0.09	0.908	0.13	0.696	0.08
Leather & footwear	cannot estimate		cannot estimate		0.820	0.16	1.067	0.22
Chemicals & products	0.843	0.19	0.690	0.19	0.918	0.22	0.820	0.24
Rubber products	0.851	0.18	0.722	0.14	0.534	0.14	0.440	0.09
Plastics & products	0.956	0.21	0.779	0.16	0.862	0.21	0.602	0.19
Non-metallic mineral products	1.163	0.18	1.029	0.26	1.092	0.13	0.992	0.20
Metal products	0.907	0.22	0.656	0.18	1.009	0.21	0.784	0.23
General machinery	1.286	0.29	0.937	0.25	1.323	0.34	0.982	0.35
Electric & precision machinery	1.157	0.48	0.945	0.43	1.247	0.55	1.068	0.51
Motor vehicles	1.329	0.35	1.196	0.34	1.106	0.23	0.846	0.22
Furniture	1.299	0.25	1.264	0.24	1.034	0.27	0.841	0.33
Jewellery	1.119	0.20	cannot estimate		0.875	0.26	ns	0.18

Notes: for probit estimates, dependent variable = 1 for export propensity = XP > 0%, =0 for XP = 0%, fit = R-squared; for ordered probit estimates, dependent variable = 4 for XP = 100, =3 for XP = 50–99%, =2 for XP = 1–49%, =1 for XP = 0%, fit = scaled-R-squared; additional independent variables are fixed assets per worker, the non-production worker share of employment, plant age, size, BOI promotional status; large plants are defined as plants with output of 25 million baht or more; ns = coefficient not significant at the 0.05 level; see source for detailed results, including details on equations that cannot be estimated.

Source: Ramstetter (2002: Appendix Tables C1–C2).

Table 8.3 Significant coefficients on dummy variables for MNC-ownership groups and goodness of fit from the third and fourth export propensity regressions

Industry	All plants				Large plants (output >= 25 million baht)			
	Minority-foreign	Majority-foreign	Wholly-foreign	Fit	Minority-foreign	Majority-foreign	Wholly-foreign	Fit
PROBIT ESTIMATES (third equation; excluding estimates for which equations could not be estimated)								
All manufacturing	0.898	1.409	1.504	0.28	0.720	1.208	1.307	0.27
Food	1.093	1.487	1.586	0.23	0.904	1.311	1.912	0.19
Chemicals & products	0.709	1.304	0.916	0.20	0.559	1.046	0.756	0.19
Plastics & products	0.769	1.181	1.851	0.21	0.650	1.140	1.265	0.17
Non-metallic mineral products	1.049	1.661	ns	0.19	cannot estimate			
Metal products	0.793	1.384	1.046	0.22	0.572	0.895	0.807	0.18
Electric & precision machinery	0.980	1.869	1.147	0.49	0.756	1.656	1.040	0.44
Furniture	1.471	ns	ns	0.25	cannot estimate			
ORDERED PROBIT ESTIMATES (fourth equation; excluding estimates for which equations could not be estimated)								
All manufacturing	0.761	1.173	1.412	0.30	0.575	1.007	1.256	0.35
Food	0.889	1.177	1.182	0.22	0.722	0.963	1.132	0.22
Textiles	0.390	1.206	1.659	0.18	ns	1.133	1.408	0.19
Apparel	1.268	1.317	ns	0.20	1.268	1.317	ns	0.20
Chemicals & products	0.768	1.401	0.999	0.23	0.648	1.308	0.894	0.26
Rubber products	0.585	ns	1.016	0.16	0.489	ns	1.015	0.12
Plastics & products	0.694	1.089	1.262	0.22	0.436	1.042	0.743	0.20
Non-metallic mineral products	0.895	1.674	2.045	0.13	cannot estimate			

Table 8.3 (Continued)

Industry	All plants				Large plants (output >= 25 million baht)			
	Minority-foreign	*Majority-foreign*	*Wholly-foreign*	*Fit*	*Minority-foreign*	*Majority-foreign*	*Wholly-foreign*	*Fit*
Metal products	0.823	1.408	1.464	0.22	0.594	1.042	1.299	0.24
General machinery	1.187	1.549	2.462	0.37	0.756	1.314	2.109	0.39
Electric & precision machinery	0.965	1.559	1.687	0.57	0.766	1.395	1.562	0.54
Motor vehicles	0.847	1.461	2.339	0.25	0.573	1.185	1.984	0.26
Furniture	1.097	ns	1.372	0.27	0.991	ns	ns	0.33
Jewellery	0.822	0.910	1.040	0.26	ns	ns	ns	0.18

Notes: see Table 8.2.
Source: Ramstetter (2002: Appendix Tables C3–C4).

Estimates of the third equation suggest that minority-, majority- and wholly-foreign plants all had a greater probability of exporting than local plants in most of the five to seven industry groups for which estimates could be made (Table 8.3). Moreover, these results also suggested that coefficients were generally much larger for majority- and/or wholly-foreign plants, than for minority-foreign plants. In other words, differences between majority- and/or wholly-foreign plants on the one hand, and local plants on the other, tended to be relatively large in this respect. Here again, coefficients tended to be somewhat smaller in the samples of large plants. On the other hand, it was impossible to estimate the third equation in seven industries for all plants and nine industries for large plants, because one or more of the independent variables perfectly predicted the dependent variable. Thus, evidence from estimates of this equation is less comprehensive than the evidence from other equations.

Like estimates of the second equation, results of estimating the fourth equation suggest that coefficients tended to be much larger for majority- and/or wholly-foreign plants than for minority-plants, and that coefficients were positive and significant for all ownership groups in most industries (Table 8.3). In other words, all foreign plants had a greater probability of falling into a group with a relatively high export propensity than local plants did but the differences between majority- and/or wholly-foreign plants on the one hand, and local plants on the other, tended to be relatively large compared to similar differences between minority-foreign plants and local plants. This pattern is again most conspicuous in the samples of all plants. In the samples of large plants, all coefficients again tended to be smaller and there were a few more cases of insignificant coefficients.

To summarize: the results of estimating these four equations and the patterns observed in the descriptive statistics are remarkably consistent. They suggest, first, that all groups of foreign MNCs are much more likely to export and to have relatively high export propensities than local plants. Second, they suggest that differences between majority- and/or wholly-foreign plants on the one hand, and local plants on the other, were relatively large in this regard. Conversely, differences between minority-foreign and local plants were still substantial, but relatively small. Thus, the results of estimating these four equations suggest that the patterns observed in the descriptive statistics persist even after accounting for the influence of factor intensities, age, size and BOI status.

8.4 Exports and foreign ownership in the Thai automobile industry

As late as 1996, Thailand's exports of automobiles and automobiles parts amounted to only US$1.1 billion but they increased over three times in the next five years to reach US$3.4 billion by 2001 (Table 8.4; Brooker Group 2002).[16] The share of autos and auto parts in Thailand's total exports also rose rapidly from 2.0 to 5.2 per cent during this period (Table 8.4; Bank of Thailand 2005). There was particularly rapid growth in the exports of autos, a very large portion of which were small trucks. Compilations of data from United Nations Statistics Division (various years) also indicate that Thailand may have developed a comparative advantage in small truck production during this period (Umemoto and Ramstetter, 2004).[17] Indeed, the growth of Thailand's auto and auto parts exports has been so rapid that some observers have begun describing Thailand as the 'Detroit of Southeast Asia'.[18] On the other hand, Thailand's auto and auto parts industries were still characterized by relatively low labour productivity and total factor productivity in 1996 and 1998 (Chapter 6; Ito 2004). In addition, Thailand's auto and auto parts industries remained highly protected in 2002 and Thailand still appeared to have a substantial comparative disadvantage in most segments of the industry as late as 2001 (Umemoto and Ramstetter, 2004). Moreover, automobile manufacturers were among the largest beneficiaries of incentive schemes offered by the Thai BOI. In short, the sharp increase in exports of autos and auto parts was clearly subsidized by Thai consumers and taxpayers during this period.

Nonetheless, there were also large structural changes in the Thai auto industry. Some of the most conspicuous structural changes occurred in the corporate landscape of the industry. Perhaps the largest change was the initiation of large-scale production and exports by affiliates of the two largest US makers, General Motors (Thailand) and AutoAlliance (Thailand), a Ford affiliate (Table 8.4). Another important change was the initiation of large-scale exports by Toyota Motor Thailand and more modest increases in exports by two other large Japanese makers: Honda Automobile (Thailand) and Isuzu Motor Thailand. As a result of these changes and the continuation of large exports by MMC Sittipol (Mitsubishi), exports of the top six exporters grew much more rapidly that than total exports, from US$0.7 billion in 1997 to US$2.4 billion in 2001. Correspondingly, the ratio of exports by the largest six exporters to total industry exports increased from 41 per cent in 1997 to 70 per cent in 2001.

Table 8.4   Exports of autos and auto parts by firm (US$ millions)

Commodity, company	1997	1998	1999	2000	2001	2002 q1–3
Total Thai exports-Bank of Thailand	57,604	54,340	58,581	69,152	64,971	50,018
Manufactures, broad definition	48,182	44,857	49,273	59,765	55,467	42,944
Manufactures, narrow definition	41,195	39,480	43,631	52,668	48,801	37,778
Autos, trucks & parts, total	1,579	1,750	2,505	3,165	3,409	–
Autos, trucks & parts, 13 firms	661	806	1,590	2,047	2,429	1,785
6 large exporters	654	802	1,548	1,976	2,394	1,751
MMC Sittipol (Mitsubishi)	505	637	714	735	717	616
AutoAlliance (Thailand)	0	10	444	580	484	415
General Motors (Thailand)	0	0	0	90	656	318
Toyota Motor Thailand	84	59	205	321	309	225
Honda Automobile (Thailand)	36	66	130	140	141	129
Isuzu Motor Thailand	30	29	56	110	86	48
7 smaller exporters	6	4	42	71	35	35
Autos & trucks (CBU), total	587	697	1,238	1,556	1,765	–
Autos & trucks (CBU), 10 firms	518	671	1,327	1,551	1,888	1,358
6 large exporters	517	669	1,292	1,492	1,866	1,339
MMC Sittipol (Mitsubishi)	499	618	682	679	640	564
AutoAlliance (Thailand)	0	10	405	444	359	313
General Motors (Thailand)	0	0	0	90	656	318
Toyota Motor Thailand	13	13	116	148	102	77
Honda Automobile (Thailand)	5	28	81	68	72	54
Isuzu Motor Thailand	0	0	8	63	37	13
4 smaller exporters	0	1	35	59	22	19
Auto & truck parts, total	991	1,053	1,267	1,609	1,645	–
Auto & truck parts, 12 firms	143	136	262	497	541	427
5 large exporters	137	133	256	484	528	412
MMC Sittipol (Mitsubishi)	6	20	32	55	77	52
AutoAlliance (Thailand)	0	0	39	137	125	102
Toyota Motor Thailand	71	47	89	173	207	148
Honda Automobile (Thailand)	31	38	49	72	70	75
Isuzu Motor Thailand	30	28	48	47	49	35
7 smaller exporters	6	3	6	13	13	16

Sources: Bank of Thailand (2005); Brooker Group (2002); Media Overseas (2003); International Monetary Fund (2005).

The vast majority of these exports consisted of completely built-up units (CBUs) for autos and trucks, and exports of the six largest exporters always amounted to the vast majority of these exports: 88 per cent in 1997 and 96 per cent or more in 1998–2001 (Table 8.4).[19] In contrast, exports of auto parts by the twelve firms for which data could be compiled were only 14 per cent of the industry total in 1997 and 33 per cent in 2001, though the exports of these twelve firms grew extremely rapidly (3.8-fold) over this period. Five of the six large exporters (all but General Motors) also had substantial exports of parts. Parts exports were much smaller than exports of autos and trucks for MMC Sittipol and AutoAlliance but of similar magnitude for Toyota, Honda and Isuzu.

The rapid increase in the exports of the six integrated producers with large exports resulted in an even larger increase of the mean export propensity for the group – from 13 to 52 per cent in 1997–2001 (Table 4.5).[20] Not surprisingly, the mean export propensity was much smaller among ten small exporters – 0.1 per cent in 1997 and 3.7 per cent in 2001. In 1997, the variation of export propensities was large among large exporters with the standard deviation exceeding the mean by more than 1.5 times. As a result, simple t-tests suggest that the difference between export propensities of large and small exporters was statistically insignificant in 1997 despite the large difference in mean propensities.[21] By 2001, variation among large exporters became much smaller relative to the mean, and the t-test correspondingly indicates that the difference in export propensities was statistically significant at standard levels (0.05 or less) in 2001. Perhaps more important in this context is the fact that foreign ownership shares were higher among the large exporters than in the small exporters – 80 versus 45 per cent in 1997 and 96 versus 61 per cent in 2001 – and that these differences were statistically significant in both years.

Unlike the tests presented in the previous section, these t-tests do not account for the influences of related characteristics such as factor intensities, vintage and size, and accounting for these influences might change the results of the tests. Small sample size makes it impossible to account for these influences in this analysis and makes the results sensitive to the addition or subtraction of firms from the samples. Nonetheless, it is important that these samples suggest large exporters have much higher export propensities and foreign ownership shares than small exporters, in a pattern that is broadly consistent with patterns observed in the analyses of the census data in the previous section.[22]

Table 8.5 also presents information for nine specialized parts exporters that initiated exports between 1997 and 2001 and nineteen other specialized parts makers that had no exports in these two years. The scale of exports was still very small among exporters in the latter sample – only US$6.5 million – and mean export-sales ratios were also much lower than among the six large exporters at 16 per cent. However, both of these figures were markedly larger than among the ten small exporters of autos and trucks. Moreover, the nine parts exporters always had higher mean foreign ownership shares than the nineteen non-exporters: 43 versus 25 per cent in 1997 and 61 versus 36 per cent in 2001. In 1997 this difference was statistically significant at standard levels and in 2001 the difference was significant if a slightly lower cutoff (0.08) is used. Thus, parts exporters also appear to be characterized by relatively high foreign ownership shares even in this sample where firms had relatively low exports, export-propensities and foreign ownership shares.[23]

Another pattern emerging from these data is an apparent correlation between increases in exports and export propensities on the one hand, and increases in foreign ownership shares on the other. For example, between 1997 and 2001, foreign ownership shares increased markedly in half of the six large exporters (from 48 to 100 per cent in MMC Sittipol, from 70 to 86 per cent in Toyota, and from 62 to 91 per cent in Honda; Umemoto and Ramstetter 2004: 46) and were 99 or 100 per cent in the other three large exporters. Correspondingly, the 38 percentage point increase in the mean export propensity was accompanied by a 16 percentage point increase in the mean foreign ownership shares, making this group of firms almost wholly-foreign owned by 2001. A similar pattern is also observed in parts exporters where the mean export propensity increased 16 percentage points and the mean foreign ownership share increased 18 percentage points, though both export propensities and foreign ownership shares remained much lower in this group. This pattern is also consistent with the notion that relatively high foreign ownership shares may be required for many parents to allow high export propensities in their foreign affiliates, because these parents want to ensure control over their international marketing networks.

It is also important to recognize that increases in foreign ownership during this period were often related to financial duress in local partners that was caused by the fallout of the 1997–98 financial crisis. For example, equity was heavily negative in 1997 in MMC Sittipol (–44 per cent of total assets), but this turned slightly positive by 2001 (2 per cent

Table 8.5   Characteristics of large automobile firms in 1997 and 2001 (US$ millions except as noted)

Major activity, company	Exports		Sales		Sales/ employee		Fixed assets/ employee		Exports/sales, %		Foreign owner, %		Age, years
	1997	2001	1997	2001	1997	2001	1997	2001	1997	2001	1997	2001	2001
INTEGRATED PRODUCERS OF AUTOMOBILES, TRUCKS, AND/OR PARTS													
6 Large Exporters, mean	109.0	399.0	541.8	834.7	0.26	0.43	0.17	0.13	13.5	51.6	80.0	96.0	23
-standard deviation	196.2	263.2	604.6	423.8	0.16	0.14	0.16	0.12	20.5	35.7	23.0	6.0	17
-number	6	6	6	6	5	6	5	6	6	6	6	6	6
10 Small Exporters, mean	0.3	1.5	134.9	60.1	0.37	0.15	0.04	0.05	0.1	3.7	44.5	60.6	23
-standard deviation	1.4	4.3	203.9	143.9	0.52	0.19	0.03	0.03	0.4	7.8	34.9	42.7	14
-number	9	10	9	10	9	9	9	9	9	10	9	10	10
Large–Small Exporters, mean	108.8	397.4	406.9	774.6	−0.11	0.28	0.13	0.08	13.3	48.0	35.5	35.4	−0.2
-significance level	0.23	0.01	0.16	0.00	0.57	0.01	0.15	0.17	0.17	0.02	0.03	0.03	0.98
SPECIALIZED PRODUCERS OF AUTOMOBILE PARTS													
9 Exporters, mean	0.0	6.5	29.4	43.6	0.13	0.22	0.05	0.03	0.0	16.4	43.4	61.3	9
-standard deviation	0.0	6.7	26.7	25.1	0.09	0.21	0.01	0.01	0.0	17.4	19.3	31.6	6

-number	7	9	7	9	7	9	4	5	7	9	6	9	9
19 Non-Exporters, mean	0.0	0.0	60.1	78.2	0.11	0.13	0.06	0.03	0.0	0.0	21.0	35.6	17
-standard deviation	0.0	0.0	54.2	73.3	0.12	0.19	0.08	0.04	0.0	0.0	24.5	39.6	10
-number	19	19	19	19	19	19	17	10	19	19	17	18	17
Exporters–Non Exporters, mean	0.0	6.5	–30.7	–34.6	0.01	0.10	–0.01	0.00	0.0	16.4	22.4	25.6	–8
-significance level	–	0.02	0.07	0.08	0.74	0.25	0.63	0.87	–	0.02	0.04	0.08	0.02

Notes: – = not applicable; when data were not available for 1997 or 2001, data for 1996 and 2000, respectively, were used as proxies; italics indicate differences significant at the 0.05 level or better; for automobiles, trucks, and parts, the six large exporters were MMC Sittipol (Mitsubishi), General Motors (Thailand), AutoAlliance (Thailand), Toyota Motor Thailand, Honda Automobile (Thailand), and Isuzu Motor Thailand, while the ten small exporters were Siam-Nissan Automobile, Hino Motors Thailand, Nissan Diesel Thailand, Thai-Swedish Assembly, Bangchan General Assembly (2000), BMW Manufacturing, Siam Motors and Nissan, Thai Rung Union Car PLC, Thonburi Automotive Assembly Plant, and Volvo Truck & Bus; for automobile parts, the nine exporters were Thai Storage Battery PLC, Takata-Toa, Thai Stanley PLC, Ford Operations (Thailand), Keihin Auto Parts (Thailand), Summit Showa Manufacturing, Thai Automotive Industry, Koyo Steering (Thailand), and Siam DK Technology, while the nineteen non-exporters were Asian Autoparts, Denso, Enkei Thai, Goodyear Thailand, Isuzu Engine Manufacturing, Keihin (Thailand), MSC Engine, Siam Battery Industry, Siam Toyota Manufacturing, Sumitomo Electric Wiring Systems, Summit Auto Body Industry, Summit Auto Seats Industry, Summit Laemchabang Auto Seats Manufacturing, Thai Summit Autoparts Industry, Thai Summit Harness, Thai Summit Laemchabang Autoparts, Thai Summit PKK, Thermstar, and Yuasa Battery (Thailand).

Sources: Advanced Research Group (various years); Board of Investment (1999); Comm Bangkok (various years); Cosmic Publications (various years); Dun & Bradstreet (1999); Kompass (various years); Media Overseas (2003); Brooker Group (1997, 2002); The Nation (various years); Toyo Keizai (various years).

of total assets; Umemoto and Ramstetter 2004: 46). The conversion of this from a minority-owned to a wholly-foreign affiliate during this period was probably related to the need to increase equity or see the affiliate go into bankruptcy, combined with the inability of local partners to come up with the needed capital. Such problems were not uncommon and several of the firms in these samples had negative equity in either or both years.[24]

Increases in foreign ownership shares were also related to changes in Thai laws and related BOI policies that removed most previous restrictions on foreign ownership. Prior to these changes foreign ownership shares were in principle limited to 49 per cent. However, there were many exceptions to this principle. For example, through the mid-1990s, firms who were promoted by the BOI were often granted exceptions to foreign ownership restrictions if they met criteria such as employing a large number of workers, locating their factories outside of the Greater Bangkok area, and/or exporting a high percentage of their output. Another example was the exception granted for US firms under the provisions of the Treaty of Amity and Economic Relations between the two countries. A third example appears to have occurred when one foreign-controlled Thai affiliate owns part of a second Thai affiliate, which often results in foreign shares in excess of 49 per cent. As a result of these exceptions, a substantial number of the firms examined here (eight of the sixteen integrated producers and one of the nineteen specialized parts makers) had foreign ownership shares that exceeded 49 per cent even in 1997, before the ownership restrictions were relaxed.

The fact that exceptions to ownership restrictions were granted for large exporters complicates the interpretation of the correlation between export propensities and foreign ownership shares somewhat, because it suggests that foreign ownership shares might be determined by export propensities rather than the reverse. However, it is probably more accurate to say that foreign ownership shares are more influenced by the expected export propensity of a project in the future, rather than the actual export propensity in a given year. For example, AutoAlliance and General Motors have always been wholly-foreign affiliates even though they exported very little before 1999 or 2000, respectively. In short, as has been reiterated several times in this chapter, the evidence presented here and in the previous section is consistent with the notion that MNCs often insist on control of an affiliate before they allow it to export on a large scale through the MNC's international marketing networks.

8.5   Conclusions

This chapter has examined the relationship between foreign ownership shares and trade propensities in a large sample of Thai manufacturing plants taken from the census for 1996, and in a more limited sample of automobile firms in 1997–2001. The results of analysing the 1996 census data suggest that foreign MNCs are more likely to have high export propensities than local plants and majority- and wholly-foreign MNCs are more likely to have high trade propensities than minority-foreign plants. These differences persist after controlling for plant-level differences in factor intensities, size, vintage, BOI-promotion status and industry affiliation. A closer examination of automobile firms in 1997–2001, some of which experienced very rapid export growth during this period, suggested that exporters tended to have high foreign ownership shares and that increases in foreign ownership shares accompanied increases in exports in some large exporters. Differences in export propensities thus appear to be very pervasive between MNCs and local firms, as well as among MNC ownership groups. They are observed more consistently than corresponding differences in wages (Chapter 3) and much more often than the infrequent observation of productivity differentials (Chapters 5, 6).

There are very good theoretical reasons to expect that MNCs will not allow their affiliates to export large amounts without closely controlling their entry into foreign markets and these empirical results are consistent with this view. Combined with similar results for Indonesian manufacturing and manufacturing MNCs in Vietnam, these findings suggest that the relationship between foreign ownership shares and export propensities is an important aspect of foreign MNC activity in Southeast Asia.

Notes

1. The term MNCs is used to refer to foreign-owned MNCs in this chapter.
2. Although this sample contains most foreign MNCs, the coverage of local firms is far less comprehensive and there is thus the possibility that previous results for Thailand pertain only to the rather limited set of firms included in the 1990 data set.
3. There is substantial disagreement in the theoretical literature about the meaning of this trait, however. For example, according to Dunning (1981, 1993) ownership advantages such as the possession of firm-specific assets is one of three requirements (internalization advantages and location advantages being the others) for a firm to become an MNC. In contrast, others (e.g. Buckley and Casson 1991; Casson 1987; Rugman 1980, 1985) argue that internalization alone explains the existence of the MNC and that the

possession of firm-specific assets simply reflects the internalization process. For more comprehensive reviews of the theoretical and empirical literature see Caves (1996), Dunning (1993) and Markusen (1991).

4. In addition, evidence from MNC projects in Vietnamese manufacturing suggests that export propensities tend to be highest in MNCs with relatively large foreign ownership shares (Phan and Ramstetter 2004b).

5. First, all but one in each of set of duplicate or near-duplicate records was removed. Second, records reporting non-positive values for production workers, non-production workers, intermediate consumption, or value added were removed. Third, records for plants with 10–19 employees were also removed. For details, see Chapter 5 as well as Ramstetter (2001, 2002b, 2003).

6. See Table 5.1 and Appendix Table A5.1 for more details on this sample and the figures cited below.

7. See Ramstetter (2002a: Appendix Tables B1–B4) for more details on the sample by trade propensity, industry, owner and size group.

8. In fact, MNCs in these samples actually tended to have relatively high capital- and non-production-worker intensities (Ramstetter 2001, 2002a), suggesting that they should have relatively low export propensities in general. On the other hand, MNCs also tended to be relatively large and promoted by the BOI much more often than local plants, suggesting relatively high export propensities. However, it is important to note that these general correlations can be reversed at the plant level or by simultaneously accounting for the effects of all influences on export propensities.

9. This is equation (a) in Ramstetter (2002b).

10. This is equation (c) in Ramstetter (2002b).

11. The third specification is equation (e) and fourth is equation (g) in Ramstetter (2002b).

12. Note that it is impossible to estimate some of the industry-level equations because one or more of the explanatory variables perfectly predicts one of the choices represented by the dependent variables.

13. As detailed in Ramstetter (2002b: Appendix Tables C1–C4), results for other coefficients were generally as expected in that vintage, size and BOI-promotion were all positively and significantly correlated with export propensities in most equations and samples. Non-production-worker intensity was also negatively and significantly correlated with export propensities as expected in many cases. However, the relationship between capital intensity and export propensities was often insignificant and sometimes significantly positive, in contrast to expectations.

14. Unfortunately, it is very difficult to correct for this problem using these estimation techniques. For example, these estimates were performed using the probit and ordered probit procedures in TSP version 4.5, which does not include options to address the problem of heteroscedasticity when using these techniques.

15. In a previous study of Indonesian manufacturing (Ramstetter 1999b) the effects of a possible policy bias were addressed by dropping plants with very high export propensities (80 per cent or more) from the samples and showing that these limited samples generated the same qualitative results as the overall samples. A similar procedure is not meaningful in this case because of the way export propensities are defined in the data.

16. This estimate of total auto and auto parts exports implies a rather broad definition of auto parts exports.
17. For example, the revealed comparative advantage index for trucks under 5 tons, defined as the sum of sections 870421 and 870431 of the harmonized system (HS) increased from 0.5 in 1996 to over 2.7 in 1999–2001.
18. See, for example, 'Thailand – the Detroit of Southeast Asia', *Canada Export on-line*, 21 Sept. 2001 (http://webapps.dfait-maeci.gc.ca/canadexport/view. asp?id = 373411&language = E).
19. Firm-level compilations are not always consistent with the commodity-based compilations used to estimate industry totals because of differences in the way exports are classified and/or how the timing of exports is reported. This is most likely why the data in Table 8.4 indicate that the five largest exporters exported more autos and trucks than Thailand in 1999 and 2001.
20. As noted in Table 8.5, the 1996 data are used as a proxy for 1997 and 2000 data are used as a proxy for 2001 for some variables and/or firms in the sample.
21. The t-test used allows both sample sizes and variances to differ among the groups compared (Sachs 1984: 270), large exporters and small exporters in this case.
22. The six large exporters also had relatively large sales per firm, in another pattern that is consistent with those observed in the census data. In contrast, there was little difference in vintage and large exporters had higher capital intensity (fixed assets per worker), but neither of these differences was significant.
23. In these samples, the nine exporters also tended to have relatively large sales per firm and be relatively new firms, similar to patterns generally observed in the census data. However, there was little difference in capital intensity (fixed assets per worker) and none of these differences were significant.
24. See Umemoto and Ramstetter (2004: 46–7) for further details.

References

Advanced Research Group Co. Ltd. (various years) *Thailand Company Information*, 1997–8, 1998–9, 1999–2000, 2000–1, 2001–2 issues, Bangkok: Advanced Research Group Co. Ltd.

Bank of Thailand (2005) Data from the 'Economic Data' section of the Bank of Thailand website, downloaded in January 2005. Bangkok: Bank of Thailand (http://www.bot.or.th/bothomepage/databank/EconData/EconData _e.htm).

Blomström, Magnus and Ari Kokko (1998) 'Multinational Corporations and Spillovers', *Journal of Economic Surveys*, 12: 247–77.

Board of Investment (2001) Database on promoted projects as of November 1999, Bangkok: Board of Investment.

Brooker Group (1997) *Profiles of BOI-Promoted Companies and Sectors – 1997*, Bangkok: Board of Investment (including accompanying diskette).

Brooker Group (2002) *Thailand's Automotive Industry*. Bangkok: Brooker Group.

Buckley, Peter J. and Mark Casson (1991) *The Future of the Multinational Enterprise*, second edition, London: Macmillan.

Casson, Mark (1987) *The Firm and the Market: Studies on the Multinational and the Scope of the Firm*, Cambridge, MA: MIT Press.

Caves, Richard E. (1996) *Multinational Enterprise and Economic Analysis*, second edition, Cambridge: Cambridge University Press.

Comm Bangkok Co. Ltd. (various years) *Factory Directory in Thailand*, Vol. 2 (May 1998), Vol. 3 (November 1999), Vol. 4 (May 2001), Vol. 5 (November 2002), Bangkok: Comm Bangkok Co. Ltd.

Cosmic Publications Co. Ltd. (various years) *Thailand Investment: a Directory of Companies Promoted by the Board of Investment*, 1997 and 1998–9 issues, Bangkok: Cosmic Publications Co. Ltd.

Dun & Bradstreet (1999) *Dun & Bradstreet Business Information Report: Thailand 1999*, Bangkok: Dun & Bradstreet.

Dunning, John H. (1981) *International Production and the Multinational Enterprise*, London: Allen & Unwin.

Dunning, John H. (1993) *Multinational Enterprises and the Global Economy*, Workingham, UK: Addison-Wesley Publishing Co.

International Monetary Fund (2005) *International Financial Statistics*, January CD-ROM, Washington, DC: International Monetary Fund.

Ito, Keiko (2004) 'Foreign Ownership and Plant Productivity in the Thai Automobile Industry in 1996 and 1998: a Conditional Quantile Analysis', *Journal of Asian Economics*, 15: 321–53.

Kompass (various years) *Thailand Company Information*, 1998, 1999 and 2002/2003 issues, Bangkok: Kompass.

Markusen, James R. (1991) 'The Theory of the Multinational Enterprise: a Common Analytical Framework', in Eric D. Ramstetter, ed., *Direct Foreign Investment in Asia's Developing Economies and Structural Change in the Asia-Pacific Region*, Boulder, Co: Westview Press, pp. 11–32.

Media Overseas Co. Ltd. (2003) *Thailand Automotive Industry Directory 2003–2004*, Bangkok: Media Overseas Co. Ltd.

Moran, Theodore (2001) *Parental Supervision: the New Paradigm for Foreign Direct Investment and Development*, Washington, DC: Institute for International Economics.

National Statistical Office (1999) *Report on the 1997 Industrial Census of the Whole Kingdom*, Bangkok: National Statistical Office.

Phan, Minh Ngoc and Eric D. Ramstetter (2004a) 'Foreign Multinationals and Local Firms in Vietnam's Economic Transition', *Asian Economic Journal*, 18: 371–404.

Phan, Minh Ngoc and Eric D. Ramstetter (2004b) 'Foreign Ownership Shares and Exports of Multinational Firms in Vietnamese Manufacturing', Working Paper 2004–32, Kitakyushu: International Centre for the Study of East Asian Development.

Ramstetter, Eric D. (1993) 'Production Technology in Foreign and Local Firms in Thai Manufacturing', Discussion Paper No. 8, Nagoya: Graduate School of International Development, Nagoya University.

Ramstetter, Eric D. (1994) 'Comparisons of Japanese Multinationals and Other Firms in Thailand's Non-oil Manufacturing Industries', *ASEAN Economic Bulletin*, 11: 36–58.

Ramstetter, Eric D. (1997) 'International Trade, Multinational Firms, and Regional Integration in Thailand', in Wendy Dobson and Chia Siow Yue, eds, *Multinationals and East Asian Integration*, Toronto: International Development Research Centre and Singapore: Institute of Southeast Asian Studies, pp. 107–30.

Ramstetter, Eric D. (1998) 'Export Propensities and Foreign Ownership Shares in Southeast Asian Manufacturing', in F. Gerard Adams and Shinichi Ichimura, eds, *East Asian Development: Will the East Asian Miracle Survive?*, Westport, CN: Praeger, pp. 171–92.

Ramstetter, Eric D. (1999a) 'Comparisons of Foreign Multinationals and Local Firms in Asian Manufacturing Over Time', *Asian Economic Journal*, 13: 163–203.

Ramstetter, Eric D. (1999b) 'Trade Propensities and Foreign Ownership Shares in Indonesian Manufacturing in the Early 1990s', *Bulletin of Indonesian Economic Studies*, 35: 43–66.

Ramstetter, Eric D. (2001) 'Labor Productivity in Foreign Multinationals and Local Plants in Thai Manufacturing, 1996 and 1998', Working Paper 2001–13, Kitakyushu: International Centre for the Study of East Asian Development.

Ramstetter, Eric D. (2002a) 'Does Technology Differ in Local Plants and Foreign Multinationals in Thai Manufacturing? Evidence from Translog Production Functions for 1996 and 1998', Working Paper 2002–04, Kitakyushu: International Centre for the Study of East Asian Development.

Ramstetter, Eric D. (2002b) 'Trade Propensities and Foreign Ownership Shares in Thai Manufacturing, 1996', Working Paper 2002–03, Kitakyushu: International Centre for the Study of East Asian Development.

Ramstetter, Eric D. (2003) 'Labor Productivity, Wages, Nationality, and Foreign Ownership Shares in Thai Manufacturing, 1996–2000', Working Paper 2003–15, Kitakyushu: International Centre for the Study of East Asian Development.

Ramstetter, Eric D. and Sadayuki Takii (2005) 'Exporting and Foreign Ownership in Indonesian Manufacturing 1990–2000', Working Paper 2005–15, Kitakyushu: International Centre for the Study of East Asian Development.

Rugman, Alan M. (1980) 'Internalization as a General Theory of Foreign Direct Investment: a Re-appraisal of the Literature', *Weltwirtschaftliches Archiv*, 116: 365–79.

Rugman, Alan M. (1985) 'Internalization is Still a General Theory of Foreign Direct Investment', *Weltwirtschaftliches Archiv*, 121: 570–5.

Sachs, Lothar (1984) *Applied Statistics: a Handbook of Techniques*, second edition, New York: Springer-Verlag (translated by Zenon Reynarowych).

The Nation (various years) *Top 1000 Companies*, 1997–1998 issues; *Top 1000*, 1999 issue; *1000 Top Companies*, 2000 issue; *Top 1000 Thai Companies*, 2001–2 issue, Bangkok: The Nation.

Toyo Keizai (various years) *Kaigai Shinshutsu Kigyo Soran [A Comprehensive Survey of Firms Overseas]*, CD-ROMs with data from 1990–2003 issues (data for 1988–2001), Tokyo: Toyo Keizai (in Japanese).

Umemoto, Masaru and Eric D. Ramstetter (2004) 'The Boom in Vehicle Exports from Thailand: Protection, Markets, and Multinationals', Working Paper 2004–01, Kitakyushu: International Centre for the Study of East Asian Development.

United Nations Statistics Division (various years) Comtrade Database, 1996–2000 and 1997–2001 CD-ROMs and online data, New York: United Nations Statistics Division (http://www.un.org/stats/).

Index